THE HISTORY
OF LAND TITLES
IN WESTERN
NORTH CAROLINA

George H. Smathers

Southern Historical Press, Inc.
Greenville, South Carolina

Please direct all correspondence and book orders to:
SOUTHERN HISTORICAL PRESS, Inc.
PO Box 1267
Greenville, SC   29602-1267

THE HISTORY
OF LAND TITLES
IN WESTERN
NORTH CAROLINA

A History of the Cherokee land laws affecting the title to land lying west of the Meigs and Freeman line, and laws affecting the title of land lying east of the Meigs and Freeman line back to the top of the Blue Ridge, including all the land on the waters of French Broad River in what was formerly Buncombe County as created by the Act of 1792, which at that time included all the land west of the Blue Ridge in this State, prepared by Geo. H. Smathers, Attorney, of Asheville, N. C., for the use and benefit of the Champion Paper and Fibre Company of Canton, N. C., and the members of the legal profession in Western North Carolina and others who have subscribed to its publication.

by

GEORGE H. SMATHERS

Attorney-at-Law

Designed and Printed by

THE MILLER PRINTING COMPANY

Asheville, North Carolina

1938

THE AUTHOR, GEORGE H. SMATHERS, AT EIGHTY-FOUR YEARS OF AGE, AND, (INSERT) AT THIRTY-EIGHT YEARS OF AGE.

George H. Smathers

An Autobiographical Sketch

EORGE HENRY SMATHERS, the author of this History, was born at Turnpike, North Carolina, on January 29th, 1854, and celebrated his eighty-fourth birthday in Asheville, N. C., on January 29th, 1938.

The Author is the son of John Charles Smathers and Lucilla E. Smathers. His father was born February 5th, 1826, and died July 21st, 1919, at the age of ninety-two years, five months and six days; and his mother was born October 16th, 1829, and died May 5th, 1911, at the age of eighty-one years, six months and nineteen days.

The Author was named for his two grandfathers, George for George Smathers on his father's side, and Henry for Henry Johnson on his mother's side.

John C. and Lucilla E. Smathers were married May 4th, 1848, and spent all the remainder of their lives at Turnpike, except for a period of four years spent in Waynesville, N. C., from 1872 to 1876. Of their thirteen children, nine, four sons and five daughters are still living.

In the year 1844 John C. Smathers purchased a rather large property on the old Turnpike Road from Asheville to the western counties, on both sides of the Haywood and Buncombe County line, and when the first toll-gate west of Asheville was established at the county line the name of Turnpike was adopted, and a few years later was made a post office. John C. Smathers was a most active man. At Turnpike he built and operated a store, blacksmith shop, saw-mill, wagon works, cabinet factory, and a complete grist and flouring mill, the second flouring mill to be built in Haywood County. At the same time he ran an extensive hotel business; first for travelers on the Turnpike Road, and later for summer visitors. At Clyde, on Pigeon River, he built and operated a second grist mill and flour mill, and a store; and at Waynesville, where he lived from 1872 to 1876, he built and operated a store and ran a hotel business. His various activities made him one of the best known men in Western North Carolina.

Except for his later study of the law, and wide reading, the Author received his education before his fifteenth year, largely in private schools taught by a well-known teacher named Mary Ann Hutsell; first in Asheville during the year 1861, at what was known as the Old Brick Academy on the present site of the Montford Avenue School, next, in 1863 and 1864, at the Sand Hill Academy near the present town of Enka, and later on, during the year 1868, at Pleasant Hill School House about one and a half miles below Turnpike; all under the same teacher.

After leaving school he joined his father in his various business enterprises, first in the store at Turnpike, then at Clyde, and later at Waynesville, where he was in charge of the business from 1872 to 1876. During this period the Author was active in the live-stock business, in which his father was also interested, and made numerous trips with droves of cattle, sheep, and hogs from the mountains out to the railway at Greenville and Spartanburg, S. C., where the stock was shipped to Columbia and Charleston, S. C., and marketed there. He also made trips with wagon trains, hauling out flour, bacon, apples, and other produce for sale, and bringing back salt, sugar, coffee, dry-goods, etc., for his father's stores. On one of these wagon trips, when twelve years old, he saw his first railway train, at Greenville, S. C.

The Author's first public office was that of United States Store Keeper and Guager, to which he was appointed by Pinkney Rollins, then U. S. Collector of Internal Revenue for the Western District of North Carolina, in which capacity he served for a few months in the year 1876.

During the year 1880, the Author decided to enter the practice of the law, and joined the well-known law school of Dick and Dillard, at Greensboro, N. C., securing his license to practice law from the Supreme Court of North Carolina in June 1881.

During the year 1882 he opened a law office in the town of Waynesville, N. C., where he continued to reside and practice law until about the year 1913, when he moved to Asheville.

In 1886 the Author was elected Mayor of the town of Waynesville, and served for two terms, during which modern improvements were started in the town.

During the year 1896 when William McKinley was elected President of the United States, the Author and Major W. W. Rollins were elected the two State Senators from the senatorial district then comprising Haywood, Buncombe, and Madison Counties, and the Author served as Chairman of the Senate Judiciary Committee during the session of 1897.

At this session the Author, in cooperation with J. W. Ferguson, member of the House from Haywood County, secured the passage of the first act providing for the levying of a tax for keeping up the public roads in Haywood County in addition to public labor. Prior to the passage of this act the roads in Haywood County were kept up entirely by labor. The act provided for the levying of a tax of ten cents on the hundred dollars for keeping up the public roads in the county. The Author was a Republican and Mr. Ferguson was a Democrat, and some of the followers of each were strongly in favor of the act, while others condemned the same. Under the provisions of the act, J. M. Tate was appointed Superintendent of Roads for the county, and the Board of County Commissioners contested the vaidity of the act and refused to levy the tax. The Author represented J. M. Tate who brought suit against the Board of County Commissioners to force them to levy the tax. The court below sustained the act and held it valid, and the case was carried by the Commissioners on appeal to the Supreme Court of North Carolina, which, in an opinion delivered by Associate Justice Clark, sustaining the opinion of the court below, and held the tax valid, and the Board of County Commissioners was forced to levy the tax. See case of Tate vs. Commissioners reported in 122nd N. C. R., page 661. See also the Act sent out as Chapter 249, Public Laws of North Carolina of 1897, page 414. This was the first act passed by the General Assembly of North Carolina that levied a tax for road purposes west of the Blue Ridge.

During the year 1899, at the request of the Eastern Band of Cherokee Indians, the Author was appointed by Attorney General Miller, under the administration of President Benjamin Harrison, as Special Assistant United States Attorney, to take charge of two suits then pending in the United States Court for the Western District of North Carolina, entitled The Eastern Band of Cherokee Indians vs. Wm. H. Thomas, et al, and The Unitd States vs. Wm. H. Thomas et al, which had as their purpose the removal of about two hundred trespassers from the lands of the Cherokee Indians, and the clearing up of the title of the Indians to lands which had been decreed by the Court to belong to the Indians in the first above entitled suit. President Cleveland, who succeeded Mr. Harrison, refused to remove the Author from his position in spite of considerable political pressure, and the work was continued under both President Cleveland and President McKinley. After about fourteen years of intensive litigation, title was finally perfected in the Indians to what is now known as the Qualla Indian Boundary, comprising some 77,000 acres of land in Jackson and Swain Counties, North Carolina, and to part of the sixty-eight scattered tracts in Jackson, Swain, Cherokee, and Graham Counties, conveyed to the Indians by the Sibbald deed of August 14th, 1880, the whole running into a value of about one million dollars. Some of these 68 tracts are still in litigation in the United States Court at Asheville.

Soon after the service of the Author as Special Assistant U. S. Attorney and attorney for the Indians was terminated in 1903, the Indians engaged the legal services of Messrs. Bryson and Black, then attorneys at law of Bryson City, N. C. During the year 1906, one W. W. Frazier, of Pennsylvania, instituted an action against the Eastern Band of Cherokee Indians to recover about five thousand acres of land up on Lufty River in the Qualla Boundary in Swain County, N. C., and at the request of Messrs. Bryson and Black the Author was employed to aid them in the trial of this case for the Indians. In the suit in the lower court, the Indians won out, and the plaintiff carried the case on appeal to the Supreme Court, which affirmed the judgment of the lower court, the opinion of the court being delivered by His Honor Chief Justice Clark. See case of Frazier vs. Cherokee Indians, reported in 146th N. C. R. page 477 et seq. See also note added to the opinion of the court by Chief Justice Clark, commenting on the kind treatment of North Carolina to the Cherokees generally.

So much of the Author's time had been devoted to land matters by this time that he decided to specialize in title work and land litigation, and he has confined his work largely to those lines ever since the year 1903.

Before completing his work for the Cherokee Indians, the Author was employed by the executors and heirs of R. Y. McAden, who owned large timber tracts in Haywood, Jackson, Swain, Macon, Clay, Cherokee, and Graham Counties, and he represented them in their land matters and litigation for many years, until most of their lands were finally disposed of. He also did considerable work for Charles D. Fuller, of Kalamazoo, Michigan, who purchased a number of timber tracts on Lufty River in Swain County during the years 1902-3, with the intention of building a pulp mill at Ela Station on the Murphy Branch of the Southern Railway. He was also employed by the Haywood Lumber and Mining Company, the William Ritter Lumber Company, and the Whitewater River Lumber Company, which owned large boundaries in the states of North and South Carolina and Georgia, known as the O'Conner Lands, for which he acted as attorney up to a few years ago. In fact, there is hardly a large timber tract in North Carolina west of Buncombe County with which the writer has not had some connection.

During the month of February, 1905, the Author met Mr. Peter G. Thomson, Sr., of Cincinnati, Ohio, at the Dickey House in Murphy, who was looking over the country for a site for a large pulp mill and tannin extract plant, and upon learning of the Author's wide knowledge of timber conditions, and especially of spruce boundaries in which he was especially interested, Mr. Thomson engaged him to aid both in the location of the plants, the securing of sufficient timber tracts to supply material for at least twenty-five years, and in the investigation of land titles, both of the timber tracts and of the lands needed for the plants. After the selection of Canton, North Carolina, as a location for the plants, Mr. Thomson, in 1906, proceeded to organize the Champion Fibre Company, and the Author has been in the employ of that company, and its successor the Champion Paper & Fibre Company ever since the year 1906, and is still in charge of most of their land title work.

In addition to the necessary land at Canton for the construction of the plants and mill village, Mr. Thomson, and later the Champion Fibre Company, purchased first a large boundary of hardwood and spruce timber on the head of Pigeon River above Canton, and later tracts on Scott's Creek in Jackson County, on Valley River, Hanging Dog and Owl Creeks in Cherokee County, on Snowbird and Santeetlah Creeks in Graham County, on the West Fork of French Broad River in Transylvania County, and other tracts in Tennessee and South Carolina, as well as stumpage on many smaller boundaries, title to practically all of which was investigated by the Author.

During the years 1916 to 1920, the Champion Fibre Company purchased from various parties a boundary of land comprising approximatey one hundred thousand acres in the Great Smoky Mountains in Swain County, North Carolina, and Sevier County, Tennessee. Title to this land had hardly been cleared up when a strong movement arose on the part of the public and the United States Government to have the land set apart and condemned for the proposed Great Smoky Mountain National Park, and the states of North Carolina and Tennessee created Park Commissions for the purpose of acquiring this and adjoining lands for delivery to the United States government.

In 1930 suits were filed in both states by their Park Commissions against the Champion Fibre Company, et al., seeking to condemn the lands, and after considerable litigation in Tennessee as to the value of the lands in that state a meeting of the representatives of the two states and Mr. Logan Thomson, now President of the Champion Coated Paper Company, Mr. Reuben B. Robertson, President and General Manager of the Champion Fibre Company, and Mr. W. J. Damtoft, Assistant Secretary of the Champion Fibre Company, was held at Washington, D. C., in April of 1931, at which an agreement was reached by which the two states agreed to pay the Fibre Company the sum of three million dollars for its holdings in the two states; and it was agreed that the Champion Fibre Company would furnish the services of the Author to assist the attorneys of the two states in clearing the title to the lands from the claims of numerous parties which had developed in the course of the condemnation actions. Rather contrary to the agreement, the burden of this litigation was thrown largely upon the Champion Fibre Company and the Author, but after two or three years work in the courts of North Carolina and Tennessee the three or four hundred adverse claims were beaten or compromised, and during the year 1933 title to the entire boundary was vested in the two states, which transferred the lands to the Federal Government. This boundary comprises one of the finest spruce and hardwood timber tracts in the Southern Appalachian Mountains, and the scenic highway from Smokemont on Lufty River up to Newfound Gap, and down the Tennessee side of the Geat Smoky Mountains to near Gatlinburg on the Little Pigeon River in Tennessee, traverses this boundary for eighteen miles.

After the settlement of this matter, on account of his advanced age, the Author retired from the general practice of the law, and has since then confined his work to the matters of the Champion Fibre Company and the Champion Paper & Fibre Company.

In connection with the Great Smoky Mountain National Park, the Author was a delegate to a convention held during the year 1899 at the old Battery Park Hotel in Asheville, which took the first steps toward the creation of a National Park in the Southern Appalachian Mountains. The proceedings of this convention were fully reported by the Asheville Citizen at that time, and the report was reproduced in an article published by the Asheville Citizen-Times in the issue of Sunday, June 17th, 1934, with a group picture showing thirty-two of the one hundred delegates, taken in front of the Vanderbilt Mansion on a trip made by the delegates over Biltmore Estate at the invitation of Mr. Charles McNamee, manager of the estate, who attended the convention.

Among the prominent men attending the convention, most of whom are shown in the group picture, of which the Author has a framed original, were N. G. Gonzales, then Editor of the Columbia State, and who was later killed by the Nephew of United States Senator Ben Tilman of South Carolina, and who presided as Chairman of the convention; Josephus Daniels, now United States Ambassador to Mexico; Marion Butler, former United States Senator from North Carolina; W. T. Crawford, late Member of Congress, of Waynesville, N. C.; H. G. Ewart, late Member of Congress from this district; Pleasant A. Stovall, late Editor of the Savannah Evening News, and United States Minister to Switzerland under President Wilson; Charles A. Webb, Publisher of the Asheville Citizen-Times; Doctor C. P. Ambler and George S. Powell, of Asheville; M. V. Richards, Industrial Agent of the Southern Railway; Moses H. Cone, of Greensboro and Blowing Rock, N. C.; Samuel Wittkowski, of Charlotte, N. C.; S. C.

Satterthwaite, of Waynesville, N. C.; Charles McNamee, Manager of the Biltmore Estate; Doctor C. A. Schenck, then Forester of Biltmore Estate, now living in Darmstadt, Germany; and E. T. McKissick, then Proprietor of the Battery Park Hotel, who took an active part in the organization of the convention. As far as can be learned, the only surviving members of the group picture are Charles A. Webb, Josephus Daniels, Marion Butler, Doctor Schenck, and the Author.

In January of 1938, the Author was elected President of the Buncombe County Bar Association, and is now serving in that capacity for the present year.

The Author was married on January 6th, 1892, at Montgomery, Alabama, to Daisy Rice Glaze, daughter of Judge Samuel F. Rice, who was made Chief Justice of the Supreme Court of Alabama prior to the Civil War at the age of thirty-eight years, and who was one of the noted lawyers of the South. His only daughter, Ellen Rice Wiley, and one grandson, Allison C. Clough, Jr., reside in New York City. The Author now resides with his wife and her daughter, Mrs. May Rice Bartlett, at Kimberly Inn, in Asheville.

CONTENTS

INTRODUCTION

I N VIEW OF THE FACT that my practice of the law, covering a period of fifty-six years, has been confined largely to land title matters in Western North Carolina and adjoining States, and to my attorneyship as Special Assistant United States Attorney in the two old suits respectively of the Eastern Band of Cherokee Indians vs. William H. Thomas, William Johnston, et al, and the United States vs. William H. Thomas, William Johnston, et al, prosecuted by the United States in behalf of the Cherokee Indians from the year 1889 to 1903, commencing under the administration of President Harrison and continuing during the administrations of President Cleveland and President McKinley, in clearing up the title of the Cherokees to the Qualla Boundary and certain other tracts in Jackson and Swain Counties outside the Qualla Boundary and land in Cherokee and Graham Counties, N. C.; and later on in land title work for the R. Y. McAden estate, the Champion Fibre Company, the Haywood Lumber and Mining Company, the William M. Ritter Lumber Company, et al, it has been urged upon me by my good friends of the legal profession in Western North Carolina that before retiring from active practice, I should write a history of the various treaties made between the state of North Carolina and the United States with the Cherokee Indians, whereby additional lands were from time to time thrown open to settlement, together with a report or discussion on the effect of these treaties upon land titles, and the various laws enacted by the Legislature of North Carolina governing the granting of these lands to private citizens.

With the assistance of a number of prominent members of the legal profession in Western North Carolina in research and discussion of certain questions upon which they were particularly well informed, I have undertaken this work with much pleasure, hoping that it may prove valuable to all members of the legal profession, as well as others, and of real value to the younger attorneys and to those who handle title matters only occasionally. For the convenience of the latter I have added a brief discussion of our title laws in general in this State.

The History of Land Titles in Western North Carolina

HAT is known as the Cherokee Country included all that boundary of land that now lies west of Pigeon River in this State and a part of which lies on the south side of Tennessee and French Broad Rivers in what was then North Carolina but now Tennessee, reserved to the Cherokee Indians by the fifth section of the Act of 1783, hereinafter referred to and set out. The Cherokee Land Laws, however, only relate to the land lying west of what is known as the Meigs and Freeman line in this State.

After the title of the Cherokees was extinguished by the Treaty of 1819 to the land lying in between the Meigs and Freeman line and Tennessee River, an act was passed at the next session of the General Assembly of North Carolina, prohibiting the entry and grant of land within this area and providing that so much of the land as would sell at a certain price per acre should be surveyed out, classed and sold by commissioners, and a part of the land within this area was sold and disposed of under the Act of 1819 and acts amendatory thereof. Later on the unsurveyed land within this area was made subject to entry and grant under the general entry and grant laws of this State, and a part granted under the Act of 1835, which act, with some modifications, continued in full force and effect until the same was repealed by the Act of 1852.

After the title of the Cherokees was extinguished to all the lands lying west of Tennessee River in this State by the Treaty of 1835, the next session of the General Assembly of North Carolina after this treaty, passed an act prohibiting the entry and grant of the lands within this area and providing the same should be surveyed, classed and sold by commissioners for the prices therein stated, and a part of the land within this area was sold and disposed of by commissioners' sale under the Act of 1836. Later on all the unsurveyed and unsold land within this area was made subject to entry and grant under the Cherokee Land Laws by the Act of 1852, and acts amendatory thereof, as well also as all the land lying west of the Meigs and Freeman line in this State was made subject to entry and grant under the Cherokee Land Laws of 1852, and a part of the land lying west of the Meigs and Freeman line in this State was entered and granted under the Cherokee Land Laws under the Act of 1852 and acts amendatory thereof, which acts continued in full force and effect until repealed by the Act of 1883, after which time the lands lying west of the Meigs and Freeman line in this State became subject to entry and grant as other vacant lands in the State; but as before stated, the Cherokee Land Laws only related to the lands lying west of the Meigs and Freeman line, and all the land lying to the east of the Meigs and Freeman line back to the top of the Blue Ridge was granted to individuals under the general entry and grant laws of this State, some of which was granted before, but most of which was granted after the title of the Cherokees was extinguished to the same.

See acts relating to the Cherokee land laws passed up to the time of the Treaty of 1835, set out on pages 188 to 214 inclusive of the Second Volume of Revised Statutes of North Carolina of 1836 under the head of "Cherokee Lands".

See also acts pertaining to Cherokee lands set out on pages 65 to 108 inclusive of Second Volume of Code of North Carolina of 1883 under Chapter 11, entitled "Cherokee Lands," which includes practically all the acts relating to Cherokee land laws up to the time of the repeal of the same in 1883.

See Act of 1883, repealing acts pertaining to the Cherokee land laws, set out in section 2478 on page 108 of the Code of 1883, which made the Cherokee lands subjects to entry and grant as other public lands.

Prior to the adoption by the states of the Articles of Confederation and the Constitution of the United States, there was an inherent power in the State of North Carolina to make and conclude all treaties with the Indian Tribes within her borders, but this power was surrendered by the State of North Carolina to the general government to a limited extent when the states adopted the Articles of Confederation, and completely surrendered to the general governmnt upon the adoption by the states of the Constitution of the United States.

See Subsection 3 of Section 8 of Article 1, of the Constitution of the United States.

Notwithstanding the fact that the Cherokees and other Indian Tribes were in possession of the territory occupied by them when explorers under British Authority landed at Roanoke Island in Eastern North Carolina, Jamestown, Virginia, and other sections of the country along the Atlantic Coast, the State of North Carolina, the original thirteen states and the United States, following the policy of the European Governments, never recognized the Indian Tribes as having any right to the soil or the land they occupied except a possessory right, and although after the adoption of the Articles of Confederation and the Constitution of the United States, the power was surrendered by the states to the general government to make treaties with the Indian Tribes, as soon as the Indian title was extinguished to land within any of the original thirteen states, the land reverted to and became a part of the public domain of that state and subject to be disposed of in such manner as the legislative department of the state might see proper.

Not only th Cherokees but the other Indian Tribes at first insisted that they were the absolute owners of the territory occupied by them and the states and the United States had no right to the same unless acquired by purchase or treaty from the Indians. But, later on by various and sundry treaties made and entered into between the Commissioners appointed by the United States and the Cherokee Indians, the Indians were forced to admit they were wards of the United States and under the control and protection of the United States. I will presently refer to and set out these treaties.

It appears that the colonial governors of this state under British authority recognized in the Cherokee and other Indian Tribes within her borders a greater interest in the soil they occupied than was recognized by the government of this state after the Declaration of Independence, and the adoption of the constitution of the state, as shown by the opinion delivered by Judge Adams, Associate Justice of the Supreme Court of North Carolina, in the case of Brown vs. Smathers reported in the 188th N. C. R., at page 172, in words as follows:

"When the maritime powers of Europe discovered this continent they found it necessary to establish some principle by which, as between themselves, their respective rights should be determined, and they agreed that 'discovery gave title to the government by whose subjects or by whose authority it was made, against all other European governments, which title might be consumated by possession'. Accordingly, Great Britain granted charters to certain subjects who were associated for the purpose of carrying into effect the policy of the crown; and while these charters, or some of them, purported to convey the soil, they were generally understood to transfer only such title as the sovereign might rightfully convey. This, said Chief Justice Marshall, was the exclusive right of purchasing such lands as the natives were willing to sell. Fletcher vs. Peck, 6 Cranch, 87, 143; 3 Law Ed., 162, 180; Worcester vs. Georgia, 6 Peters; 515; 8 Law Ed., 483. So, before the Revolution, the colonists dealt with the Indians as a tribe or nation capable of holding property, and entered into treaties with them, defining their respective rights; but after the renunciation of colonial dependence, the soil was declared to be the property of the people who composed the state. And, although the policy of observing treaties 'secured by any former or future legislature' was enjoined by the Constitution of 1776 (Declaration of Rights, sec. 25), North Carolina, after this time and before the adoption of the Federal Constitution, had the inherent right, except as affected by the Articles of Confederation, to conclude treaties with the Indians living within her borders. Weston vs. Lumber Co., 163 N. C., 78. The Indian title, unless otherwise defined, was thus treated as a mere possessory right, or right of occupancy, unquestionable until it was extinguished by treaty, conquest, or voluntary cession. If extinguished, the title reverted to the State, for all 'lands lying within the boundary of the State, acknowledged by the Federal Government when received into the Union, must remain the lands of the State until she cedes them away'. Strother vs. Cathey, 5 N. C., 162; Eu-che-lah vs. Welch, 10 N. C., 155; Danforth vs. Wear, 9 Wheaton, 673; 6 Law Ed., 188; Fletcher vs. Peck, supra, p. 3; Brown vs. Brown, 103 N. C. 222, 223; S. c., 106 N. C., 454."

It appears that the contention of the United States that the Cherokees only had a right of occupancy in the boundary of land reserved to them by the 5th section of the Act of 1783 west of Pigeon River in this state here-in-after referred to and set out, was fully and completely sustained by the decision of the Supreme Court of the United States in the case of Latimer vs. Poteet, reported in 14th Peters U. S. R., Pages 3 et seq, and cases cited. The court held in this case, which involved the title to land covered by Grant No. 226 to William Cathcart calling to contain 49,920 acres, that the State of North Carolina could have granted the fee in the land subject to the Indian right of occupancy, and when the Indian title was extinguished by treaty that this would have relieved the land from the encumbrance; but that in this case, as the title of the Cherokees had not been extinguished to the land in controvrsy by the treaty of Holston of July 2nd, 1791, and as the 6th Section of the Act of 1783 prohibiting the entry and grant of lands reserved to the Cherokees by the 5th Section of the same Act had not been repealed and was in full force and effect on the date of the issuing of the grant, that the entire grant was absolutely void. I will take up and discuss this matter later on, after I set out in full the 5th and 6th Sections of the Act of 1783.

I find, however, that a grant issued by Colonial Governor Eden by and with the advice of the Lord Proprietors to a boundary of land lying on the south side of Morrahock (now Roanoke) River to King Blount, for himself and the Tuscarora tribe of Indians, on the 5th of June, 1717, was held by our Supreme Court to be a fee simple title and did not require the residence of the Indians on the land. See the decision of our Supreme Court rendered in the case of Sacaruse & Longboard vs. William King's heirs, etc., 2 L. R., 451, at January term, 1816, reported in 4th N. C. R., pages 316, et seq. See this decision as well as numerous decisions effecting the title of the Cherokees and individual Cherokees to land reserved to the Cherokees by the treaty of 1819, and the title of the Cherokees generally set out in the 7th Col. Enc. Dig. of N. C. Reports, pages 472-5, entitled "Indians."

In fact, this state being the owner of the fee in the land, could grant the fee in the land subject to the Indian right of occupancy, and when the Indian right of occupancy was extinguished by treaty or otherwise, the land would be relieved from the encumbrance. But it was the fixed and determined policy of the State of North Carolina from its early history not to permit any lands set apart and reserved to the Cherokees to be made subject to entry and grant until the Indian title or right of occupancy was extinguished by treaty or otherwise; or at least this was so as to the boundary of land west of Pigeon River reserved to the Cherokees by the act of 1783, as manifested by numerous acts of the General Assembly of North Carolina, hereinafter referred to and set out.

The following are acts of the General Assembly of North Carolina and decisions of the Supreme Courts of North Carolina and the United States bearing on this point:

Acts 1778, 1 Pot. Rev. ch. 132, p. 354;

Acts 1782, Pot. Rev. ch. 172, p. 413;

Acts 1783, 1 Pot. Rev. ch. 185, p. 435, The Code, pp. 2346-2347.

Acts 1783 brought forward and re-enacted in sections 2346 and 2347 of the Code of North Carolina of 1883.

Acts 1809, Pot. Rev. ch. 774.

Strother vs. Cathey, 1st Murphy, N. C. R., p. 162;

Latimer vs. Poteet, 39 U. S. R. (14th Pet.), p. 4;

Westfelt vs. Adams, 159 N. C. R., p. 409, etc.

The following are the treaties made and concluded between the State of North Carolina and the United States and the Cherokee Indians that affect the title to land that lies west of the Blue Ridge in this State, to-wit:

(1)   Joint treaty made and concluded between the States of Virginia and North Carolina and the Cherokees at the Long Island of Holston, on July 20, 1777.

(2)   The Treaty of Hopewell, of November 28, 1785.

(3)   The Treaty of Holston, of July 2, 1791.

(4)   The Treaty of Tellico, of October 2, 1798.

(5)   The Treaty of February 27, 1819.

(6)   The Treaty of New Echota, Georgia, on December 29, 1835. By this Treaty the Cherokees relinquished their claim of title to all land lying east of the Mississippi River.

In order to avoid confusion, I will here call attention to the fact that there were two Holston Treaties:

First, joint treaty between the States of Virginia and North Carolina entered into between the Commissioners appointed by the States of Virginia and North Carolina and the Chiefs and head men of the Cherokee Nation at the Long Island of Holston of July 20, 1777, entered into before the treaty-making power was surrendered by the states to the general government under the Articles of Confederation and the adoption of the Constitution of the United States.

Second, the Treaty of Holston of July 2, 1791, made and entered into between Commissioners appointed on behalf of the United States and the Chiefs and head men of the Cherokee Nation at White's Ford on French Broad River near what was then and is now Knoxville, Tenn., which treaty was made and entered into after the treaty-making power was surrendered by the states to the general government under the Articles of Confederation and the adoption of the Constitution of the United States.

The Treaty of Hopewell was made and entered into by and between Commissioners appointed by the United States acting under the Articles of Confederation and the Chiefs and head men of the Cherokee Nation; but the subsequent treaties above referred to were all made after the adoption of the Constitution of the United States.

All the above mentioned treaties together with the correspondence and the data relative to the same, are set out in a book, prepared and published in pursuance to Act of Congress, and entitled, "Annual Report of the Bureau of Ethnology, J. W. Powell, Director, 1883-84." Said treaties will be hereafter referred to in said book. Accompanying this book and made a part thereof is a map prepared by C. C. Royce, showing the treaty lines, run and established in pursuance to said treaties, giving dates and showing, by color, when the Indian title or right of occupancy was extinguished to the lands within the states formerly occupied by the Cherokee Nation or Tribe of Indians.

The Royce map can be found in a pocket in the back of Powell's book, which book and map are referred to and made a part hereof. See:

Joint treaty entered into by the States of Virginia and North Carolina and the Cherokees, set out in Powell's book on page 150 aforesaid: Hopewell Treaty set out in Powell's Book on page 153, etc.

Holston Treaty of July 2, 1791, set out in Powell's Book, on pages 158, etc. See also 7 U. S. Stat. 39;

Tellico Treaty of October 2, 1798, set out in Powell's Book on pages 174, etc. See also 7 U. S. Stat. 62.

Treaty of July 8, 1817, set out in Powell's Book on pages 212, etc. See also 7 U. S. Stat. 156;

Treaty of February 27, 1819, set out in Powell's Book on page 219, etc. See also 7 U. S. Stat. 195.

Treaty of December 29, 1835, entered into between the United States and the Cherokee Indians at New Echota, Georgia, set out in Powell's Book, 1883-4, on pages 253 to 297 inclusive.

See also these treaties set out in Whitney's Land Laws of Tennessee.

North Carolina being one of the original thirteen states, was the owner of all the vacant lands within her borders, and the power was given by the people to the legislative department to provide the manner for disposing of the vacant lands within the state. This disposition of vacant lands has been made by the Legislature in different ways, but the most general method has been and is now that of allowing the citizens of the state to enter and grant the same.

Following the adoption of the Constitution of this state and the Declaration of Rights, December 17 - 18, 1776, the first act of the General Assembly of this state providing for the entry and grant of the vacant lands of this state was passed in the year 1777.

See: Acts 1777, 1 Pot. Rev. ch. 114, p. 274.

Up to the time of the passage of this act, no treaty had been made and entered into between North Carolina, as a state, and the Cherokee Indians, nor any reservation made by the General Assembly of the State of North Carolina to the Cherokees; but a joint treaty was made and concluded by and between the States of Virginia and North Carolina and the Cherokee Indians at the Long Island of Holston on July 20, 1777, by Messrs. Preston, Christian and Shelby, who were appointed commissioners on the part of Virginia, and Messrs. Avery, Sharp, Winston and Lanier, who were appointed commissioners on the part of North Carolina, and the Chiefs and head men of the Cherokee Nation, by the terms of which there was reserved and set apart for the Cherokee Indians as a hunting ground, occupancy, etc., all the lands west of the Blue Ridge in what is now North Carolina and a part of the land in what is now Tennessee, and which included among other lands the French Broad Valley.

The Long Island of Holston, referred to in the treaty of July 20, 1777, is on the Holston River just below the Virginia line and what was then in North Carolina but now the State of Tennessee. North Carolina ceded to the United States what is now the State of Tennessee during the year 1790. See act of General Assembly of North Carolina passed during the year 1789 authorizing this deed of cession set out on pages 171 to 174 inclusive of the Second Volume of the Revised Statutes of North Carolina of 1836, entitled "An Act For The Purpose of Ceding To The United States of America Certain Western Lands Therein Described." See deed of cession set out in L. U. S., page 85.

See report of this treaty set out on page 381, First Volume of Dr. Sondley's History of Buncombe County, N. C.

See full contents of treaty of Long Island of Holston on the 20th of July, 1777, set out in full on pages 150, etc., of Powell's book of 1883-4.

At the next session of the General Assembly of North Carolina following the making of this treaty, an act was passed ratifying and confirming the same and prohibiting the entry and grant of any lands within the boundary reserved to the Cherokees. See this act referred to and set out on page 150 of Powell's book aforesaid.

By the fifth section of an act passed and ratified by the General

Assembly of North Carolina in the year 1783, Ch. 185, entitled, "An act for opening the land office for the redemption of specie and other certificates and discharging the arrears due to the Army," a boundary of land was reserved for the use, enjoyment, and as a hunting ground for the Cherokee Indians in words as follows:

"And be it further enacted, that the Cherokee Indians shall have and enjoy all that tract of land bounded as follows, to-wit: Beginning on the Tennessee where the southern boundary of the state intersects the same nearest to the Chickamauga towns, thence up the middle of the Tennessee and Holston to the middle of French Broad, thence up the middle of the French Broad River (which lines are not to include any island or islands in the said river) to the mouth of Big Pigeon River, thence up the same to the head thereof, thence along the dividing ridge between the water of Pigeon River and Tuckaseegie River to the southern boundary of this state; and that the lands contained within the aforesaid bounds shall be and are hereby reserved unto the said Cherokee Indians and their nation forever, anything herein to the contrary notwithstanding."

And the sixth, or next section of the same act prohibited the entry and grant of any of the lands reserved to the Indians aforesaid, in words as follows:

"And be is further enacted, that no person shall enter and survey any land within the bounds set apart for the Cherokee Indians under the penalty of fifty pounds specie for every such entry so made, to be recovered in any court of law in this state by and to the use of any person who will sue for the same, and all such entries and grants thereupon, if any, should be made, shall be utterly void."

(In referring to this act hereafter, I will refer to the fifth section as the "fifth section of the Act of 1783," and refer to the sixth section as the "sixth section of the Act of 1783".)

This act was passed before the State of Tennessee was ceded by North Carolina to the United States, and a part of the land set forth in the boundary set apart to the Cherokee Indians above described is now in the State of Tennessee.

The effect of the above act was to repeal the act of 1778 prohibiting the entry and grant of land reserved to the Cherokees by the Treaty of the Long Island of Holston on July 20, 1777, from the top of the Blue Ridge back to Pigeon River; but to prohibit the entry and grant of any land lying within the boundary reserved to the Cherokees by the Act of 1783 west of Pigeon River in this state.

Rowan County was created by an act of the General Assembly of North Carolina during the year 1753 and was taken from a part of Anson County by the name of Rowan County and St. Luke's Parish. See this act set out on pages 158-59, Second Volume of Revised Statutes of North Carolina of 1836. By reference to this act it will be seen that the boundary of Rowan extended westward as far as inhabited.

The following is a copy of the Act creating Rowan County:

AN ACT FOR ERECTING THE UPPER PART OF ANSON COUNTY INTO A COUNTY AND PARISH, BY THE NAME OF ROWAN COUNTY AND ST. LUKE'S PARISH; AND FOR AP-POINTING A PLACE FOR HOLDING A COURT IN SAID COUN-TY. (Passed in the year 1753.)

2. "We pray it may be enacted, *And be it enacted, by the Honorable Matthew Rowan, Esq., President, by and with the advice and consent of His Majesty's Council, and the General Assembly of this province, and by the authority of the same,* That Anson County be divided by a line, to begin where Anson line was to cross Earl Granville's line, and from thence, in a direct line, north, to the Virginia line; and that the said county be bounded to the north by the Virginia line, and to the sounth by the southernmost line of Earl Granville's land; and that the upper part of the said county, so laid off and divided, be erected into a county and parish, by the name of Rowan County and St. Luke's Parish; and that all the inhabitants to the westward of the said line, and included within the before mentioned boundaries, shall belong and appertain to Rowan County; and that the said county and parish shall enjoy all and every the privileges, which any other county in this province holds or enjoys."

It is a well-known historical fact that Samuel Davidson was the first white man who attempted to settle on lands in this state west of the Blue Ridge and who settled on land at the foot of Jones Mountain on Christian Creek, a tributary of Swannanoa River, and built his cabin there during the latter part of the year 1784 and was murdered during the same year by the Cherokee Indians. For full particulars as to the attempted settlement by Samuel Davidson on the land above referred to and his being murdered by the Cherokee Indians, see report made by Dr. Sondley in reference to this matter, set out on pages 396, etc., First Volume of Dr. Sondley's History of Buncombe County. While there might have been, and no doubt were, hunting parties that crossed over the Blue Ridge from the east side and hunted on lands west of the Blue Ridge in this state prior to the year 1784, Samuel Davidson appears to have been the first white man who attempt-ed to settle on any land west of the Blue Ridge in this state. But on the seventh day of August, 1787, a grant was issued by the state to William and James Davidson for 640 acres of land lying in Burke County on both sides of Savannah River, which afterwards took the name of Swannanoa River, in the locality of what is now Biltmore, and another grant was issued on the same date to William Moore for 450 acres of land on Hominy Creek, lying on the road between the

Sand Hill Church and Enka, as well as some other grants for land up on French Broad River near the mouth of Cathey's Creek in what is now Transylvania County, N. C., and the grantees no doubt took possession of the land about the time or before the granting of the same. I will later on set out copies and descriptions of some of these grants and comment on the same.

Burke County was created in 1777 taken from Rowan County by an act of the General Assembly of North Carolina. See this act set out on pages 108, etc., of the Second Volume of the Revised Statutes of North Carolina of 1836. The following is a copy of the act creating Burke County:

AN ACT FOR DIVIDING ROWAN COUNTY, AND OTHER PURPOSES THEREIN MENTIONED. (Passed in the year 1777.)

"Whereas the large extent of the county of Rowan, renders it grievous and troublesome to many of the inhabitants thereof, to attend the courts and general elections, and other public meetings appointed therein;

1. BE IT THEREFORE ENACTED BY THE GENERAL ASSEMBLY OF THE STATE OF NORTH CAROLINA, AND BY THE AUTHORITY OF THE SAME, That from and after the first day of June next, the said county of Rowan be divided by a line beginning at the Catawba River, on the line between Rowan and Tryon Counties; thence running up the meanders of said river to the north end of an island, known by the name of the Three Cornered Island; thence north to the ridge that divides the Yadkin and Catawba waters, then westerly along the ridge to the mountain which divides the eastern and western waters, commonly known by the name of the Blue Mountain. And that all that part of the late county of Rowan, which lies to the east of the said dividing line, shall continue and remain a distinct county by the name of Rowan; and all that other part of the said county thenceforth be erected into a new and distinct county, by the name of Burke."

By reference to this act it will be seen that none of the calls in the act creating Burke County extended west of the Blue Ridge, but the last call or closing line of the act was left out and that Rowan County lay east of Burke County. I will comment later on on the effect of the failure to include the closing line of this act.

Rutherford County was created in 1779 and was taken from what was formerly known as Tryon County, but the name of which was changed to Lincoln. See this Act set out on Page 159, Second Volume of Revised Statutes of North Carolina of 1836. The following is a copy of this Act:

AN ACT FOR DIVIDING TRYON COUNTY INTO TWO DISTINCT COUNTIES BY THE NAMES OF LINCOLN AND RUTHERFORD, AND FOR OTHER PURPOSES THEREIN MENTIONED. (Passed in the year 1779.)

1. "Whereas the large extent of the County of Tryon renders the attendance of the inhabitants on the extreme parts of the said county to do public duties extremely difficult and expensive; For remedy whereof,

2. BE IT ENACTED, ETC., That from and after the passing of this act, the County of Tryon shall be divided into two distinct counties, by a line beginning at the south line near Broad River, on the dividing ridge between Buffalo Creek and Little Broad River, thence along the said ridge to the line of Burke County, thence along the said line to the old Cherokee line, thence a due west course to the top of a dividing ridge between the eastern and western waters, thence along the said ridge to the old line claimed by South Carolina; and all that part of the said county which lies on the east side of the said line shall be called and known by the name of Lincoln County, and all that part of the county which lies on the other or west side thereof, shall be called and known by the name of Rutherford County."

By reference to this act it will be seen that Rutherford County lay to the south of Burke County and only extended to the top of the Blue Ridge.

During the year 1788 an act was passed for establishing the dividing line between the counties of Burke and Rutherford. See this act set out on page 109, Second Volume Revised Statutes of North Carolina of 1836. The following is a copy of this act:

AN ACT FOR ESTABLISHING THE DIVIDING LINE BETWEEN THE COUNTIES OF BURKE AND RUTHERFORD. (Passed in the year 1788.)

"Whereas the dividing line between the Counties of Burke and Rutherford hath not yet been established, in consequence of which the lands west of the Appalachian Mountain have been indiscriminately entered in the respective counties, contrary to the intent and meaning of an act of assembly in that case made and provided:

1. BE IT THEREFORE ENACTED, ETC., That the lines as laid out, marked and extended by Joseph M'Dowell, junior, in the year one thousand seven hundred and eighty five, viz.: Beginning at the west point of the line that formerly divided the above said counties, thence west to the Indian boundary as in the act of assembly of the seventeenth of May, one thousand seven hundred and eighty three; which line is hereby established to be the dividing line between the counties of Burke and Rutherford."

The Indian boundary above referred to was the boundary reserved to the Cherokees by the fifth section of the Act of 1783, as this act was ratified on the 17th of May, 1783.

When I read over carefully the act creating Burke County, before cited, it appeared to me that under the calls set out in the act that Burke County would not extend west of the Blue Ridge, or at least it was questionable, and as I had always heard that Burke County extended westward to the Mississippi River or at least to the western limits of North Carolina, I decided to consult some of the leading attorneys in the City of Asheville in reference to this matter and get their opinion on this subject; and accordingly I consulted Mr. Kingland Van Winkle, Mr. J. G. Merrimon, Mr. Joseph F. Ford, and Mr. J. J. Alexander, one of the title examiners in the United States Forest Service here in the City of Asheville.

In discussing the matter with these gentlemen I submitted to them the reasons why it appeared to me that Burke County would not extend west of the Blue Ridge in this state, and that the General Assembly of North Carolina in creating Burke County did not intend that the same should extend west of the Blue Ridge in this state, or at least that it was questionable, which reasons were given by me as follows:

First, that during the same year that Burke County was created in 1777 the Treaty of the Long Island of Holston was entered into between the States of Virginia and North Carolina and the Cherokees on the 20th of July, 1777, by the terms of which all the lands lying west of the Blue Ridge in what is now this state and a part of what is now Tennessee was reserved to the Cherokees for use of the Cherokees as a hunting ground and occupancy, and the next session of the General Assembly of North Carolina following this treaty in 1778 ratified and confirmed the same and prohibited the entry and grant within the boundary reserved to the Cherokees; and I was strongly impressed with the idea that it was not the intention of the General Assembly of North Carolina in creating Burke County to extend the same west of the Blue Ridge so as to interfere with the right of the Cherokees.

Second, this view of the matter was strengthened by the provisions of the first act of the Legislature of North Carolina during the year 1777, providing a method by which the vacant lands of the state might be entered and granted. This act provided among other things that it was "the duty of the justices of the peace of each county to elect an entry taker, who shall receive entries for any lands lying in such county, which have not been granted by the Crown of Great Britain or the Lords Proprietors of Carolina or any of them in fee before the 4th day of July, 1776, or which accrued or shall accrue to the state by treaty or conquest"; and it was not intended to create any county that would interfere with any territory reserved by the state to the Cherokees until the title of the Cherokees was extingushed by treaty or purchase.

Third, that when Rowan County was created during the year 1753 it only extended westward so far as the same was inhabited.

Now it is evident that the act creating Rowan County only intended to extend westward to the extent that the same was inhabited by white citizens and not include any part of Western North Carolina not settled by white citizens and especially any part of North Carolina west of the Blue Ridge; for it was a well-known historical fact that at that time a good part of the land lying for some distance east of the Blue Ridge was not settled by white citizens and that all the land west of the Blue Ridge in this state was then occupied by the Cherokee Indians, and that neither the persons nor property of the Cherokees was subject to the control and jurisdiction of the State of North Carolina, and the Cherokees exercised their own self-government; and it was not until after the Treaty of New Echota, Georgia, on December 29, 1835, and the bulk of the Cherokees were moved to the Indian territory that the courts of the State of North Carolina began to exercise jurisdiction over the persons and property of the Indians, and then only to a limited extent.

See State vs. To-cha-na-tah, reported in 64 N. C. R., pages 521, etc.

By reference to the opinion of the court in this case it will be seen that neither the civil nor criminal laws of this state were extended over the persons and property of the Cherokees until the year 1838, this being the year that the Cherokees were forcibly removed from the territory occupied by them in this and other states east of the Mississippi River to the Indian territory under the Treaty of New Echota, Georgia, of December 29, 1835; and I fail to find any records of legislation of our state or decisions of our Supreme Court where the civil and criminal laws of the state were extended over the persons and property of the Cherokees prior to the time of their forcible removal to the Indian territory in 1838, except to prevent encroachment by the whites on the land reserved to the Cherokees by the Treaty of the Long Island of Holston of July 20, 1777, and the boundary of land reserved to the Cherokees west of Pigeon River in this state by the fifth section of the Act of 1783 aforesaid.

In support of the position that even after the removal of the Cherokees to the Indian territory in 1838 the courts of this state only extended to a limited extent the civil and criminal laws over the persons and property of the Cherokees, I call attention to an article written by the noted writer, Charles Lanman, in 1848, who paid a visit to the Qualla Town Indians in what is now Jackson and Swain Counties. This article describes the status, habits, and life of these Indians during that period, and appears on page 79, Volume 2, Boyd's History of North Carolina, and is in words and figures as follows:

"About three-fourths of the entire population can read in their own language, and, though the majority of them understand English, a very few can speak the language. They practice, to a considerable extent, the science of agriculture, and have acquired such a knowledge of the mechanic arts as answers them for all ordinary purposes, for they manufacture their own clothing, their own plows, and other farming utensils, their own axes, and even their own guns. Their women are no longer treated as slaves, but as equals; the men labor in the fields and their wives are devoted entirely to household employments. They keep the same domestic animals that are kept by their white neighbors, and cultivate all the common grains of the country. They are probably as temperate as any other class of people on the face of the earth, honest in their business intercourse, moral in their thoughts, words, and deeds, and distinguished for their faithfulness in performing the duties of religion. They are chiefly Methodists and Baptists, and have regularly ordained ministers who preach to them on every Sabbath, and they have also abandoned many of their more senseless superstitions. They have their own court and try their criminals by a regular jury. Their judges and lawyers are chosen from among themselves. They keep in order the public roads leading through their settlement. By a law of the state they have a right to vote, but seldom exercise that right, as they do not like the idea of being identified with any of the political parties. Excepting on festive days they dress after the manner of the white man, but far more picturesquely. They live in small log houses of their own construction, and have everything they need or desire in the way of food. They are, in fact, the happiest community I have yet met with in this southern country."

Mr. Lanman, who wrote this article, was at one time Private Secretary of Daniel Webster when he was United States Senator from the State of Massachusetts, and who wrote a number of articles on Western North Carolina about that time.

See reference made to Charles Lanman by Dr. Sondley on pages 409, etc., First Volume Sondley's History of Buncombe County.

THE FOLLOWING IS INFORMATION OBTAINED FROM JOSEPH F. FORD, PERTAINING TO THE LOCATION OF BURKE COUNTY

In the Library there is a printed pamphlet containing records of early settlers of Rowan County, written by Eugene H. Dean, 1914, in which he treats of the establishment and records of Burke County with respect to its establishment and location. He says that Rowan County was established with the same eastern boundary as Anson County (79½° Long., 35½° Lat., as the southern boundary), the Virginia line as the northern boundary and the western waters as the western boundary. From 1777 to 1836 it was (referring to Burke County) continually sliced until it was left in area as it is today. The boundary of Anson County lay north of the Granville line.

Ashe's History Of North Carolina

Ashe says that Rowan County, established in 1753, was part of Anson County, which lay north of Granville's line (this refers to the part of Rowan County sliced from Anson County, 1773). Anson was cut off to form Rowan. Boundaries of these new counties extended to the Blue Ridge Mountains and beyond.

Mr. Ford says that appearing in the Asheville Times, December 4, 1936, is a copy of the History of Burke County as given in a talk over radio by Miss Beatrice Cobb. The following is taken from this talk: "1777 Burke County formed. For the time it embraced not only all of Western North Carolina and extended as we have been wont to say, to the Mississippi River, but as a matter of fact, it had no western boundary."

When I first took up and discussed this matter with Mr. Van Winkle he said that the reason why the last call or closing line was omitted from the act creating Burke County was to extend the western limits of Burke County westward as far as the same would extend under the act creating Rowan County and counties from which Rowan was taken, but admitted that there was a question as to whether or not it was intended to extend Burke County any further than was inhabited by white people, and on account of there being a question in the mind of Mr. Van Winkle as to how far Burke County extended westward he went to work and found an act creating Washington County, which now covers all of what is the State of Tennessee, and which act also defined the boundary lines of Burke County, and which act is in words and figures as follows:

Chapter 31, Laws Of 1777.

"An Act for erecting the district of Washington into a county, by the name of Washington County.

1. Be it enacted by the General Assembly of the State of North Carolina, and it is hereby enacted by the authority of the same, That the late district of Washington, and all that part of this state comprehended within the following lines, shall be erected into a new and distinct county, by the name of Washington County, viz. Beginning at the most northwesterly part of the County of Wilkes, on the Virginia line; thence running with the line of Wilkes County, to a point thirty-six miles south of the Virginia line; thence due west, to the ridge of the Great Iron Mountain which heretofore divided the hunting grounds of the Overhill Cherokees, from those of the Middle Settlements, and Valley; thence running a southwesterly course, along the said ridge to the Unacoy Mountain, where the trading path crosses the same from

the Valley to the Overhills; thence south with the line of this state, adjoining the State of South Carolina; thence due west, to the great river Mississippi; thence up the said river the courses thereof, to a point due west from the beginning; thence due east with the line of this state, to the beginning. And it is hereby declared, that all that part of this state comprehended within the lines aforesaid, shall from henceforth be and remain the County of Washington, and shall be, and is hereby declared to be part of the District of Salisbury.

II. And be it further enacted by the authority aforesaid, and it is hereby declared, That all that part of this state lying west of Rowan County, and south of the County of Washington, shall be, and is hereby declared to be part of the County of Burke."

But by reference to this act it will be seen that unless Burke County extended westward to the Mississippi River under the act creating Burke County in 1777, before cited, the western limits of Burke County only extended westward to about the present western limits of the State of North Carolina, and that Burke County included all the territory east of Washington County back to Rowan County and that all the area between what is now the western limits of this state and the Mississippi River was included in Washington County, which covered practically all of what is now the State of Tennessee. And after Mr. Van Winkle called my attention to the act creating Washington County, which act defined the boundaries of Burke County, the writer admitted that all the territory west of the Blue Ridge in what is now North Carolina was a part of Burke County.

Mr. Van Winkle, in reply to my suggestion that it was not the intention of the General Assembly of North Carolina to include in any county any land occupied by the Cherokees until the title of the Cherokees was extinguished by treaty, called my attention to the fact that when Buncombe County was created, hereafter set out, during the year 1792, that the same included all the territory west of the Blue Ridge in what is now this state, and at that time the title of the Cherokees had only been extinguished to the land occupied by them under the fifth section of the Act of 1783 up to the Holston Treaty line; and furthermore, that at the time of the passage of the Act in 1777 creating Washington County and defining the boundary lines of Burke County, a good part of what is now the State of Tennessee was occupied by the Cherokees.

So the writer and the general public is indebted to Mr. Van Winkle for information relative to the boundary lines of Burke County that does not seem to have been discovered by Mr. Ashe, Mr. Connor, and other historians referred to in the communication of Mr. Ford, or historians not mentioned by Mr. Ford. I can very well understand, however, why these historians failed to secure the information as to the boundary lines of Burke County, as it would hardly be expected for them to look to an act creating Washington County for information relative to the location of Burke County.

When I discussed the matter of the western limits of Burke County with Mr. J. G. Merrimon, he said he had always understood that the western limits of Burke County was the Mississippi River and that when Buncombe County was created it was taken from Burke and Rutherford Counties and included all the territory now west of the Blue Ridge in this state. Mr. Merrimon said that up to that time he had been too busy to make an investigation of the matter, but said he was under the impression that Dr. Sondley in his History of Buncombe County had gone into a full discussion of the creation of Burke and other counties in Western North Carolina, and suggested that I see what Dr. Sondley had to say about the matter, and I then made a thorough investigation of Dr. Sondley's history, but I failed to find where he made any specific report on the western limits of Burke County.

I next took up and discussed the matter with Mr. J. J. Alexander, one of the Title Examiners in the office of the United States Forest Service here in Asheville, knowing that Mr. Alexander had made a thorough study of the acts of the Colonial goverment and the acts of the General Assembly of this state in the creation of counties in the state and the history of land titles generally in this state, and he prepared and furnished me with a history of the acts of this state from the formation of the County of Anson in 1749 to the formation of the County of Buncombe in 1791, and their relation to the Earl of Granville's southern boundary of 1728, entitled "A SKETCH OF THE ORIGIN OF COUNTIES AND THEIR DESCRIPTIONS FROM THE FORMATION OF THE COUNTY OF ANSON IN 1749 TO THE FORMATION OF THE COUNTY OF BUNCOMBE IN 1791, AND THEIR RELATION TO THE EARL OF GRANVILLE'S SOUTHERN BOUNDARY LINE OF 1728."

This history is in words and figures as follows:

"King Charles II of England on March 24, 1663, granted to eight of his Lords all the territory between North Latitude 31° and 36°, and William Drummond was their first governor (Proprietary). In the year 1665 a second charter to the same Proprietors extended the limits to 36° 30' North.

In the year 1728, seven of the Lords Proprietors sold their interests to George II, then King of England. The eighth Proprietor, the Earl of Granville, or John Lord Carteret, retained his one-eighth interest, which was set off to him in a strip of land seventy miles wide south of and next to the southern boundary line of the State of Virginia. This line is approximately North Latuted 35° 30' and may be designated on the map of the State of North Carolina running east to west through the Town of Selma, Johnston County, the southern boundary line of the present Randolph County, the northern boundary line of Cabarrus County and directly west, just south of Candler, Buncombe County, and also south of Canton, Haywood County, and north of Waynesville, Haywood County, to the Tennessee state line. This, he, or his heirs, owned at the time of the Revolutionary War, except that portion of same that had been theretofore granted. This line plays an important part in the following years in the creation of North Carolina counties, especially in the western portion of the state.

The County of Anson was formed in the year 1749 from the County of Bladen, which county was formed from New Hanover in 1734. The description of Bladen County is vague and indefinite, but states that the line runs west to the bounds of the government. The description of the County of Anson is as follows:

'That Bladen County be divided by a line, beginning at the place where the south line of this province crosseth the westermost branch of Little Pee-Dee River, then by a straight line to a place where the commissioners for running the southern boundary of this province crosseth that branch of Little Pee-Dee River, called Drowning Creek, thence up that branch to the head thereof; then by a line, to run, as near as may be, equidistant, from Saxaphaw River, and Great Pee-Dee River; and that the upper part of the said county and parish so laid off and undivided, be erected into a county and parish, by the name of Anson County, and St. George's Parish, and that all the inhabitants to the westward of the aforementioned dividing line, shall belong and appertain to Anson County.'

The eastern boundary of the County of Anson runs east from the South Carolina line to the southwestern corner of Hoke County, thence with the western boundary line of said county to Drowning Creek, thence up Drowning Creek to a point just north of Candor, Montgomery County, thence a line directly north through the Counties of Randolph, Guilford and Rockingham to the Virginia state line. Anson County, by this description, included land lying north and south of the boundary of the Earl of Granville.

The County of Rowan was created in the year 1753 and is described as follows:

'That Anson County be divided by a line, to begin where Anson line was to cross Earl Granville's line, and from thence, in a direct line, north, to the Virginia line, and that the said county be bounded to the north by the Virginia line, and to the south by the southermost line of Earl Granville's land; and that the upper part of said county, so laid off and divided, be erected into a county and parish by the name of Rowan County, and St. Luke's Parish; and that all the inhabitants of the westward of the said line, and included within the beforementioned boundaries, shall belong and appertain to Rowan County:'

The County of Mecklenburg was formed from Anson County in the year 1762 and is described as follows:

'The said County of Anson shall be, and is hereby divided into two distinct counties, by a line beginning at Lord Carteret's line, six miles northeast from Captain Charles Hart's plantation on Buffalo Creek, and to run from thence to the mouth of Clear Creek which empties itself into Rocky River, below Captain Adam Alexander's; and from thence due south, to the bounds of the Province of South Carolina; and that all that part of the said county which lies to the eastward of the said dividing line, shall be a distinct county, and remain and be called by the name of Anson County; and that all that part of the said county lying to the westward of said dividing line, shall be thenceforth one other distinct county, and called by the name of Mecklenburg. . . .'

The description of Mecklenburg County, when created, included all that portion of Anson County lying south of the boundary of the Earl of Granville and west of the western line of Stanley County to where same intersects with Union County direct south to the State of South Carolina.

The County of Tryon was formed from Mecklenburg in the year 1768 and is described as follows:

'. . . the said County of Mecklenburg shall be, and is hereby divided into two distinct counties and parishes, by a line beginning at Earl Granville's line, where it crosses the Catawba River; and the said river to be the line to the South Carolina line; and that all that part of the said county which lies to the eastward of the said dividing line shall be a distinct county and parish, and remain and be called by the name of Mecklenburg County, and St. Martin's Parish; and that all that part of the county lying to the westward of the said dividing line shall be one other distinct county and parish, and be and remain by the name of Tryon County and St. Thomas's Parish. . . .'

The description of Tryon County covers all that portion of Mecklenburg County lying between the southern boundary line of the Earl of Granville and the State of South Carolina, and west of the Catawba River. The boundary line between Rowan, Mecklenburg and Tryon was authorized to be run in the year 1770 and is in language as follows:

'. . . to run the dividing line between the said County of Rowan, and the Counties of Mecklenburg and Tryon; beginning at Cold Water, where John Patterson's upper line crosses the creek; thence due west until it intersects the Cherokee Indian line; which said line, when run by the commissioners aforesaid, or a majority of them, shall by them be entered on record in the court of each of the said counties, and shall hereafter be deemed and taken to be the dividing lines between the said counties.'

The County of Burke was formed from Rowan County in the year

1777 and is described as follows:

'. . . Beginning at the Catawba River, on the line between Rowan and Tryon Counties, thence running up the meanders of said river to the north end of an island, known by the name of the Three Cornered Island; thence north to the ridge that divides the Yadkin and Catawba waters; thence westerly along the ridge to the mountain which divides the eastern and western waters, commonly known by the name of the Blue Mountain. And that all that part of the late County of Rowan which lies to the east of the said dividing line, shall continue and remain a distinct county, by the name of Rowan; and all that other part of said County of Rowan which lies west and south of the said dividing line, shall thenceforth be erected into a new and distinct county, by the name of Burke. . .'

It is clear from this description of Burke County that same lies north of the Counties of Mecklenburg and Tryon and does not extend south of Earl Granville's southern line, which was the southern boundary line of the County of Rowan from which Burke County was created.

The County of Washington, the present State of Tennessee, was formed from what was known as the Washington District in 1777. Roughly it was that section of Tennessee west of the County of Wilkes, east of the Mississippi River and south of the Virginia state line. This territory had beeen allowed three representatives in the General Assembly of North Carolina in the year 1776, and was the territory ceded to the United States in the year 1790 and is described as follows:

'. . . Beginning at the most northwesterly part of the County of Wilkes, on the Virginia line; thence running with the line of Wilkes County, to a point thirty six miles south of the Virginia line; thence due west, to the ridge of the great iron mountain which heretofore divided the hunting grounds of the Overhill Cherokees, from those of the Middle Settlements and Valley; thence running a southwesterly course, along the said ridge, to the Unacoy Mountain, where the trading path crosses the same from the Valley to the Overhills; thence south with the line of this state, adjoining the State of South Carolina; thence due west, to the great river Mississippi; thence up the said river the courses thereof, to a point due west from the beginning; thence due east with the line of this state, to the beginning: And it is hereby declared, that all that part of this state comprehended within the lines aforesaid shall from henceforth be and remain the County of Washington, and shall be, and is hereby declared to be part of the District of Salisbury.

II. And be it further enacted by the authority aforesaid, and it is hereby declared, That all that part of this state lying west of Rowan County, and south of the County of Washington, shall be, and is hereby declared to be part of the County of Burke.'

It will be noted from reading the foregoing description that same is vague and indefinite. There have been some who in the past contended that the eastern boundary line of the County of Washington should run directly south from the Unicoi Mountains in Madison County, which line would run near the mouth of Big Laurel Creek and between the towns of Hot Springs and Marshall in Madison County, North Carolina, to the South Carolina line. I feel that we can safely assume that the eastern boundary line of the County of Washington is the same boundary line, though more accurately described, in the Deed of Cession from the State of North Carolina, to the United States covering the present State of Tennessee, dated February 25, 1790. The description in this Deed of Cession states that it follows Iron Mountain to where Nolachucky River runs through the same, thence to the top of the Bald, thence along the extreme height of said mountain to the Painted Rocks on the French Broad River, thence along the ridge of said mountain to the place where it is called the Great Iron or Smoky Mountains (this point lies within the Great Smoky Mountain National Park), thence along the extreme height of the said mountain to the place where it is called Unicoi or Unaka Mountain between the Indian towns of Cowee and Old Chota, thence along the main ridge of said mountain to the southern boundary of this state.

I am of the opinion that the Iron Mountain mentioned in the act establishing the County of Washington is the Great Iron or Smoky Mountain which divides the hunting grounds of the Overhill Cherokees from those of the Middle Settlements and Valleys and that the Unicoi Mountain mentioned in the act is the Unaka or Unicoi Mountain forming the northern and western boundaries of the present Counties of Cherokee and Graham in the southwestern corner of the State of North Carolina as the Indian town of Cowee was located near Murphy, the county seat of Cherokee County, and the Indian town of Old Chota was in the State of Tennessee near the town of Loudon, and that the trading path referred to in said act is the approximate location of the present highway between Murphy, North Carolina, and Madisonville, Tennessee. This highway crosses said mountain at the point where the line between the States of North Carolina and Tennessee runs directly south to the line of the State of Georgia.

The County of Tryon established in 1768 was abolished during the year 1779 and from its boundaries two counties were formed: Lincoln County on the east and Rutherford County on the west. A description of the Counties of Lincoln and Rutherford is as follows:

'. . . the County of Tryon shall be divided into two distinct counties, by a line beginning at the south line, near Broad River, on the dividing ridge between Buffalo Creek and Little Broad River, thence along said ridge, to the line of Burke, thence along said line unto the old Cherokee line, thence a due west course into the top of a dividing ridge between the Eastering and Westering waters, thence along said ridge unto the old line claimed by South Carolina, and all that part of the said county which lies on the east side of the said line shall be called, and known by the name of Lincoln County, and all that part of the county which lies on the other or west side thereof, shall be called and known by the name of Rutherford County. . .'

The eastern line and the first line called for in this description crosses the present County of Cleveland and runs almost directly north from the Town of Earl, through Bellwood, to Earl Granville's southern boundary line or the line of Burke County. Then this line runs west to the dividing ridge between the eastern and western waters, which is evidently the Blue Ridge, thence along said ridge to the South Carolina line. The calls here stop and the act states that all land lying east of this line shall be Lincoln County and all land lying west, Rutherford County. While it is not clear from the act itself, it is evident that the line referred to as the dividing line between the Counties of Lincoln and Rutherford is the first line called for and is not the Blue Ridge.

The dividing line between Burke and Rutherford was authorized to be established in 1788,

'. . . That the line as laid out, marked and extended by Joseph M'Dowell, Junior, in the year one thousand seven hundred and eighty-five, viz: Beginning at the west point of the line that formerly divided the above counties, thence west to the Indian boundary as in the Act of Assembly of the seventeenth of May, one thousand seven hundred and eighty-three; which line is hereby established to be the dividing line between the counties of Burke and Rutherford; . . .'

The County of Buncombe was formed from the Counties of Burke and Rutherford in the year 1792, and includes roughly all that section of North Carolina lying west of the Blue Ridge, south of Toe River and between the States of Tennessee, Georgia and South Carolina.

In conclusion I will state that I am inclined to the opinion that it was never intended that Burke County extend south of the Earl of Granville's southern boundary line notwithstanding the second paragraph of the act creating the County of Washington that states that all that part of this state lying west of Rowan County and south of the county line of Washington should be declared to be the County of Burke. The land lying directly west of the County of Rowan would not extend south of this line though the land lying south of the County of Washington may cover the portion south of this line.

A further reason for this conclusion is that the line run by Joseph McDowell in 1785 to Pigeon River was only an extension of the Burke and Rutherford County line and no land was taken from Burke and added to Rutherford County."

While a good part of the history given by Mr. Alexander as to the creation of counties in this state does not have any special bearing on the title to lands west of the Blue Ridge in this state, I have incorporated the same in my report for the reason that it contains a lot of historical data that the public is interested in.

Dr. Sondley in Chapter XI on pages 306, etc., in the First Volume of his History of Buncombe County goes into a full discussion of the Granville line referred to by Mr. Alexander in his report. On pages 319 and 320 of his History of Buncombe County, Dr. Sondley in commenting on this line and the claim of those succeeding to the title of Lord Granville uses the following language:

"The Granville line after the first section would constitute the southern boundary of Chatham and prolonged from Haw River would constitute the southern boundaries of Randolph, Davidson, Rowan, and original Burke and the northern boundaries of Moore, Montgomery, Stanly, Cabarrus and Mecklenburg Counties, and pass through parts of Lincoln, Cleveland, and Rutherford Counties. If extended still further west it would pass through the southern portion of the original McDowell County and through Buncombe County near Buena Vista, through the middle of Haywood County and the northern part of Swain County into the State of Tennessee.

Soon after obtaining title in severalty to his land in North Carolina, the Earl of Granville established a land office at Edenton, North Carolina, and sold lands through his agents there. Then came in 1775 and 1776 the American Revolution and stopped all sales of the Granville lands, already lagging. During that war North Carolina passed several acts confiscating property therein of British subjects. Claimants to the Granville lands were British subjects, having acquired their claims under John Earl of Granville who died January 2, 1763, and under his son and heir Robert Earl of Granville, who died in 1776, by purchase. In none of these acts of confiscation were the Granville lands mentioned in express terms. Still the State of North Carolina assumed ownership and control of these lands in various statutes. After the close of the Revolutionary War two ejectment suits for the assertion of title to these lands by claimants of British citizenship were brought in the United States District Court at Raleigh, North Carolina, by "George William, Earl of Coventry, successor by devise to the Earl of Granville, against Nathaniel Allen and Josiah Collins and against William R. Davie, in 1801. On trial before Henry Potter, District Judge, at June term 1805 of that court judgments were rendered in the cases against the British claimants, plaintiff; and those judgments were carried by writ of error to the Supreme Court of the United States where, after pending some years the writs of error were dismissed, February 4, 1817, some writers say for want of bond, others say for want of prosecution, others say for the death of the plaintiff, Earl of Coventry. In 1823 the Supreme Court of the United States mentioned this Granville claim as an instance of forfeiture.

The Supreme Court of North Carolina has repeatedly decided that the Granville lands were forfeited to the State of North Carolina in the Revolutionary War as claims and property of an alien enemy. These North Carolina cases are most incorrect and not always consistent, however, in the statements of the facts. It is said that the British claimants to these Granville lands were, later on, indemnified for their loss by about two hundred and fifty thousand dollars in value. About half the counties of North Carolina being within the territory so allotted in severalty to John Lord Carteret, these suits produced much consternation in the state. The matter is now one of history only."

I will here state that Mr. J. J. Alexander appears to be of the opinion that when Joseph McDowell, Jr., ran the dividing line between Burke and Rutherford Counties from the top of the Blue Ridge to Pigeon River duing the year 1785 that he started from a point on top of the Blue Ridge where the Granville line struck the same and extended the Granville line the same course as located east of the Blue Ridge, which was practically an east and west line from the top of the Blue Ridge to Pigeon River; and Mr. Alexander and Mr. Moffett both seem to think that Dr. Sondley's location of the Granville line near Buena Vista is about right. Mr. Alexander is of the opinion that Joseph McDowell, Jr., when he ran the dividing line between Burke and Rutherford Counties during the year 1785 adopted the Granville line; in other words, that the dividing line run by Joseph McDowell, Jr., in 1785 between Burke and Rutherford Counties from the top of the Blue Ridge to Pigeon River and the Granville line are one and the same line; but Dr. Sondley locates the Joseph McDowell, Jr., line of 1785 four or five miles to the north of where he locates the Granville line at Buena Vista, as shown by my report later on, on page 28, etc.

I am of the opinion that in view of the fact that the Act of 1778 prohibiting the entry and grant of land reserved to the Cherokees by the Treaty of the Long Island of Holston of July 20, 1777, was repealed by the Act of 1782 above cited as to the lands lying west of and in between the Blue Ridge and Pigeon River that after the creation of Burke County by the Act of 1777 aforesaid, all the land lying west of and in between the Blue Ridge and Pigeon River became subject to entry and grant under the general entry and grant laws of this state, and all grants taken out within this area in Burke County between the time of the creation of Burke County in 1777 up to the year 1788 when the dividing line between Burke and Rutherford Counties was established according to the survey made by Joseph McDowell, Jr., during the year 1785, if properly described and properly authenticated would be valid grants, which would include among others, the grant to William and James Davidson for 640 acres of land, in the locality of Biltmore, issued on the 7th of August, 1787, hereinafter referred to and set out, and the grant to William Moore for 450 acres of land on Hominy Creek, issued on August 7, 1787, and grant No. 964 to

Joseph Morgan for 200 acres in Burke County, dated August 7, 1787, up on French Broad River in Transylvania County, N. C., hereinafter referred to and set out, and grant No. 1100 to James Miller for 640 acres of land in Burke County up on French Broad River in Transylvania County, N. C., dated December 15, 1787, hereinafter referred to and set out, and other grants issued within this area prior to the Act of 1788 above cited; and this, too, notwithstanding the fact that the title of the Cherokees may not have been extinguished to all the land granted to parties within this area by the Hopewell Treaty of November 28, 1785, and the Holston Treaty of July 2, 1791, hereinafter referred to and set out, as there was no prohibition against the entry and grant of lands lying between the Blue Ridge and Pigeon River in this state after the repeal of the Act of 1778 by the Act of 1782, above cited, and the state had the right to grant the fee in the land subject to the right of occupancy by the Cherokees; and when the title of the Cherokees was extinguished, this would relieve the land of the encumbrance according to the principle enunciated by the decision of the Supreme Court of the United States in the case of Latimer vs. Poteet reported in 14th Pt., page 4, (39 U. S. R.) I will take up and comment on the effect of this decision later in my report.

But as the act creating Rutherford County did not extend west of the Blue Ridge, all grants taken out in Rutherford County between the top of the Blue Ridge and Pigeon River during the interval between the creation of Rutherford County during the year 1779 and the Act of 1788 extending the line of Rutherford County from the top of the Blue Ridge back to Pigeon River according to the survey made by Joseph McDowell, Jr., in 1785, are absolutely void on account of the same having been granted for land as being in Rutherford County when Rutherford County did not, prior to the Act of 1788, extend west of the top of the Blue Ridge.

I think my view of this matter is sustained by the decision of our Supreme Court in the case of Avery vs. Strother rendered at June term 1802 of said court, reported in 1st N. C. R., page 560, which is directly in point in support of the fact that all grants taken out by persons on land in Rutherford County in between the top of the Blue Ridge and Pigeon River prior to the passage of the Act of 1788 were absolutely void.

The case of Avery vs. Strother involved a controversy as to the title to a 640-acre tract of land on the west side of Pigeon River that lay inside of the boundary reserved to the Cherokee Indians by the Act of 1783; and the defendant, Strother, contended that the grant under which the plaintiff, Avery, claimed title was void for two reasons:

First. The land was entered as being in Rutherford County when Rutherford County at that time only extended up to Pigeon River and not west of it, and the land in controversy was on the west side of

Pigeon River.

Second. That the land in controversy lay on the west side of Pigeon River and inside of the boundary of land reserved to the Cherokee Indians by the Act of 1783 and the paintiff's grant was taken out in violation of the 6th section of this act and was void.

The Supreme Court in this case sustained the contention of the defendant, Strother, on both grounds. For like reason, if the land lying in between the top of the Blue Ridge and Pigeon River was not in Rutherford County prior to the passage of the Act of 1788, then any grants taken out by persons in Rutherford County between the top of the Blue Ridge and Pigeon River prior to the Act of 1788 were absolutely void.

After the Act of 1788 was passed and ratified, above cited, accepting and adopting the line run by Joseph McDowell, Jr., from the top of the Blue Ridge to Pigeon River during the year 1785 as the dividing line between Burke and Rutherford Counties, all the territory lying to the north of this line was in Burke County and all to the south in Rutherford County; and after the passage and ratification of the Act of 1788 above cited, grants issued for land in Burke County south of this line would be void, and any grants issued for land in Rutherford County north of this line would be void, except as to grants issued for land in either county, a part of which lay in Burke and a part of which lay in Rutherford County, and in cases like this the grants have been validated by acts of our legislature.

I had occasion to look into this matter some years ago, and found the following authorities and decisions of our Supreme Court thereunder validating such grants:

See Section 7586 under chapter 128 entitled "State Lands", set out on page 1953 of the Code of 1927 of N. C.

Under Section 7586 grants issued upon such entries are declared to be good and valid against any entries thereafter made or grants issued thereon.

See decisions of our Supreme Court cited under Section 7586 in words as follows:

"Found in Two Counties. This section only extends to cases where the entry of land lying partly in two counties, which is unknown to the grantee, is made only in one county. In such cases the statute cures the defect. Harris vs. Norman, 96 N. C. 59, 2 S. E. 72."

But in cases where grants were issued for land for the entire tract in the wrong county, that is where the entire tract lay in another county, I failed to find any act validating such grants, and such grants have been held to be void in the cases cited under Section 7586 aforesaid in words as follows:

"Entry in County Where No Part of Land Lies. Land can only be entered in the county where it lies, and entry and grant in another county is void. Lunsford vs. Bostion, 16 N. C. 483; Harris vs. Norman, 96 N. C. 59, 2 S. E. 72; Avery vs. Strother, 1 N. C. 558."

I will now set out the information I have been able to secure from records and otherwise as to the point where Joseph McDowell, Jr., during the year 1785 started to run and ran the dividing line between Burke and Rutherford Counties from the top of the Blue Ridge back to Pigeon River.

I have heretofore called attention to the fact that the last call or closing line in the act creating Burke County was omitted and there does not appear to be anything in the acts creating either Burke or Rutherford Counties that will enable one to a certainty to locate the point where the southern boundary of Burke County would connect and tie on to Rutherford County on top of the Blue Ridge.

Now the 3rd call in the act creating Rutherford County is in words as follows: "thence a due west course to the top of a dividing ridge between the eastern and western waters", and I think it can be said that the point where this line struck the top of the Blue Ridge was the corner of Burke and Rutherford Counties at that date; and I think the chances are that this is the point from which Joseph McDowell, Jr., started to run the dividing line between Burke and Rutherford Counties, but the question is, where is this point on top of the Blue Ridge?

I find an act was passed by the General Assembly of North Carolina in 1786, which took from Burke County and gave to Rutherford County the territory formerly in Burke County, that lay to the south of the ridge dividing the waters of Little Broad River and Cane Creek. See this act set out on pages 159-160, Second Volume of Revised Statutes of N. C. of 1836.

It will be observed that this act was passed in 1786, about a year after Joseph McDowell, Jr., ran the dividing line between the Counties of Burke and Rutherford to Pigeon River in 1785; so it appears to me that when Joseph McDowell, Jr., ran the dividing line between Burke and Rutherford Counties, he started his survey on the line from the point between Burke and Rutherford Counties on top of the Blue Ridge and before that part of Little Broad River was taken from Burke and given to Rutherford County, and the line would start from the point on top of the Blue Ridge, which formerly divided Burke and Rutherford Counties before the passage of the Act of 1806, above cited.

I find that Dr. Sondley on page 441 in the First Volume of his History of Buncombe County, in referring to grants that were issued to William and James Davidson for land on Swannanoa River and to William Moore for land on Hominy Creek during the year 1787, and in referring to the dividing line between Burke and Rutherford Counties run by Joseph McDowell, Jr., during the year 1785 says:

"The earliest grants now known which issued for lands in that mountain country were dated August 7, 1787, and were for lands described as in Burke or in Rutherford County. Numerous other grants prior to that time have been issued for lands on the Swannanoa River and nearby, since the lands granted by them in that vicinity are mentioned in the grants of 1787; but such other grants are not registered in Buncombe County. In fact it seems that those of 1787 have not been so registered. These are a grant to William and James Davidson on what is now some of the southern part of Asheville, and a grant to William Moore for land on Hominy Creek.

At a period before this time the Swannanoa River was recognized as the dividing line down to French Broad of the territories west of the Blue Ridge between Burke County on the north and Rutherford County on the south. In 1785 Joseph McDowell, Jr., ran this dividing line, 'Beginning at the west point of the line that formerly divided the above said counties, (Rutherford and Burke), thence west to the Indian boundary as in the Act of Assembly of the seventeenth of May one thousand seven hundred and eighty-three.' This 'Indian boundary' was Big Pigeon River. McDowell's line crossed Swannanoa River from south to north about a half mile above Biltmore Avenue. In 1788 this survey was adopted by the state legislature."

Now it appears to me from what Dr. Sondley says, that prior to the time that Joseph McDowell, Jr., ran the dividing line between Burke and Rutherford Counties in 1785 from the top of the Blue Ridge back to Pigeon River, that Swannanoa River was recognized as the dividing line between the Counties of Burke and Rutherford down to the mouth of French Broad River; but when Joseph McDowell, Jr., ran or located this line during the year 1785, he did not recognize Swannanoa River as the dividing line between the two counties, as Dr. Sondley says that this line so run by Joseph McDowell, Jr., crossed Swannanoa River from "south to north" about a half mile above Biltmore Avenue. This statement in the History of Dr. Sondley must be a typographical error, for any line running from the corner of Burke and Rutherford Counties on top of the Blue Ridge to Pigeon River would be in a westerly direction, and a "south to north" line would be absolutely impossible, for it would run into Tennessee and never reach Pigeon River at any point. I think the chances are that Joseph McDowell, Jr., in locating the dividing line between Burke and Rutherford Counties from the top of the Blue Ridge to Pigeon River, commenced his survey on the corner of Burke and Rutherford Counties as the corner existed at that date on top of the Blue Ridge, and at the same point where the Granville line struck the top of the Blue Ridge, as the Granville line east of the top of the Blue Ridge was the dividing line between Burke and Rutherford Counties, and that Joseph McDowell, Jr., extended the dividing line between Burke and Rutherford Counties in the same course from the top of the Blue Ridge to Pigeon River, and the Granville line and the Joseph McDowell line are one and the same line. And from my knowledge of the geography of this section of country, this point would be between Hickory Nut Gap and Swannanoa Gap, as indicated on Moffett map; and I am inclined to think that this line would be about where Dr. Sondley locates the Granville line at Buena Vista, and that this line would strike Pigeon River about a mile above the Town of Canton.

At the time that Joseph McDowell, Jr., is said to have run or located the dividing line between Burke and Rutherford Counties during the year 1785 from the top of the Blue Ridge to Pigeon River there were very few, if any, whites settled west of the Blue Ridge; and as before stated, it is a well known historical fact that Samuel Davidson was the first white man who attempted to settle on lands west of the Blue Ridge, and this was in the fall of 1784; but if McDowell actually ran or located the line, this fact was no doubt made known to people who contemplated the entering and granting of lands in French Broad Valley; and parties hereinafter referred to and set out entered and granted lands on Swannanoa River, Hominy Creek, and French Broad River, under the impression that Rutherford County extended west of the Blue Ridge and took in all the territory that lay south of the line run by Joseph McDowell, Jr., in 1785; in fact, some parties hereinafter referred to, entered and granted lands up on French Broad River about the mouth of Cathey's Creek in what is now Transylvania County, N. C., about five miles above the Town of Brevard during the year 1783; but I fail to see how anyone by reading the act creating Rutherford County in 1779 would be able to locate any part of the county west of the Blue Ridge; but as before stated, when Washington County was created in 1777, which defined the boundary lines of Burke County, it (Burke County) included all the territory in what is now North Carolina west of the Blue Ridge until the act was passed in 1788 adopting the line run by Joseph McDowell, Jr., in 1785 as the dividing line between the two counties, after which time all the land lying south of that line was in Rutherford County, and all the land north of that line was in Burke County.

In the work I did in the investigation of the title for the Champion Fibre Company for its property at Canton during the years 1905-6, I found that a grant was issued by the state on August 22, 1795, being Grant No. 1251 to John and Joseph McDowell, calling to contain 640 acres of land in Burke County on both sides of Pigeon River, known as the Beaverdam Survey, that covers the lower part of the Town of Canton and a part of what is now known as the Town of Fibreville, and I found and located the original grant to this property. The following is a description of this tract of land containing 640 acres:

"Beginning on a white oak marked IND and runs west with the lower line of Joseph McDowell's tract of 640 acres three hundred poles to the river crossing same course one hundred and fifty-two poles to a stake, then north two hundred and twenty-seven poles to a stake, then east four hundred and fifty-two poles crossing the river to a stake, then south two hundred and twenty-seven poles crossing Beaverdam Creek to the beginning."

I failed, however, to locate any grant issued to Joseph McDowell for the 640-acre tract referred to in the first call set out in the description in Grant No. 1251 to John and Joseph McDowell, but was informed that it was a well known fact that this tract was granted to Joseph McDowell and was known as the Locust Oldfield survey and covered the land where the old Locust Oldfield Church formerly stood, and lay to the south of Grant No. 1251 to John and Joseph McDowell, Beaverdam Survey. The plants and most of the property of the Champion Paper and Fibre Company at Canton, N. C., are located on the Locust Oldfield Survey, and most of the Town of Canton is located on this survey, but a part is located on the Beaverdam Survey; and the chances are that this grant for 640 acres was issued to Joseph McDowell for land in Burke County, and I find that the grant issued to the plaintiff, Avery, for 640 acres of land on the west side of Pigeon River, which was the subject of litigation in the suit between Avery and Strother, above cited, called for land in Rutherford County, and which tract was on the west side of Pigeon River about two miles above the Town of Canton; and the chances are that when the grants were taken out by John and Joseph McDowell and by Avery, which was soon after the dividing line between Burke and Rutherford Counties was run by Joseph McDowell, Jr., in 1785, that these parties knew or were advised as to the location of the dividing line run by Joseph McDowell, Jr., in 1785, and that the grant issued to John and Joseph McDowell for 640 acres, and the grant issued to Joseph McDowell for 640 acres lying south of the same were both in Burke County and lay on the north side of the line run by Joseph McDowell, Jr., in 1785, and the land lying to the south of the Joseph McDowell tract was probably in Rutherford County; and Avery evidently laid his entry upon the idea that the Joseph McDowell line would be extended westward, west of Pigeon River, and the land granted by him would be in Rutherford County. This appears to be about the best evidence I have been able to find as to the location of the dividing line between Burke and Rutherford Counties.

I will here state that after such a long lapse of time and without more definite knowledge as to where the dividing line between Burke and Rutherford Counties was run by Joseph McDowell, Jr., in 1785, that where grants were issued to parties for land in either Burke or Rutherford Counties after the passage and ratification of the Act of 1788, that it would be very difficult for anyone to attack the validity of such grants on account of the entries having been laid and the grants obtained in the wrong county.

I think the chances are that Joseph McDowell, one of the grantees in Grant No. 1251, above referred to, was the same Joseph McDowell that ran the dividing line in 1785 between Burke and Rutherford Counties, and this same Joseph McDowell was a Major of the Catawba Militia who took an active part in the Battle of King's Mountain in 1780. See page 145 of Volume three of Theodore Roosevelt's work on the "Winning of the West," under head of chapter five, "King's Mountain, 1780."

I will here state that Avery, the plaintiff in the suit of Avery vs. Strother, above cited, was Waightstill Avery, who was the first Attorney-General of North Carolina and one of the most prominent lawyers of the state in his day and time, and was the same party who challenged Andrew Jackson to a duel, and who, it appears, fought a sham duel on the "hill on the southside of Jonesboro, Tenn.," about the time the State of Tennessee was admitted as a state into the Union. I say "sham" duel for the reason that when they met for the duel, it seems to have been arranged that neither party desired to injure the other, and both fired into the air, pistols being the weapons used. John Adair was Avery's second, Jackson's being unknown.

See report of this duel by Arthur on pages 357, etc., in his History of Western North Carolina, under head of "Duels".

I find that grants were issued by the State of North Carolina to persons between the years 1783 and 1788 for land between the Blue Ridge and Pigeon River as follows:

Grant No. 1031 to William Moore, issued on the 7th day of August, 1787, calling to contain 450 acres of land in Burke County on both sides of Hominy Creek. This grant was recorded in Book 187, page 296, records of Buncombe County, N. C., on November 3, 1913. The following is a copy of this grant as recorded in Buncombe County:

"STATE OF NORTH CAROLINA, No. 1031

To all whom these presents shall come, greeting.

KNOW ye that we for and in consideration of the sum of ten pounds for every hundred acres hereby granted paid unto our treasury by William Moore, have given and granted, and by these presents do give and grant unto the said William Moore, a tract of land, containing four hundred and fifty acres lying and being in our County of Burke on both sides of Hominy Creek and both sides of the path that leads from the fording of French Broad River to the Cherokee nation, beginning on a post oak, on the north side of the creek in a hollow, then west seventy five chains to a stake and two post oaks, then south crossing a large branch, the path and creek aforesaid above the ford Rutherfords Cross sixty chains to a stake, then east seventy five chains to a stake, then north passing the corner of his lower survey and crossing Stanning Creek to the beginning. As by the plat hereunto annexed doth appear; together with all woods, waters, mines, minerals, hereditaments and appurtenances, to the said land belonging or appertaining; to hold to the said William Moore, his heirs and assigns forever. Yielding and paying to us such sums of money yearly, or otherwise as our General Assembly from time to time may direct, provided always, that the said William Moore shall cause this grant to be registered in the Register's Office of our said County of Burke within twelve months, from the date hereof, otherwise the same shall be void and of none effect.

IN TESTIMONY whereof we have caused these our letters to be made patent and our Great Seal to be hereunto affixed. Witness Richord Caswell, Esquire, our Governor, Captain-General and Commander-in-Chief at Kinston the seventh day of August in the XI year of our Independence, and in the year of our Lord one thousand seven hundred and eighty seven."

Registered November 3, 1913, at 10 A. M., in Book No. 187, page 296, Records of Buncombe County, North Carolina.

Grant No. 912, issued by the state on the 7th day of August, 1787, to William and James Davidson for a tract of land calling to contain 640 acres in Burke County on both sides of Savannah. It appears that what is now Swannanoa River was known at the date of the issuing of this grant as Savannah, or Savana River. See copy of this grant set out on page 838 of Second Volume of Dr. Sondley's History of Buncombe County, and his comments on the location of the same, of which the following is a copy:

State Grant To William And James Davidson "Swannanoa Tract"
"STATE OF NORTH CAROLINA,

No. 912. Know ye that we have given and granted unto William and James Davidson a tract of land containing six hundred and forty acres lying and being in our County of Burke on both sides of Savannah, bounded on the west by William Steward and on the east by John McDowell, beginning at a water black oak the north side of Savannah near a small creek in a bottom, thence west three hundred and seventy two poles to a stake fifty two poles to a water oak said Steward's corner, thence south thirty degrees east forty poles to an oak saplin on the north bank of Savana, Steward's corner, thence south crossing Savanah thirty one and a half poles to a stake on Steward's line, thence east three hundred and fifty poles to a stake, thence north crossing the Savana to the beginning. To hold to the said William and James Davidson, their heirs and assigns forever. Dated 7th day of August, 1787.
"Rd CASWELL.

"J. GLASGOW, Secretary."

This is as the grant appears in the office of the Secretary of State of North Carolina, Book 65, page 358. This grant includes within its boundaries the southern portion of the present City of Asheville in the parts formerly constituting Kenilworth and Biltmore and also other lands in the vicinity of these portions. It will be seen that this grant was not recorded in Buncombe County, but appears in the office of the Secretary of State of North Carolina.

I have always heard that the William Moore tract was the first tract that was granted by the state to anyone for land west of the Blue Ridge in this state, but it appears that while this grant was issued on the same day as the grant that was issued to William and James Davidson that the number of the grant to William and James Davidson is 912, and that to William Moore is 1031. Besides, I find that Grant No. 54 was issued by the state to William Porter on October 11, 1783, for fifty acres of land in Rutherford County on Cabin Branch of Cathey's Creek, and that several other grants were issued to parties for land in Rutherford County during the year 1785 that lie on French Broad River in the locality of Cathey's Creek, about five miles above the Town of Brevard in what is now Transylvania County, N. C., which are several years older than Moore Grant No. 1031; and some other grants were issued to parties in that locality for land in Burke County during the year 1787. The dates of said grants, the names of the grantees, the description of said grants and the acreage contained therein are set out below.

Mr. J. J. Alexander, title examiner in the U. S. Forest Service Office here in Asheville, was kind enough to furnish me with copies of abstracts of grants, which the Forest Service Office had secured from the office of the Secretary of State, giving descriptions with plats attached of seven grants issued by the state to persons for land on French Broad River around the mouth of Cathey's Creek, up in what is now Transylvania County, N. C., bearing dates as follows:

State of North Carolina to William Porter, Grant No. 54, for 50 acres of land in Rutherford County, N. C., dated October 11, 1783, recorded in Book 45, page 317, in the Office of the Secretary of State.

State of North Carolina to Robert Gilkey, Grant No. 113, for 50 acres of land in Rutherford County, N. C., dated September 28, 1785, recorded in the Office of the Secretary of State in Book 58, page 129.

State of North Carolina to William Gilbert, Grant No. 127, for 100 acres of land in Rutherford County, N. C., dated September 28, 1785, recorded in the Office of the Secretary of State in Book 58, page 143.

State of North Carolina to William Gilbert, Grant No. 141, for 300 acres of land in Rutherford County, N. C., dated September 28, 1785, recorded in the Office of the Secretary of State in Book 58, page 157.

State of North Carolina to James Miller, Grant No. 73, for 200 acres of land in Rutherford County, dated December 16, 1785, recorded in the Office of the Secretary of State in Book 61, page 19.

State of North Carolina to Joseph Morgan, Grant No. 964, for 200 acres of land in Burke County, dated August 7, 1787, recorded in the

Office of the Secretary of State of N. C., in Book 65, page 373.

State of North Carolina to James Miller, Grant No. 1100, for 640 acres of land in Burke County, dated December 15, 1787, recorded in the Office of the Secretary of State of N. C., in Book 65, page 448.

The above named grants issued to parties for land in Rutherford County are void for the reason that Rutherford County at the date of the issuing of these grants did not extend west of the Blue Ridge and it was not until the Act of 1788, above cited, that the line of Rutherford County was extended from the top of the Blue Ridge back to Pigeon River; but the grants above mentioned, issued for land in Burke County were valid as well as other grants issued to parties for land in Burke County between the top of the Blue Ridge and Pigeon River prior to the Act of 1788, above cited.

The following are descriptions of these grants with plats attached:

STATE OF NORTH CAROLINA	RUTHERFORD COUNTY, N. C.
TO	GRANT No. 54—50 Acres
WILLIAM PORTER	Dated Oct. 11, 1783
	Entered (date not given)
	Recd. Office Sec. of State
	Book 45, page 317.
DESCRIPTION:	On Cabin Branch of Cathey's Creek.
	BEGINNING at a pine on the N. side of the creek in his own line thence

N. 64 poles to a red oak thence
E. 127 poles to a stake thence
S. 64 poles to a stake in his own line thence
W. along his own line 127 poles to the BEGINNING.

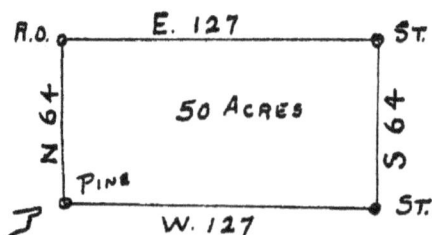

STATE OF NORTH CAROLINA	RUTHERFORD COUNTY, N. C.
TO	GRANT No. 113—50 Acres
ROBERT GILKEY	Dated Sept. 28, 1785
	Entered (date not given)
	Recorded Of. Sec. of State
	Book 58, page 129.
DESCRIPTION:	On Cathey's Creek.
	BEGINNING at a post oak in his own line a corner of James Cook's land running then

S. 68 E. 64 pole˙ ˙o a stake in said Cook's line then
N. 22 E. 127 poles to a pine then
N. 68 W. 64 poles to a stake then
S. 22 W. 227 (127) poles to the BEGINNING.

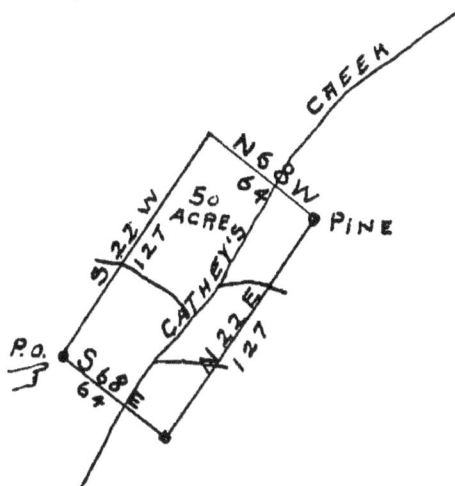

STATE OF NORTH CAROLINA

TO

WILLIAM GILBERT.

RUTHERFORD COUNTY, N. C.
GRANT No. 127—100 Acres
Dated Sept. 28, 1785
Entered (date not given)
Rec'd. Office Sec. of State
Book 58, page 143.

DESCRIPTION: On the waters of Cathey's Creek.
BEGINNING at a post oak by the side of the
road leading from his house to Col. Hampton's
in or near his own line running then with said line

S. 50 W. 164 poles to a post oak then
N. 40 W. 98 poles crossing said road to a pine then
N. 50 E. 164 poles to a red oak then
S. 40 E. 98 poles to the BEGINNING.

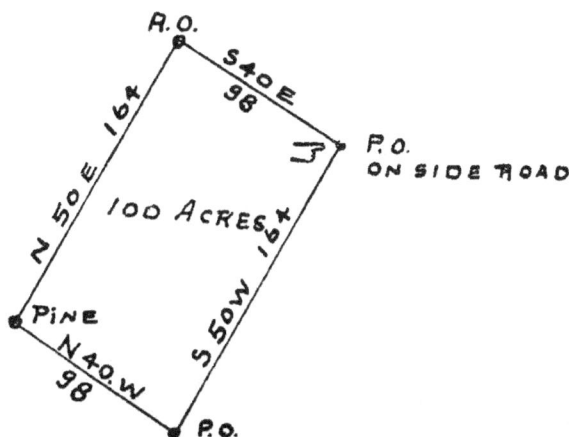

STATE OF NORTH CAROLINA
TO
WILLIAM GILBERT.

RUTHERFORD COUNTY, N. C.
GRANT No. 141—300 Acres
Dated Sept. 28, 1785
Entered (date not given)
Rec'd. Office Sec. of State
Book 58, page 157.

DESCRIPTION:

On a branch of Cathey's Creek joining his own land.
BEGINNING at a post oak on the
S. side of the creek and running
then

N. 80 E. 155 poles to a pine then
S. 10 E. 310 poles to a hickory then
S. 80 W. 155 poles to a stake in his own line then along said line
N. 10 W. 310 poles to the BEGINNING.

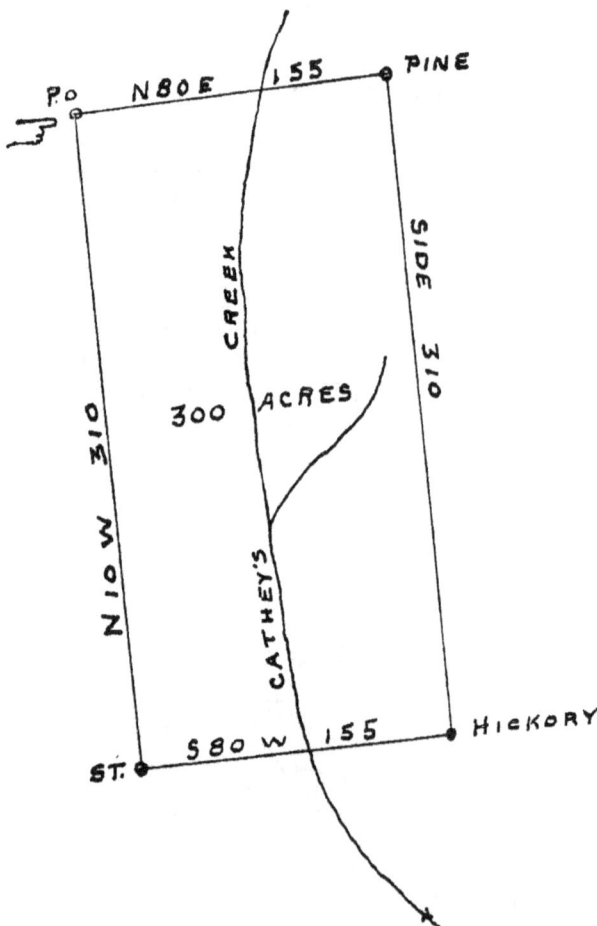

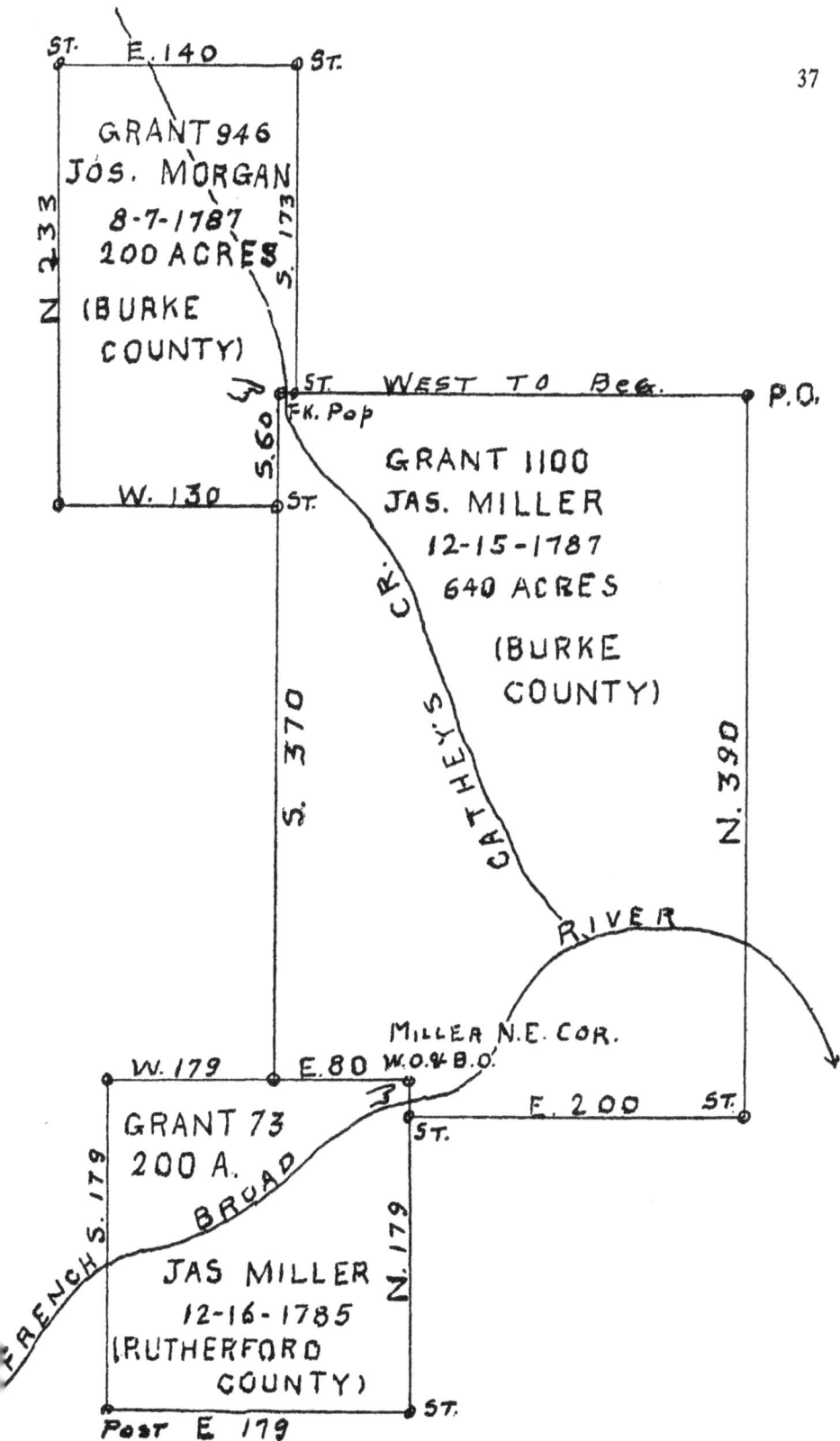

ST. E. 140 ST.

GRANT 946
JOS. MORGAN
8-7-1787
200 ACRES

(BURKE
COUNTY)

N 233

S. 173

W. 130 ST.

S. 60

ST. WEST TO BEG. P.O.
FK. Pop

GRANT 1100
JAS. MILLER
12-15-1787
640 ACRES

(BURKE
COUNTY)

S. 370

CR.

CATHEY'S

RIVER

N. 390

MILLER N.E. COR.
W.O.& B.O.

W. 179 E. 80

GRANT 73
200 A.

E. 200 ST.

ST.

BROAD

N. 179

JAS MILLER
12-16-1785
(RUTHERFORD
COUNTY)

FRENCH S. 179

POST E 179 ST.

STATE OF NORTH CAROLINA
TO
JAMES MILLER.

RUTHERFORD COUNTY, N. C.
GRANT No. 73—200 acres
Dated Dec. 16, 1785
Recorded Office Sec. of State
Book 61, page 19.

DESCRIPTION:

On the Western Waters on both side of the main fork of French Broad River, above the mouth of Cathey's Creek, being known by the name of James Lindsays Entry

BEGINNING on a White Oak and a Black Oak on the river below the mouth of a small branch on the North Side of the river opposite to a high round hill and runs

West 179 poles to a stake and pointers; thence
South 179 poles crossing the river to a post; thence
East 179 poles to a stake, thence
North to the BEGINNING.

See Plat shown on page 37.

STATE OF NORTH CAROLINA
TO
JOSEPH MORGAN.

BURKE COUNTY, N. C.
GRANT No. 964—200 acres
Dated Aug. 7, 1787
Recd. Office Sec. of State
Book 65, page 373.

DESCRIPTION:

Two Hundred acres lying and being in our County of Burke on the Western waters on both sides of Cathey's Creek a branch of French Broad River.

BEGINNING at James Miller's N. W. corner forked poplar on the West side of said Creek and runs with his line

South 60 poles to a state near an old Indian Path; thence
West 130 poles to a stake; thence
North 233 poles to a stake and pointers; thence
East 140 poles crossing the creek to a stake; thence

South 173 poles to a stake in the upper line of said Miller's survey;
thence with said line
West 10 poles to the BEGINNING.

See Plat shown on page 37.

STATE OF NORTH CAROLINA	BURKE COUNTY, N. C.
TO	GRANT No. 1100—640 acres
JAMES MILLER.	Dated Dec. 15, 1787
	Recd. Office Sec. of State
	Book 65, page 488.

DESCRIPTION: On the Western waters on both sides
of French Broad River and on both
sides of Cathey's Creek:

BEGINNING at a large forked
poplar on the bank of said creek on
the West side about 50 poles above
an old Indian path and runs
South 370 poles to a stake on the line of said Miller's No. 20 survey;
thence with said line
East 80 poles to his N. E. corner White Oak on the River Bank thence
with his
South line 20 poles crossing the river to a stake; thence
East 200 poles crossing the end of a mountain to a stake; thence
North 390 poles crossing the river to a post oak; then
West crossing the Creek to the BEGINNING.

See Plat shown on page 37.

I don't imagine that the information I have given as to grants
issued to parties for land in Rutherford County between the top of
the Blue Ridge and Pigeon River prior to the Act of 1788 would be of
any special benefit to the legal profession for the reason that the lands
granted by the state after the year 1783 and before the passage of the
Act of 1788, were of the very best quality; and it is reasonably certain
that the parties who obtained grants for the five tracts above referred
to took possession of the same, immediately after the issuing of the
grants or before, and the title has long since been divested out of the
state and the parties who now occupy the same have no doubt acquired
a good title to the same by possession under grants and deeds as color
of title; but I have called attention to the facts relating to these old
grants as a matter of historical interest.

I will here state that that part of Grant No. 912, issued to William and James Davidson, that lies on the north side of Swannanoa River, is included in Grant No. 253 issued by the state to John Gray Blount on the 28th of November, 1796, for 320,640 acres of land, hereinafter referred to and set out, but the grant to William and James Davidson is not mentioned as one of the excepted tracts in the Blount grant.

I will next set out a list of grants that were issued by the state to parties during the years 1790-91 for land in Burke and Rutherford Counties west of the Blue Ridge on the waters of French Broad River that are recorded in the office of the Register of Deeds of Buncombe County, N. C., giving book and page where recorded, which appear to have been entered and granted after the passage of the Act of 1788, and which appear to be valid grants. Other grants may have been issued during this period for land on the waters of French Broad River that can be found on file in the office of the Secretary of State of North Carolina, and may or may not be recorded in Burke or Rutherford Counties.

Grant No. 518, dated 11-16-1790, John McKnitt Alexander et al, Book 1, Page 37, for 400 acres near Green River, Rutherford County.

Grant No. 559, dated 11-16-1790, John McKnitt Alexander et al, Book 1, Page 36, for 640 acres, Henry's Creek, Rutherford County.

Grant No. 1405, dated 12-15-1791, John McKnitt Alexander et al, Book 1, Page 38, for 100 acres Sandy Mush Creek, Burke County.

Grant No. 579, dated 11-16-1790, John McKnitt Alexander et al, Book 1, Page 40, for 200 acres Mills River, Rutherford County.

Grant No. 1400, dated 12-15-1791, John McKnitt Alexander et al, Book 1, Page 39, for 100 acres Sandy Mush Creek, Burke County.

Grant No. 1406, dated 12-15-1791, John McKnitt Alexander et al, Book 1, Page 41, for 100 acres Sweetens Creek, Burke County.

Grant No. 1399, dated 12-13-1791, Abner Sharpe, Book 1, Page 23, for 200 acres, Sandy Mush Creek, Burke County.

Grant No. 553, dated 11-16-1790, William Sharpe, Book 1, Page 22, for 300 acres on Swannanoa in Rutherford County.

Grant No. 1404, dated 12-15-1791, William Sharpe, Book 1, Page 24, for 400 acres French Broad River, Burke County.

Grant No. 1403, dated 12-15-1791, William Sharpe, Book 1, Page 32, for 200 acres Sandy Mush Creek, Burke County.

Grant No. 1402, dated 12-15-1791, William Sharpe, Book 1, Page 33, for 250 acres Sandy Mush Creek, Burke County.

Grant No. 1401, dated 12-15-1791, William Sharpe, Book 1, Page 34, for 250 acres Sandy Mush Creek, Burke County.

Grant No. 559, dated 11-16-1790, William Sharpe, Book 1, Page 36, for 640 acres Henry's Creek, Rutherford County.

Grant No. 518, dated 11-16-1790, William Sharpe et al, Book 1, Page 37, for 400 acres near Green River, Rutherford County.

Grant No. 1405, dated 12-15-1791, William Sharpe et al, Book 1, Page 38, for 100 acres Sandy Mush Creek, Burke County.

Grant No. 1400, dated 12-15-1791, William Sharpe, et al, Book 1, Page 39, for 100 acres Sandy Mush Creek, Burke County.

Grant No. 579, dated 11-16-1790, William Sharpe et al, Book 1, page 40, for 200 acres Mills River, Rutherford County.

Grant No. 1406, dated 12-15-1791, William Sharpe et al, Book 1, Page 41, for 100 acres Sweetens Creek, Burke County.

Buncombe County was created by an act of the General Assembly of North Carolina, passed and ratified on January 14, 1792, and was taken from Burke and Rutherford Counties, and an organization of the county was effected by the commissioners named in the act for that purpose on April 16, 1792. See this act set out on pages 107-8 of the Revised Statutes of N. C. of 1836. The following is a copy of this act:

AN ACT FORMING THE WESTERN PARTS OF BURKE AND RUTHERFORD COUNTIES INTO A SEPARATE AND DISTINCT COUNTY. (Passed in 1791).

"Whereas the western parts of Burke and Rutherford Counties are very inconvenient to the court houses in the said counties, which renders the attendance of jurors and witnesses very burthensome and expensive, and almost impossible in the winter season; and in order to remedy the same,

1. BE IT ENACTED, ETC., That all that part of the Counties of Burke and Rutherford, circumscribed by the following lines, viz. Beginning on the extreme height of the Apalachian Mountain, where the southern boundary of this state crosses the same, thence along the extreme height of said mountain to where the road from the head of Catawba River to Swannanoe crosses, then along the main ridge dividing the waters of South Toe from those of Swannanoe unto the Great Black Mountain, then along said mountain to the northeast end, then along the main ridge between South Toe and Little Crabtree to the mouth of said Crabtree Creek, then down Toe River aforesaid to where the same empties into the Nollichucky River, then down the said river to the extreme height of the Iron Mountain and cession line, then along said cession line to the southern boundary, then along the said boundary to the beginning, is hereby erected into a separate and distinct county by the name of Buncombe."

By reference to the act creating Buncombe County it will be seen that Buncombe County at that time included practically all the territory that lies west of the Blue Ridge in this state.

See also a fuller and more complete account of the act creating Buncombe County set out on pages 444 etc., under head of Chaper XV, in the First Volume of Dr. Sondley's History of Buncombe County.

See also proceedings had by the proper officials in the organization of Buncombe County, set out in Chapter 16 on pages 457 etc., in the Second Volume of Dr. Sondley's History of Buncombe County.

By reference to the proceedings had by the commission creating Buncombe County, it will be seen that proper officers were elected for the county. It appears, however, that at that time the Justices of the Peace of the county elected the entry taker, and the Justices of the Peace elected for Buncombe County did elect an entry taker to receive entries of grants, as held by our Supreme Court in the case of Strother vs. Cathey, reported in 5th N. C. R., star page 162.

In addition to Grant No. 912 issued by the state to William and James Davidson for 640 acres of land on both sides of what is now Swannanoa River above referred to and set out on pages 838-39, Second Volume of Dr. Sondley's History of Buncombe County, Dr. Sondley on page 838 sets out a copy of Grant No. 64 to John Burton for 200 acres of land in Buncombe County, issued on the 7th day of July, 1794, which covers the northern part of what is now the City of Asheville. The following is a copy of this grant as recorded in Book 55, Page 430, Records of Buncombe County, N. C.

STATE GRANT TO JOHN BURTON, TOWN TRACT
"STATE OF NORTH CAROLINA,

No. 64. Know ye that we have granted unto John Burton two hundred acres of land in our County of Buncombe lying about two miles and a half from Colo. Davidsons on the other side of Swannanoa joining Gillihans entry, beginning at a black oak Burtains southeast corner and runs south towards Swannanoa two hundred and fifty three poles to a stake near three W. oaks marked as pointers then west crossing the branch one hundred and twenty seven poles to a stake, north two hundred and fifty three poles to Burtains southwest corner, then east along Burtains line to the beginning.

"To hold to the said Burtain his heirs and assigns forever. Dated the 7th July 1794.

"RICHD DOBBS SPAIGHT.

"J. Glasgow, Secretary."

This is as the grant appears in the office of the Secretary of State of North Carolina. Registered in Buncombe County, Records of Deeds, Book 55, page 430.

Dr. Sondley also sets out on pages 838 to 843 inclusive of same Volume, copy of Grant No. 253, issued by the state to John Gray Blount, calling to contain 320,640 acres of land, in Buncombe County, N. C., with a list of exceptions contained in this grant, issued on the 28th day of November, 1796. A copy of this grant with exceptions and comments of Dr. Sondley on the same as appear on pages 839 to 843 inclusive are here set out. This grant covers that part of the present City of Asheville that lies north of Swannanoa River and a good portion of that part of what is now Buncombe County on the northeast side of French Broad River down to the Madison County line and a portion of what is now Madison County from the Buncombe and Madison County line down to the painted rock, and also covers a good part of Yancey County. This grant is exceptionally well located, calling for streams, mountains, and natural objects that fix the location of the same without question.

It now appears that the map or plat made a part of this grant has disappeared and can not be found on file in the office of the Secretary of State and that the 131 exceptions set out by Dr. Sondley have also disappeared. I here call attention to the last clause of the description contained in this grant: "Within which bounds there are thirteen thousand seven hundred and thirty five acres of land entered by persons whose names are hereto annexed since the date of said Blount entries and by his permission, but as they are not yet surveyed, their situation cannot be dehiveated."

"STATE OF NORTH VAROLINA.   Grant No. 253

"Know ye that we have granted unto John Gray Blount three hundred and twenty thousand six hundred and forty acres of land in Buncombe County, on the northeast side of French Broad River, beginning at a hickory in Burke County line on the top of the Blue Ridge where the wagon road leading from Buncombe Court House to Morganton crosses the said ridge running thence along the same road westerly to flat creek thence down the various courses of said creek to Swananock (Swannanoa) River thence down the various courses thereof to French Broad River, thence down that river the various windings thereof to the painted rock below the warm springs, which is the territorial or the Tennessee state line, thence with the said line to the highest pinnacle of the bald spot on the Bald Mountain, thence north thirty-two degrees, east two thousand and twenty poles to Nolachucky River where it breaks through the Unaka Mountain, thence up the various courses of Nolachucky and Toe River to the mouth of Crabtree Creek, thence with the Burke County line along the top of the Black Mountain and Blue Ridge to the beginning, within which bounds there are thirteen thousand seven hundred and thirty five acres of land entered by persons whose names are hereto annexed since the date of said Blount entries and by his permission, but as they are not yet surveyed their situation cannot be dehiveated.

"To hold to the said John Gray Blount his heirs and assigns forever. Dated the 28th of November 1796.

"SAM ASHE.

"J. GLASGOW, Secretary."

A list of lands which were entered within the bounds of the annexed plat, by permission of John Gray Blount, since the date of his entries therein, and which entries are excluded therefrom for the benefit of those who made the same

	Acres
William Kyle	150
John Baker	100
Thomas Hopper	100
William Jones	100
Mark Forrester	300
Saml. Smith, Charles Lane and John Craig	100
John Jiles	100
Abney Barrett	100
John Renfrow	100
Samuel Pittle	100
Phillip Hoodingpile	200
Phillip Hoodingpile	100
Phillip Hoodingpile	25
Geo. Baker and Mark Forrester	300
Geo. Baker and Mark Forrester	100
Stephen Bennett	100
Henry Roberts	200
Phillip Hoodingpile and George Baker	100
Isaac Burlurson	100
William Roberts	100
Benjamin Gregory	50
John Page	100
John Page	100
John Roberts	200
John Roberts	100
William Munday	100
John Roberts	150
John Roberts	200
Edward Blurtin	50
Benjamin Gregory	100
Joseph Gash	10
Charles Gad	50
Henry Dewise and John Ramsey	200

Henry Dewise	200
Garrett Dewise	100
James Boys	50
Silus Gillaspy	100
William Forrester	100
Thomas Wray	100
Thomas Wray	100
David Hinton	50
David Hinton	50
Jacob Biffle	100
William Murphy	100
David Vance and George Baker	100
David Vance and George Baker	100
David Vance and Hickman Hencely	100
David Vance and George Baker	100
Cornelius Guin	100
Josiah Phips	100
Benjamin Gregory	150
Adam Biffle	100
Jacob Wagoner	100
Isaac Pratan	100
Gabriel Elkins	100
Jacob Wagoner	500
Merry Webb	100
George Cunningham	100
John Weaver	100
John Weaver	150
Mashack Boehm	150
James Dickson	50
William Ussery	200
Joseph Hughey	300
Samuel Hughey	50
Meriday Edwards	100
John Cubey	200
Edward Blurton	200
Philip Mason	100
Thomas Love	100
John Webb	100
George Penland	100
James Peeters	50
James Peeters	150
William Ramsey	100
William Holloway	100
John Roberts	100
John Holcom	100

Benjamin Brigarts _____ 200
George Baker _____ 200
James Sanford _____ 50
Wm. Robert Hinton _____ 100
William Gillaspy _____ 640
William Hunter _____ 100
in the office of the Secretary of State of North Carolina,
William Penland _____ 100
John Patton _____ 100
James Bobbit _____ 150
Thomas Dillard _____ 100
Robert Harvis _____ 100
William Gregory _____ 200
William Beeley _____ 100
Edward Land _____ 200
Spencer Pendergrass _____ 100
George Revis _____ 100
Cornelius Quinn _____ 50
Robbert Pattan _____ 50
Gabriel Ragsdall _____ 100
William Gudger _____ 100
Mathew Patton _____ 50
James Ballinger _____ 60
Josiah Ballinger _____ 250
Bedant Beard _____ 100
Eanos Shields _____ 100
Jabes Jarvis _____ 100
Jacob Beeler _____ 50
Jacob Beeler, 100 and 50 _____ 150
John Dillard _____ 100
William Sase _____ 100
James Greenlea _____ 100
Mathew Patton Senr. _____ 50
William Davis _____ 100

Acres _____ 13735
Thomas Wilson _____ 100
William Wilson _____ 100

The foregoing is a copy of the state grant to John Gray Blount mentioned and the exceptions thereto as they appear produced here through the courtesy of Mr. Brandon Patton Hodges, Lawyer, Asheville, North Carolina. The grant is No. 253 and, without the exceptions, is on the Record of Deeds of Buncombe County Book S1-2, p-462. The exceptions are said to be missing now from the office of the

Secretary of State.
No. 64.

STATE OF NORTH CAROLINA,
TO ALL TO WHOM THESE PRESENTS SHALL COME GREETINGS:

"Know ye that we for and in consideration of the sum of thirty shillings for every hundred acres hereby paid into our treasury by John Burtain have given and granted and by these presents do give and grant unto the said John Burtain a tract of land containing two hundred acres lying and being in our County of Buncombe on Gleans Creek the waters of French Broad River, beginning at a water oak on the north side of Glens fork and including said fork runs south two hundred and fifty three poles to a stake and B oak then east one hundred and twenty seven poles to a stake and B. O., north crossing the creek two hundred and fifty three poles to a stake, then west crossing the creek to the beginning, as by the plat hereunto annexed doth appear:

Together with all woods, waters, mines, minerals, hereditaments and appurtenances to the said land belonging or appertaining to hold to the said John Burtain, his heirs and assigns, forever, yielding and paying to us such sums of money yearly or otherwise, as our General Assembly from time to time may direct, provided always that the said John Burtain shall cause this grant to be registered in the Register's office of our said County of Buncombe, within the time allowed by law, otherwise the same shall be void and of no effect.

In Testimony Whereof we have caused these our Letters to be made patent and our Great Seal to be hereunto affixed.

Witness Richard Dobbs Spaight, Esquire our Governor, Captain General and Commander in Chief at Newbern the 7th day of July in the 19th year of our Independence and in the year of our Lord, one thousand seven hundred and ninety four."
By his Excellency's Com.

RICH. DOBBS SPAIGHT.
J. GLASCOW, Secretary.

This 4th April A. D. 1829.

(Courtesy of office of Register of Deeds of Buncombe County, North Carolina, furnished this copy, from Book 15 of the Record of Deeds of that county, of Jim Burton's two hundred acres "Gillihan Tract" immediately north of his Town Tract.)

As I understand it there is no plat or map on record of the Blount Grant in the office of the Secretary of State that shows the 131 exceptions, and this being so I made an effort to locate the 131 exceptions in the Blount Grant through Mr. Daniel Hodges, and in the talk I had with Mr. Hodges over the 'phone, he stated that he found the grant in the safe of the office of Merrimon Adams and Adams, and took the same into the office of Mr. Sneed Adams, who said that he had obtained the grant from Harriett E. Rhea, who had obtained it from the Secretary of State prior to the time that the list of exceptions had become lost in the Secretary of State's office, and it had been delivered to his father in connection with some law suits that he was trying for her. Mr. Hodges then suggested that I look into the old Rhea, Coggins, etc., suits that went to the Supreme Court, which involved a partition of land by parol, and by doing so, I would find that the exceptions were set up and established and passed upon by the Supreme Court in those cases. I have endeavored to find the decision of the Supreme Court referred to by Mr. Hodges, involving the question of parol partition, and after a careful examination, I fail to find any decision of the Supreme Court bearing on this matter; and as Mr. Hodges does not remember the decision of the Supreme Court bearing on this matter, I think the chances are that these exceptions have disappeared and will never be found.

I have examined the records in the office of the Register of Deeds of Buncombe County, N. C., to see how many of the 131 excepted tracts referred to were granted to the persons therein named, are on record in Buncombe County, and I only found grants issued to seventeen parties named in the exceptions, on record. It may be, however, that the parties assigned their entries and the grants were taken out in the name of other parties, and the chances are that some of them may have abandoned their entries.

Eight of the above mentioned seventeen parties named in the exceptions obtained grants prior to the date of the Blount Grant, for acreage as follows:

Grant No.   ?   to Phillip Hoodingpile for 100 acres on Jack's Creek in Buncombe County, recorded in Book S1-2, Page 385, dated 7-2-1794.

Grant No.   ?   to William Murphy for 100 acres on Reems Creek, in Buncombe County, recorded in Book 3, Page 6, dated 3-20-1795.

Grant No.   ?   to George Cunningham for 100 acres on Bull Creek, in Buncombe County, recorded in Book 4, Page 204, dated 10-13-1795.

Grant No. 200 to George Baker for 200 acres on Caney River in Buncombe County, recorded in Book 3, Page 145, dated 8-22-1795.

Grant No.   ?   to Wm. Robert Hinton for 100 acres on Caney River in Burke County, recorded in Book S1-2, Page 52, dated 8-13-1794.

Grant No. 217 to William Gudger for 100 acres Swannanoa River in Buncombe County, recorded in Book S1-2, Page

297, dated 12-9-1795.

Grant No. 21 to John Dillard for 100 acres on Flat Creek in Buncombe County, recorded in Book S1-2, Page 67, dated 1-6-1794.

Grant No. 1638 to James Greenlea for 100 acres between Flat Creek and Ivey River in Burke County, recorded in Book 7, Page 495, dated 11-27-1792.

Nine of the above mentioned seventeen parties named in the exceptions obtained grants after the date of the Blount Grant, for acreage as follows:

Grant No. 788 to Stephen Bennett for 100 acres on Caney River in Buncombe County, recorded in Book S1-6, Page 217, dated 9-1-1800.

Grant No. 2243 to William Roberts for 100 acres on Big Ivey in Buncombe County, recorded in Book H, Page 380, dated 4-30-1816.

Grant No. 293 to Benjamin Gregory for 50 acres on French Broad River in Buncombe County, recorded in Book 4, Page 454, dated 7-10-1797.

Grant No. ? to Thomas Wray for 100 acres Jack's Creek in Buncombe County, recorded in Book 10, Page 272, dated 11-26-1804.

Grant No. 304 to David Hinton for 50 acres on a branch of Ivy in Buncombe County, recorded in Book 4, Page 255, dated 7-19-1797.

Grant No. 3275 to Samuel Hughey for 50 acres on Harwood's Creek in Buncombe County, recorded in Book 20, Page 24, dated 5-15-1835.

Grant No. ? to Thomas Dillard for 100 acres Little Ivey in Buncombe County, recorded in Book 4, Page 192, dated 7-14-1798.

Grant No. 295 to Eanos Shields for 100 acres on Ivey in Buncombe County, recorded in Book 4, Page 11, dated 7-10-1797.

Grant No. ? to William Davis for 100 acres Warm Springs Creek in Buncombe County, recorded in Book 14, Page 141, dated 4-15-1820.

I will here state that even if the 131 exceptions to the Blount Grant can not be located, the chances are that the parties who laid the entries on the same, or most of them, took immediate possession of the land after laying their entries, and acquired a good title to the same by possession under deeds as color of title, and they would now be able to show title as against anyone claiming title under the Blount Grant; and it is a well-known historical fact that the title to the land covered by the Blount Grant has passed by successive conveyances, court proceedings, wills, etc., to individuals and corporations, who now claim and hold title to the same. I don't think any information I have given in reference to the Blount Grant and exceptions thereto will be of any special benefit to the legal profession, for the reason that the title to these lands is now pretty well settled; but I decided to give this information as a matter of historical interest.

Referring again to Grant No. 1031 for 450 acres of land on Hominy Creek, issued by the state to William Moore on the 7th day of August, 1787, above referred to; as before stated, I have always heard that this was the first tract of land granted to anyone west of the Blue Ridge, but I find that a grant was issued by the state to William Porter for 50 acres of land in Rutherford County on October 11, 1783, on Cabin Branch of Cathey's Creek, a tributary of French Broad River, which now lies about five miles above the Town of Brevard in Transylvania County, N. C., hereinbefore referred to and set out, that was about four years older than Grant No. 1031 to William Moore for 450 acres of land on Hominy Creek, and that several other grants were issued by the state to parties for land in Burke and Rutherford Counties in the same locality during the year 1785, that are about two years older than the William Moore tract. The grant issued to William Moore, above referred to, is known as the old William Moore tract and lies on both sides of Hominy Creek on the road leading from West Asheville to Enka, a short distance south from the old Sand Hill Academy, and the old Moore House, which is said to have been 150 years old, stood on the left side of the road, a short distance this side of Hominy Creek; and it was only a few years ago that the same was torn down.

I deem it proper to here state as a matter of historical interest that William Moore, the grantee of this 450 acres of land, was a Captain in the army of Gen. Griffith Rutherford, who during the Revolutionary War made an expedition with 2,400 men from Rowan County during the month of September 1776, to quell and suppress an insurrection of the Cherokee Indians in the country west of the Blue Ridge in this state, who had allied themselves with the British in the Revolutionary War. Gen. Rutherford was joined by Gen. Williamson of South Carolina with an army of about 2,000 men on Tennessee River, then known as Nequassee, near what is now the Town of Franklin, N. C.; and after the armies of Gen. Rutherford and Gen. Williamson had subdued the Cherokees and destroyed their crops on Tuckaseigee, Tennessee, and Hiawassee Rivers, Gen. Rutherford returned to his home in Rowan County, and later on Captain Moore, joined by Capt. Harden, made another expedition across the Blue Ridge and quelled an insurrection among the Indians on Tuckaseigee River, and destroyed their crops, and it was on these expeditions that Captain Moore decided to obtain a grant for the land and make his future home on the land on Hominy Creek.

See account of the expedition of Gen. Rutherford and Captain Moore and the second expedition by Captain Moore with Captain John Harden against the Cherokees set out on pages 378-79-80, First Volume of Dr. Sondley's History of Buncombe County, North Carolina.

See also account of the expedition made by Gen. Rutherford and Gen. Williamson set out on pages 101, etc., of Chapter 3, Second Volume of Theodore Roosevelt's History of the "Winning of the West."

See also account of the route taken by Gen. Rutherford in his expedition referred to as the "Rutherford's War Trace," set out on page 157 in Powell's Book of 1883-4.

Captain William Moore, soon after having obtained a grant of this tract of land, located on the same and lived there until the time of his death. Captain William Moore was the father of Capt. Charles Moore, who upon the death of his father, lived at the old William Moore homestead up to the time of his death soon after the Civil War.

Capt. Charles Moore was one of the most progressive and public-spirited citizens of his day and time, and it was through his efforts that Sand Hill Academy was established and became one of the most noted seats of learning in Western North Carolina.

Among other prominent men who received their education at Sand Hill Academy were Judge George A. Jones, late of Macon County, the father of our townsman, G. Lyle Jones; Judge George A. Shuford, late of the City of Asheville, father of our townsman, George A. Shuford, Jr.; Judge Charles A. Moore, and Judge Walter E. Moore; Herschel S. Harkins, former U. S. Collector of Revenue for this district and Postmastter of Asheville, N. C., at one time, father of our townsman, Hon. T. J. Harkins, all of whom were students at Sand Hill Academy in 1863-64 during the Civil War; and Col. V. S. Lusk, former U. S. Attorney for the Western District of N. C., and a prominent member of the Bar of Buncombe County, N. C., was also educated at Sand Hill Academy a short time prior to the year 1863. The writer was a classmate of the above named parties except Col. V. S. Lusk, and received a part of his limited education at Sand Hill Academy during the years 1863-64.

Capt. Charles Moore was the grandfather of the late Judge Charles A. Moore and Judge Walter E. Moore, and Judge Fred Moore, and Capt. Charles Moore left numerous other descendants in Buncombe and other counties in Western North Carolina and other states. The writer heard Col. A. T. Davidson say that Capt. Charles Moore was one of the most progressive and leading citizens in North Carolina in his day and time, and was one of the most hospitable men he ever met, and had perhaps entertained more prominent men, Judges of the Superior and Supreme Court, and Governors of North Carolina, than any man west of the Blue Ridge.

The following information as to Capt. William Moore and the

old William Moore house was furnished me by Mr. W. W. Candler, Attorney-at-Law of Asheville, N. C., a great-great-grandson of Capt. Charles Moore on his father's side.

Mr. Candler says that his information is that Capt. William Moore married the daughter of Gen. Griffith Rutherford, and I am informed by Mr. Candler that the old William Moore house was first built as a fort by Gen. Griffith Rutherford and Capt. William Moore, and was occupied as such for several years. Mr. Candler says he is informed that the old log house was built as a fort for the protection of the whites against the Indians and had openings in the nature of port holes where the whites could spy on the Indians and shoot them; and the old log house, which was a two-story building with four rooms, was later weather-boarded by Capt. William Moore and occupied as his residence up to the time of his death in 1812; and upon the death of Capt. William Moore, the same was occupied by his son, Capt. Charles Moore, up to the time of his death in 1876. The house was later occupied by Dr. David Gudger, the father of Owen Gudger, until the same was torn down about five years ago. Mr. Candler says the old log house was reputed to be about 150 years old.

A full account of William Moore and his descendants and the warfare that formerly existed between the whites and the Indians in the locality of the old William Moore residence, was published in the Asheville Sunday Citizen on January 12, 1930. Mr. Candler has in his possession a copy of this article.

I will now take up and discuss and show how the title of the Cherokees to land lying east of the Meigs and Freeman line was extinguished by the treaties of Hopewell of November 28, 1785, the Holston Treaty of July 2, 1791, and the Treaty of Telllco of October 2, 1798, and the line run or located in pursuance to these treaties; and I will next take up and discuss and show how the lands lying east of the Meigs and Freeman line became subject to entry and grant under the general entry and grant laws of the state; and will next take up and show how the title of the Cherokees was extinguished to lands lying west of the Meigs and Freeman line under the treaties of 1817 and 1819, and 1835, and how the same was disposed of by the state under the Cherokee land laws and the general entry and grant laws of the state.

I have a map prepared by Mr. E. M. Moffett, F. E., from U. S. geological sheets, showing all the country lying west of the top of the Blue Ridge in this state, and showing thereon all the treaty lines as run or located in pursuance to the Hopewell Treaty of November 28, 1785, the Holston Treaty of July 2, 1791, and the Treaty of Tellico of October 2, 1798, and the Treaty of 1819, and also showing on this map and designating thereon in red border the location of the following old land grants that were issued to parties during the years 1796-7 for land in Buncombe County:

Grant No. 253, issued by the state to John Gray Blount on the 28th day of November, 1796, calling to contain 320,640 acres of land after deducting excepted tracts, which covers the northern part of what is now Buncombe County, a part of Madison County, and a good part of Yancey County.

Recorded, Buncombe County, Book S1-2, Page 462. Date not shown.

Grant No. 252, issued by the state to John Gray Blount on November 29, 1796, calling to contain 176,000 acres of land after deducting excepted tracts. All of this grant lies on the waters of Jonathon's Creek and Pigeon River in Haywood County, except about 35,000 acres that lie on the headwaters of the Raven's Fork of Oconalufty River in Swain County, all of which 35,000 acres is now included in the Great Smoky Mountain Park, and the northern part of that part of this grant that lies in Haywood County is also included in the Great Smoky Mountain Park.

Recorded, Buncombe County, Book S1-2, Page 462. Date not shown.

Grant No. 251, issued by the state to David Allison on November 29, 1796, calling to contain 250,240 acres of land after deducting excepted tracts. This grant lies in what is now Buncombe, Henderson, Transylvania, Jackson, and Haywood Counties. The title to about 100,000 acres of this grant that lies on the north and west forks of French Broad River in what is now Transylvania County, N. C., passed to George W. Vanderbilt and later was purchased by the U. S. Forest Service from the Vanderbilt Estate, et al, and the title to this area is now vested in the United States and constitutes a part of what is known as the Pisgah National Forest.

This grant found indexed in Buncombe County under name of "David Blount, et al" in error. Book S1-2, Page 458. Correction was promised in February 1938. Date recorded not shown.

Grant No. 224, issued by the state to William Cathcart on July 20, 1796, calling to contain 33,280 acres of land. Most of this grant lies in what is now Jackson County, and is a part of the Qualla Boundary owned by the Eastern Band of the Cherokee Indians. All of this grant lies east of the Meigs and Freeman line.

Recorded, Buncombe County, Book 3, Page 81, 8-9-1796.

Grant No. 225, issued by the state to William Cathcart on July 20, 1796, calling to contain 49,920 acres of land. This grant lies in what is now Jackson County and most of it lies west of the Meigs and Freeman line.

Recorded, Buncombe County, Book 3, Page 82, 8-9-1796.

Grant No. 226, issued by the state to William Cathcart on July 20, 1796, calling to contain 49,920 acres of land. This grant lies within what is now Jackson County, and about two-thirds of the area lies east of the Meigs and Freeman line, and the remainder of this area lies west of it. This grant was made the subject of the litigation in the case of Latimer vs. Poteet, reported in 39 U.S.R., pages 4 etc. (14th Pet.) The Latimers lost in the suit. The main controversy in this action was as to the location of the Holston Treaty line of July 2, 1791.

Recorded, Buncombe County, Book 3, Page 83, 10-8-1796.

Grant No. 230, issued by the state to George Latimer on July 20, 1796, calling to contain 50,560 acres of land after deducting excepted tracts. About two-fifths of this grant lies on the waters of French Broad River in Transylvania County, N. C., and about six or eight thousand acres lie on the headwaters of the East Fork of Tuckaseigee River in Jackson County, N. C., on the north side of the Blue Ridge; and about three-fifths lies on the southern slope of the Blue Ridge in Transylvania and Jackson Counties, N. C., in what is known as the Toxaway Country; and all of this grant lies inside the boundary reserved to the Cherokee Indians by the Act of 1783, except that part that lies on the waters of French Broad River, and that part that lies on the waters of French Broad River lies outside of the boundary reserved to the Cherokee Indians by the Act of 1783 aforesaid, as defined by our Supreme Court in the case of W. Vance Brown et al, vs. George H. Smathers et al, reported in 188 N. C. R., pages 166 etc., with map attached. As will be seen by reference to Moffett map, most of this grant lies west of the Meigs and Freeman line.

Recorded, Buncombe County, Book 3, Page 88, 8-10-1796. (Name spelled "Latimore," but later deeds show "Latimer.")

Grant No. 279, issued by the state to John Holdeman and Jacob Eshleman on the 3rd day of April, 1797, for 200,960 acres of land that covers a good part of what is now Jackson, Swain and Macon Counties. This grant is recorded in old deed book S2-2, page 421, Records of Buncombe County, N. C.

When the General Assembly of North Carolina by the Act of 1783 aforesaid removed the boundary of the Cherokees from the top of the Blue Ridge back to Pigeon River, the Cherokees seriously protested against such action, claiming that the state had no right to change the boundary without the consent of the Cherokees, and which consent had not been given, and which resulted in the Treaty of Hopewell of November 28, 1785. See Hopewell Treaty and causes that led up to the same, and correspondence relating thereto, set out on pages 133 etc., in Powell's Book of 1883-84. By reference to this treaty it will be seen that the Cherokees relinquished their claim of title to the lands in what is now North Carolina lying to the east of lines running a southerly course from what was then the northern boundary of North Carolina, now the State of Tennessee, to the South Caroina Indian boundary line, which lines were run or at least located as shown on C. C. Royce map, running through or a little to the east of the City of Asheville. See these lines shown on C. C. Royce map, designated "East Boundary of Cherokee Nation as Defined by Treaty of November 28, 1785."

These lines are also shown on Moffett map.

So it will be seen by this treaty that the boundary between the top of the Blue Ridge and Pigeon River was divided about equally between the Indians and the whites. The Indians by this treaty extinguished their claim of title to land lying to the east of the Hopewell Treaty lines, but left the land lying west as a part of the Indian boundary.

Dr. Sondley, on pages 517, etc., of the Second Volume of his History of Buncombe County, in commenting on the Treaty of Hopewell of November 28, 1785, says that a great injustice was done to North Carolina by this treaty, and through the fraud and influence of the U. S. Commissioners, the Cherokees were persuaded to ignore an agreement formerly entered into between the State of North Carolina and the Cherokees by the terms of which the Cherokees were to relinquish their claim of title to land therein referred to in North Carolina, upon delivery to the Cherokees of certain goods amounting to the value of $3,333 1-3 which the State of North Carolina was then ready to deliver in accordance with the agreement. Dr. Sondley, in commenting on this treaty, says that by the terms of this treaty the Cherokees were given the right to murder all whites who should disregard the Treaty of Hopewell, knowing that already many whites were settled beyond the boundary thus fixed, and the Cherokees accordingly murdered many whites. Dr. Sondley also says that this treaty was entered into against the protests of North Carolina Commissioners, who were present.

I have made a careful examination of the Hopewell Treaty set out in Powell's Book of 1883-84 on pages 133 etc., and I fail to find any such stipulation in the treaty as referred to by Dr. Sondley, giving the Cherokees the right to murder whites who violated the Hopewell Treaty. It may be, however, that the Cherokees did murder whites who occupied territory reserved to them by the Treaty of Hopewell, feeling that they were authorized to do so by the fifth clause of that treaty in words as follows:

"Citizens of the United States or persons other than Indians who settle or attempt to settle on lands west or south of said boundary and refuse to remove within six months after ratification of this treaty to forfeit the protection of the United States, and the Indians to punish them or not, as they please: PROVIDED, That this article shall not extend to the people settled between the fork of French Broad and Holstein Rivers, whose status shall be determined by Congress.

It appears that the whites settled upon and occupied land in what is now the State of Tennessee and especially East Tennessee, formerly North Carolina, from five to ten years before the whites settled upon and occupied land in what is now Western North Carolina. Neither the Cherokees nor the whites were satisfied with the Treaty of Hopewell, the whites being dissatisfied on account of the failure of the United States to extinguish the title of the Cherokees to land occupied by the

whites, in Tennessee. The dissatisfaction of the Cherokees was not
so much on account of the terms of the treaty, but on account of the
failure of the United States, after the treaty was made, to enforce the
terms of the same. It was only a short time after the treaty was made
that more than 500 white families settled upon and occupied land on
French Broad and Nollichucky Rivers in what is now East Tennessee,
then in North Carolina, that was reserved to the Cherokees by the
Treaty of Hopewell. Protest was made by the Cherokees to the War
Department against the flagrant violation of the treaty as shown by
communications addressed by Gen. Knox, then Secretary of War, to
President Washington, and from President Washington to Congress and
action taken by the United States Senate in the matter as follows:

"General Knox, Secretary of War, under date of July 7, 1789, in
a communication to the President, remarked that 'the disgraceful violation of the Treaty of Hopewell with the Cherokees requires the serious
consideration of Congress. If so direct and manifest contempt of the
authority of the United States be suffered with impunity, it will be
in vain to attempt to extend the arm of government to the frontiers.
The Indian tribes can have no faith in such imbecile promises, and the
lawless whites will ridicule a government which shall, on paper only,
make Indian treaties and regulate Indian boundaries.'

He recommended the appointment of three commissioners on the
part of the United States, who should be invested with full powers to
examine into the case of the Cherokees and to renew with them the
treaty made at Hopewell in 1785; also to report to the President such
measures as should be necessary to protect the Indians in the boundaries
secured to them by that treaty, which he suggested would involve the
establishment of military posts within the Indian country and the
services of at least five hundred troops. President Washington, on the
same day, transmitted the report of the Secretary of War, with the
accompanying papers, to Congress. He approved of the recommen-
dations of General Knox, and urged upon that body prompt action
in the matter.

Congress, however, failed to take any decisive action at that session,
and on the 11th of August, 1790, President Washington again brought
the subject to the attention of that body. After reciting the substance
of his previous communication, he added that, notwithstanding the
Treaty of Hopewell and the proclamation of Congress, upwards of five
hundred families had settled upon the Cherokee lands, exclusive of
those between the forks of the French Broad and Holston Rivers. He
further added that, as the obstructions to a proper conduct of the matter
had been removed since his previous communication, by the accession
of North Carolina to the Union and the cession to the United States
by her of the lands in question, he should conceive himself bound to
exert the powers intrusted to him by the Constitution in order to carry

into faithful execution the Treaty of Hopewell, unless it should be thought proper to attempt to arrange a new boundary with the Cherokees, embracing the settlements and compensating the Cherokees for the cessions they should make.

UNITED STATES SENATE AUTHORIZES A NEW TREATY

Upon the reception of this message the Senate adopted a resolution advising and consenting that the President should, at his discretion, cause the Treaty of Hopewell to be carried into execution or enter into arrangements for such further cession of territory from the Cherokees as the tranquillity and interests of the United States should require. A proviso to this resolution limited the compensation to be paid to the Cherokees for such further cession to $1,000 per annum and stipulated that no person who had taken possession of any lands within the limits of the proposed cession should be confirmed therein until he had complied with such terms as Congress should thereafter prescribe.

Accordingly, instructions were issued to William Blount, governor of the territory south of the Ohio River and 'ex-officio' superintendent of Indian affairs, to conclude a treaty of cession with the Cherokees."

See this correspondence set out on pages 160-61, etc., of Powell's Book of 1883-84, which resulted in the Treaty of Holston of July 2, 1791, which was followed by the Treaty of Tellico of October 2, 1798.

The Treaty of Hopewell of November 28, 1785, was entered into between the commissioners appointed by the United States and the chiefs and head men of the Cherokee Nation on the Keowee River in Hopewell, South Carolina.

TREATY OF HOLSTON OF JULY 2, 1791

By the terms of the Holston Treaty of July 2, 1791, the title of the Cherokees was extinguished to that part of the boundary reserved to the Indians by the Act of 1783, to the north and east of a line running from the post known as both the Hawkins and Meigs post on the top of the Smoky Mountains S. 76° E. to the southern boundary of North Carolina where it intersects the Hopewell Treaty line of 1785. The Holston Treaty line was run by a man by the name of Benjamin Hawkins from near the mouth of Clinch River in Tennessee S. 76° E. to the top of the Smoky Mountains to the point since known as the Hawkins and Meigs post. There is a question as to whether or not the Holston Treaty line was run by Hawkins from the top of the Smoky Mountains at the Hawkins and Meigs post through North Carolina to the southern boundary of North Carolina in accordance with the provisions of the Treaty, for the reason that at that time there were very few white settlers occupying land in North Carolina between the Hopewell Treaty line of 1785 and the Holston Treaty line of 1791.

The main object of the Treaty of Holston was to extinguish the title of the Cherokees to land occupied by white settlers inside the Indian boundary in what is now East Tennessee.

But the Supreme Court of the United States in the case of Latimer vs. Poteet, 39 U.S.R. (14th Pet.) page 4, which had under consideration the Holston Treaty line in this state and its effect on the validity of Grant No. 226 to William Cathcart, calling to contain 49,920 acres of land, now in Jackson County, N. C., shown on Moffett map, which was the subject of litigation in that suit, in construing the Holston Treaty held that the Hawkins line as far as run by Hawkins from near the mouth of Clinch River S. 76° E. to the top of the Smoky Mountains was the true Holston Treaty line, but expressed a doubt as to whether or not Hawkins had run the line from the top of the Smoky Mountains southeast to the southern boundary of this state, as nothing could be found in the office of the War Department of Washington, D. C., showing that this line had been run by Hawkins through North Carolina; but the court in construing the Holston treaty held that the Hawkins line as far as run from the mouth of Clinch River to the top of the Smoky Mountains at the point which is now known as the Hawkins and Meigs post, was the correct location of the Holston Treaty line, and that this line should be extended from Hawkins' post S. 76° E. to the southern boundary of North Carolina, and that that would be the true location of the Holston Treaty line in North Carolina.

This line intersects the Hopewell Treaty line of 1785 as will be seen by reference to Royce's map.

This line is shown on C. C. Royce map designated Picken's line, and is also shown on map prepared by E. M. Moffett, and designated thereon "Hawkins' line," S. 76° E., which is the same as the Picken's line shown on Royce map.

For a full and complete history of the Holston Treaty see report of same set out on pages 158, etc., of Powell's Book of 1883-84.

The Treaty of Holston, above set out, was entered into between the commissioners appointed by the United States and the chiefs and head men of the Cherokee Nation at what was then known as White's Ford on French Broad River, near what was then and is now Knoxville, Tennessee.

Tellico Treaty Of October 2, 1798

Now as to the Tellico Treaty of October 2, 1798, the following are the lines called for in this treaty so far as the same relates to the State of North Carolina: "The Cherokees cede to the United States all lands within the following points and lines, viz:

From a point on the Tennessee River, below Tellico Block House, called the Wild Cat Rock, in a direct line to the Militia Spring near the Maryville Road leading to Tellico. From said spring to the Chill-howie Mountain by a line so to be run as will leave all the farms on Nine Mile Creek to the northward and eastward of it, and to be continued along Chill-howie Mountain until it strikes Hawkin's line. Thence along said line to the Great Iron Mountain, and from the top of which a line to be continued in a southeastwardly course to where the most southwardly branch of Little River crosses the divisional line to Tuggaloe River."

There was much difficulty encountered by the surveyors in locating the line running from Hawkin's or Meig's Post southeastwardly to the Little River called for, for the reason that there were two Little Rivers tributary to French Broad River in North Carolina, and another Little River, tributary to Keowee River, in South Carolina.

The first attempt to locate this line was made by General Butler, who surveyed a line from Hawkin's Post to Little River in South Carolina. This line is shown on the Royce map as the Butler Line, and runs about South 19° East. The Indians protested against this location, and Return J. Meigs was appointed a Commissioner on behalf of the United States to locate this line, and he in turn employed Thomas Freeman to run and locate this line. Freeman accordingly ran and located this line from the Hawkins' Post on top of the Great Smoky Mountains South 52° East, during or about the year 1802, to where the same intersected the Hopewell Treaty line of 1785, which is shown on the Royce map. This line was accepted by the War Department and by the State of North Carolina as the correct location of the Tellico Treaty line, and has since been known as the Meigs and Freeman line. For a full and complete history of the Tellico Treaty see report of same set out on pages 174 to 183 of Powell's Book of 1883-4. The Meigs and Freeman line runs through the Cherokee Training School property at Cherokee, N. C., and about a mile east of the Town of Sylva, N. C., and crosses the West Fork of French Broad River.

The Meigs and Freeman Line as run by Freeman in 1802 is a well-established line, and Messrs. Thomas A. Cox, Sr., H. R. Queen, and S. M. Parker, all surveyors of Jackson County, N. C., have run parts of this line, and found old marked trees where the timber was still standing which corresponded with the date of the survey by Freeman in 1802, and it has been recognized by the State of North Carolina as the true location of the Tellico Treaty Line, as held by the Supreme Court in the case of Brevard Land and Timber Company vs. Kinsland, reported in 154 N. C. R., star page 79.

By the terms of the Tellico Treaty, the Cherokees relinquished their claim of title to that part of the boundary of land reserved to the Indians by the Act of 1783 that lay to the east of the Meigs and Freeman Line.

The Treaty of Tellico, above referred to, was entered into between the commissioners appointed by the United States and the chiefs and head men of the Cherokee Nation at what was then and is now known as Tellico Plains on Tellico River in Tennessee.

By reference to the Moffett map it will be seen that all of Grant No. 252 to John Gray Blount, calling to contain 176,000 acres, lies inside of the boundary reserved to the Cherokee Indians by the Act of 1783, and that all of this grant now lies in what is now Haywood County, except about 35,000 acres that lie on the headwaters of the Ravens Fork of Oconalufty River in Swain County, and that a part of Grant No. 251 to David Allison lies within the boundary reserved to the Cherokees by the Act of 1783, and a part lies on the outside and that this grant covers a good part of what is now Buncombe County and a good part of what is now Haywood and Jackson Counties, and some of it lies in both Henderson and Transylvania Counties.

The Supreme Court in the case of Brown vs. Smathers, 188 N. C., page 166 with map attached, in defining the boundary of land set apart to the Cherokee Indians by the Act of 1783, left the land on the waters of French Broad River on the outside of this boundary. The Court in that case, referring to the line called for in the boundary reserved to the Cherokees by the Act of 1783, in words . . . "Thence along the dividing ridge between the waters of Pigeon River and Tuckaseegee River to the southern boundary of this State," construed this call as running with the summit of the Balsam range a southerly course to where the same intersects the summit of the Blue Ridge at the point designated on the map as "Cold Mountain," thence along the summit of the Blue Ridge a southeast course to the southern boundary of the State, and running thence with the South Carolina and Georgia line back to the beginning on Tennessee River, near the Chicamauga towns, which was then in North Carolina but now in Tennessee, thereby leaving that part of the land embraced in Grant No. 230 to George Latimer that lies on the waters of French Broad River outside the boundary reserved to the Cherokees by the Act of 1783; but the Court held in that case that the remainder of Grant No. 230 to George Latimer lay inside the boundary reserved to the Cherokees by the Act of 1783, and under the sixth section of the Act of 1783 was absolutely void.

See boundary of land reserved to the Cherokee Indians by the fifth section of the Act of 1783 and the sixth section of the same act prohibiting the entry and grant of any land within the said boundary, set out as sections 2346 and 2347 under Chapter 11, entitled "Cherokee Lands," on pages 65-6 of Second Volume of the Code of 1883 of North Carolina.

See decision of the Supreme Court in the case of Brown vs. Smathers et al, reported in 188 N. C. R., pages 166 etc., with map attached.

I have heretofore called attention to the fact that the act passed by the General Assembly of North Carolina of 1778, prohibiting the entry and grant of any lands reserved to the Cherokees by the Treaty of the Long Island of Holston of July 20, 1777, west of the Blue Ridge, was repealed by the Act of 1782, after which all the land lying on the waters of the French Broad River, if not before, became subject to entry and grant under the Act of 1792 creating Buncombe County; and

Grant No. 23♦ to George Latimer was not issued by the State until July 20, 1796, and as our Supreme Court in the case of Brown vs. Smathers et al, above cited, in defining the boundary reserved to the Cherokees by the Act of 1783 aforesaid did not include any land on the waters of French Broad River, I am of the opinion that a good title passed to George Latimer to that part of the land embraced in Grant No. 230 to George Latimer that lies on the waters of French Broad River, then in Buncombe, now in Transylvania County, N. C., and that the individuals and corporations who succeeded to the Latimer title through Grant No. 230 to George Latimer to the lands on French Broad River have acquired a good title to the same. This, too, notwithstanding an act was passed by the General Assembly of North Carolina during the year 1809 declaring all grants issued for lands west of the Meigs and Freeman line were void. It is very evident that this act was only intended to apply to lands lying west of the Meigs and Freeman line inside the boundary reserved to the Cherokees by the Act of 1783, but if otherwise intended, it could not have the effect to be retroactive and divest out of George Latimer, the grantee, the title to that part of the grant that lay on the waters of French Broad River, which grant was issued about eleven years before the passage of the act, and after the title of the Cherokees was extinguished and made subject to entry and grant under the general entry and grant laws of the State by the act creating Buncombe County in 1792, if not before, and the Meigs and Freeman line will not cut any figure in the matter.

As above stated, the title of the Cherokees was extinguished to the land lying in between the Hopewell Treaty line that runs through or a little east of the City of Asheville back to the top of the Blue Ridge by the Treaty of Hopewell of November 28, 1785, and the title of the Cherokees to the remainder of the land on the waters of French Broad River was extinguished by the Treaty of Holston of July 2, 1791.

The Act of 1809 above referred to is contained in Chapter 774 of Pot. Rev. of 1809, and a full copy is set out in the case of Adams vs. Westfelt, reported in 159 N. C. R., page 414. I will refer to and comment on this act later in my report.

Summary of things that I have heretofore called attention to affecting the title of land lying from the top of the Blue Ridge back to Pigeon River between the years 1778-1796:

1. The title of the Cherokees was extinguished to the land lying in between the Hopewell Treaty line running through or a little east of the City of Asheville to the top of the Blue Ridge by the Treaty of Hopewell of November 28, 1785.

2. The title of the Cherokees was extinguished to the land lying in between the Hopewell Treaty line which runs through or a little to the east of the City of Asheville west to the Holston Treaty line, running from the Hawkins and Meigs post on top of the Smoky Moun-

tains S. 76° E. to the South Carolina Indian boundary line by the Treat of Holston of July 2, 1791.

3. The title of the Cherokees was extinguished to the land lying in between the Holston Treaty line and the Meigs and Freeman line by the Tellico Treaty of October 2, 1798.

4. The Act of 1778 prohibiting the entry and grant of land west of the Blue Ridge reserved to the Cherokees under the Treaty of the Long Island of Holston of July 20, 1777, was repealed by the Act of 1782; and I am of the opinion that after the passage of the act creating Washington County during the year 1777, which defined the boundary lines of Burke County, that all the land lying west of and in between the top of the Blue Ridge and Pigeon River became subject to entry and grant under the general entry and grant laws of this State, and that all grants issued to parties for land in Burke County within this area up to the time of the passage and ratification of the Act of 1788, accepting and adopting the dividing line between Burke and Rutherford Counties as run by Joseph McDowell, Jr., in 1785, from the top of the Blue Ridge to Pigeon River, if properly described and properly authenticated, were valid grants; but none of the grants issued for land in Rutherford County within this area prior to the passage and ratification of the Act of 1788, above cited, were valid, and only grants issued for land in Rutherford County to parties after that date were valid.

I have heretofore given it as my opinion that none of the grants issued to parties for land in Rutherford County lying west of and in between the top of the Blue Ridge and Pigeon River prior to the passage and ratification of the Act of 1788, above cited, were valid, and only grants issued for land in Rutherford County to parties after the passage and ratification of the Act of 1788 that lay south of the dividing line between Burke and Rutherford Counties, run by Joseph McDowell, Jr., during the year 1785 were valid grants, and only grants issued to parties for land in Burke County north of this line were valid grants, except in cases where grants were issued to parties for land in one of the counties, which included land in both counties, and in such cases grants have been validated under acts of our Legislature, as held by our Supreme Court, hereinbefore cited.

I have heretofore set out a large number of grants that were issued to parties after the creation of Buncombe County in 1792 durng the year 1796 and prior and subsequent dates.

As before stated, some of the land that lies on the waters of French Broad River between the top of the Blue Ridge and the ridge dividing the waters of French Broad from Pigeon River, and from that ridge back to the main prong of Pigeon River was entered and granted in pursuance to the Act of 1788 above cited, and some entered and granted in pursuance to the act creating Buncombe County in 1792 aforesaid under the general entry and grant laws of this State, or at least a part of the land within this area was entered and granted under the acts aforesaid; and if the entries upon which grants were issued to parties for land in Burke and Rutherford Counties under the Act of 1788 above cited were laid in the proper counties of Burke and Rutherford and the grants were in proper form and properly authenticated, the State passed such title as it had to the lands therein described to the grantees therein named; and after the act creating Buncombe County in 1792, all grants issued to parties upon which entries were made after the creation of Buncombe County in 1792 if such grants were in proper form and properly authenticated, passed such title as the State had to the lands therein described to the grantees therein named.

I will later on show when and how the land reserved to the Cherokee Indians by the Act of 1783, lying in between Pigeon River and the Meigs and Freeman line became subject to entry and grant under the general entry and grant laws of this State, after concluding my report on the title to land lying in between Pigeon River and the top of the Blue Ridge.

Haywood County was created by an act of the General Assembly of North Carolina in 1808, taken from Buncombe County, and included all the territory in this State west of what is now Buncombe County. See this act set out on page 134 of the Revised Statutes of North Carolina of 1836. The following is a copy of this act:

AN ACT ERECTING THE WEST PART OF BUNCOMBE INTO A SEPARATE AND DISTINCT COUNTY, AND A PART OF BRUNSWICK AND A PART OF BLADEN COUNTIES INTO A SEPARATE AND DISTINCT COUNTY. (Passed in the year 1808.)

"Whereas the inhabitants in the west part of Buncombe County are very inconvenient to the court house in said county, which renders the attendance of jurors and witnesses very burthensome and expensive, and almost impossible in the winter season; For remedy whereof,

1. BE IT ENACTED, ETC., That all that part of the County of Buncombe, to wit: beginning where the southern boundary line of this State crosses the highest part of the ridge dividing the waters of the French Broad from those of the Tucky Siegy river, then along the said ridge to the ridge dividing the waters of Pigeon and the French Broad river, then with said ridge to the top of Mount Pisgah, thence a direct line to the mouth of the first branch emptying into Hominy creek on the north side above Jesse Belieu's, thence with said branch to the source, and thence along the top of the ridge, dividing the waters of French Broad and those of Pigeon River, to the northern boundary of this State, and with the state line to the line which shall divide this State from the state of Georgia, and with that line to the beginning, shall be and is hereby erected into a separate and distinct county, by the name of Haywood, in honor of the present treasurer of this State."

It appears that some of the members of the General Assembly of North Carolina of 1809 had had their attention called to the fact that numerous large grants had been taken out on lands during the years 1796-97 that lay inside the boundary of land reserved to the Cherokee Indians by the Act of 1783 aforesaid, and the General Assembly of North Carolina of that year passed an act prohibiting the entry and grant of any land lying west of the Meigs and Freeman line, declaring that all entries and grants obtained on land west of the Meigs and Freeman line were null and void in words as follows:

"The land lying west of the line run by Meigs and Freeman, within the bounds of this State, shall not be subject to be entered under the entry laws of this State; but the same, when the Indian title shall be extinct, shall remain and inure to the sole use and benefit of the State; any law to the contrary notwithstanding. All entries made, or grants obtained, or which may hereafter be made or obtained, shall be null and void."

See this act set out as Chapter 774 in Pot. Rev. of 1809.

Also see this act set out in the opinion of our Supreme Court in the case of Adams vs. Westfelt, reported in 159 N. C. R., page 414.

While this act does not so declare in express words, it is very evident that the same was intended to ratify and confirm Grant No. 251 issued by the State to David Allison and grants issued by the State to John Gray Blount, William Cathcart, et al, during the year 1796, that lay inside of the boundary reserved to the Cherokees by the Act of 1783, up to the Meigs and Freeman line; and I have heard it suggested that the parties who railroaded this act through the General Assembly of North Carolina during the year 1809, while they professed to be acting in the interest of the State, as a matter of fact were acting in the interest of Allison and the Cathcarts and parties claiming title through them to these old grants. It appears, however, that this act made very little impression on the Supreme Court of the United States in the case of Latimer vs. Poteet above cited as to Grant No. 226 issued by the State to William Cathcart calling to contain 49,920 acres of land on July 20, 1796, shown on Moffett map, which was the subject of the litigation in the case of Latimer vs. Poteet supra. This decision was rendered during the year 1840, about thirty-one years after the Act of 1809 was passed. By reference to the decision of the Court in this case it will be seen that the Court in construing the Holston Treaty line held that all of Grant No. 226 to William Cathcart lay west of the Holston Treaty line, as defined by the Court in that case, and that the sixth section of the Act of 1783, prohibiting the entry and grant of land within the boundary of land reserved to the Cherokees by the fifth section of the Act of 1783 was still in full force and effect, and the Court held in that case that every foot of Grant No. 226 to William Cathcart was void. It seems, however, that the Supreme Court of this State in the case of Brown vs. Brown, reported in 106 N. C. R., pages 451 etc., which was rendered about fifty years after the decision of the Court in the case of Latimer vs. Poteet supra, held that that part of Grant No. 251 to David Allison was a valid grant up to and east of the Meigs and Freeman line, but void west of it; so it will be seen that there is a conflict of opinion between the Supreme Court of the United States in the case of Latimer vs. Poteet supra, and that of our Supreme Court in the case of Brown vs. Brown, reported in 106 N. C.R., pages 451 etc., supra. The effect of the former decision was that so much of these grants as lay west of the Holston Treaty line, running from the top of the Smoky Mountains S. 76° E. to the South Carolina Indian boundary line was void, and that of our Supreme Court was that these grants were valid up to the Meigs and Freeman line; but as the decision of our Supreme Court in the case of Brown vs. Brown, reported in 106 N. C. R., supra, was rendered about fifty years after the opinion of the Supreme Court in the case of Latimer vs. Poteet supra, under the rule of practice laid down by the Supreme Court of the United States, that the United States Courts would follow the decisions of the highest court of the States involving title to land within the States, in case a controversy should arise over this matter hereafter in the United States Courts, which is not at all likely, the United States Courts would probably ignore its former decision in the case of Latimer vs Poteet, supra, and follow the later decision of the Supreme Court of this State in the case of Brown vs. Brown, reported in 106 N. C. R., supra, and this being so, it can be said that all of these old grants issued to David Allison, John Gray Blount, and the Cathcarts during the year 1796 that lie inside of the boundary reserved to the Cherokee Indians by the Act of 1783 are valid up to the Meigs and Freeman line, but not west of it.

Strange to say, notwithstanding the decision of the Supreme Court of the United States in the case of Latimer vs. Poteet, supra, holding all of Grant No. 226 to William Cathcart to be void for reasons above stated, Margaret Latimer and others who succeeded to the title of William Cathcart to Grants No. 226 and No. 225, filed a petition for partition and sale of these grants and other lands in the proper Court of Buncombe County, and the same were sold under decree of the Court and were purchased by W. J. Brown; and Brown, after his purchase, asserted title to that part of the Cathcart grants that lay east of the Meigs and Freeman line, and later sold and conveyed the same to W. H. Thomas, and W. H. Thomas sold and conveyed the same to Davies and Oram, and Davies and Oram took possession of that part lying east of the Meigs and Freeman line and such possession was kept up under deeds as color of title until they perfected the title to the same, and such title as Davies and Oram had in that part of the Cathcart grants that lay east of the Meigs and Freeman line together with that part of Grant No. 251 to David Allison that lay in Jackson County of about 35,000 acres, appears to have passed to the Highland Forest Company, who conveyed the same to the Jackson Lumber Company, who conveyed the same to the Blackwood Lumber Co., and others, and among others, the Champion Fibre Company became the purchaser of about 5,000 acres of land of what is known as the Scott's Creek Boundary near Willett's Station on the line of the Southern Railway Company, and whatever doubt formerly existed as to the title of that part of the Cathcart grants that lie east of the Meigs and Freeman line is now settled and it appears that the purchasers have acquired a good title by both possession under deeds as color of title and a good record title under the decision of our Supreme Court in the case of Brown vs. Brown, reported in 106 N. C. R., pages 451 etc.

I will now give the reason why in my opinion there was an acquiescence by the State and the citizens of that section of country to the claim of title of the parties who succeeded to the title of the Cathcart grants by the partition proceedings aforesaid, east of the Meigs and Freeman line, which is this:

That the Holston Treaty line was never run in North Carolina by Hawkins, and after the Meigs and Freeman line was run in pursuance to the Tellico Treaty of October 2, 1798, the people generally understood the Meigs and Freeman line to be the Holston Treaty line, and for that reason parties claiming title through the Allison grant and the Cathcart grants east of the Meigs and Freeman line were not contested by the State or individuals; in fact this view of the matter is supported by the decision of our Supreme Court in the case of Brown vs. Brown, reported in 106 N. C. R., pages 451 etc. By reference to the decision of the Court in that case it will be seen that the Court held that there had been a controversy about the true location of the Holston Treaty line, and that as the title of the Cherokees had long since been extinguished to the land in controversy in that suit, and neither the United States nor the Cherokees had any further interest in the matter, the State of North Carolina had the right to fix and determine for itself the true location of the Holston Treaty line, and hence accepted and recognized the Meigs and Freeman line as the true Holston Treaty line, and accordingly held that Grant No. 251 to David Allison was good up to the east of the Meigs and Freeman line, but not west of it, and the effect of this decision was to hold that Grants No. 226 and No. 225 to William Cathcart were likewise good up to the Meigs and Freeman line and not west of it, and I do not think that any question will ever be raised hereafter as to the validity of the David Allison, Blount, and Cathcart grants up to and east of the Meigs and Freeman line.

I have heretofore made my report on when and how the lands lying in between the top of the Blue Ridge and Pigeon River became subject to entry and grant under the general entry and grant laws of this State.

REPORT ON WHEN AND HOW THE LANDS LYING IN BE-
TWEEN PIGEON RIVER AND THE MEIGS AND FREEMAN
LINE IN THIS STATE BECAME SUBJECT TO ENTRY AND
GRANT UNDER THE GENERAL ENTRY AND GRANT LAWS
OF THIS STATE.

WILL NOW take up and discuss when and how the lands lying in between Pigeon River and the Meigs and Freeman line became subject to entry and grant under the general entry and grant laws of this State, and I will here state that just when and how the lands lying within this area became subject to entry and grant has been a fruitful source of litigation and conflicting opinions in the Supreme Court of our State and of conflicting opinions rendered by the Supreme Court of our State in the second and third cases of Brown vs. Brown, and the decision of the Supreme Court of the United State, as will be seen by reference to the following decisions of our Supreme Court of this State and the Supreme Court of the United States:

Strother vs. Cathey, 1st Murphy, 162 (5th N. C. R., star page 163, and cases cited).

Latimer vs. Poteet, 14th Pet., page 4, (39 U. S. R.).

Brown vs. Brown, first reported in 103 N. C. R., page 213.

Brown vs. Brown, reported second time in 103 N. C. R., page 221.

Brown vs. Brown, reported third time in 106 N. C. R., pages 451 etc.

I have already shown how the title of the Cherokees was extinguished to that part of the boundary reserved to the Cherokee Indians by the fifth section of the Act of 1783, between Pigeon River and the Meigs and Freeman line:

First, by the Holston Treaty of July 2, 1791, from Pigeon River up to the Holston Treaty line, running from the Hawkins and Meigs post on top of the Smoky Mountains South 76° East to the South Carolina Indian boundary line.

Second, by the Treaty of Tellico of October 2, 1798, from the Holston Treaty line up to the Meigs and Freeman line.

See Holston Treaty line shown on Moffett map, marked "Hawkins' Line," South 76° East, Holston Treaty, July 2, 1791.

See Meigs and Freeman line shown on Moffett map as the Tellico Treaty line, marked "Meigs and Freeman Line," South 52° East, Tellico Treaty, October 2, 1798.

Notwithstanding the conflicting opinions of the Supreme Court of our State and the Supreme Court of the United States, above cited, as to when the land lying in between Pigeon River and the Meigs and Freeman line in this State became subject to entry and grant, I have heretofore given it as my opinion that the title to Grant No. 253 to John Gray Blount, calling to contain 176,000 acres of land, and the title to so much of Grant No. 251 to David Allison, and Cathcart Grants No. 226 and No. 225, lying east of the Meigs and Freeman line, are valid, as held by our Supreme Court in the case of Brown vs. Brown, reported third time in 106 N. C. R., pages 451 etc., and the chances are that the decision of the Supreme Court in this case will stand and not be disturbed hereafter; but at the same time, the history of the Cherokee land laws would not be complete without a report on the effect which the first decision in the case of Brown vs. Brown, reported in 103 N.C.R., page 212, in over-ruling the decision of the Supreme Court in the case of Strother vs. Cathey supra, and holding that part of Grant No. 251 to David Allison that lay inside the boundary reserved to the Cherokees by the fifth section of the Act of 1783 void, had in upsetting titles temporarily to about one-half of the land in Haywood County and considerable acreage in Jackson County, and how when a wail went up by the citizens of Haywood and Jackson Counties, who held title through the Love Estate through Grant No. 251 to David Allison and Grant No. 253 to John Gray Blount, and how upon petition of the plaintiff filed for a rehearing, our Supreme Court in an honest effort to prevent upsetting titles, in rendering its second decision in the case of Brown vs. Brown, reported in 103 N. C. R., page 221, resorted to a four-line statute of 1794, hereinafter referred to, reversed its former decision, and held that this four-line statute authorized the entry and grant of land lying inside the boundary reserved to the Cherokees by the fifth section of the Act of 1783, east of the ceded territory, meaning the State of Tennessee, and how when the attention of the Court was called to the fact that this decision would validate so much of Grants No. 226 and No. 225 to William Cathcart, and Grant No. 251 to David Allison as lay west of the Meigs and Freeman line, and all of Grant No. 279, issued by this State to John Holdeman and Jacob Eshleman on the 3rd day of April, 1797, for 200,960 acres of land that covers a good part of what is now Jackson, Swain and Macon Counties, which our Supreme Court and the Supreme Court of the United States had previously held to be void on account of the prohibition of entry and grant contained in the sixth section of the Act of 1783, and also the act of our General Assembly of North Carolina of 1809, above cited, declaring same void; and would upset, if not destroy, the title of a great many of the parties who had entered and granted land under the general entry and grant laws of this State under the Act of 1835, lying in between the Meigs and Freeman line and Tennessee River, and would also upset, if not destroy, the title of a great many parties who had acquired title under the Cherokee land laws of 1819 and act amendatory thereof, and 1836 and act amendatory thereof, and 1852 and acts amendatory thereof, and would upset more titles than were cured by the second decision in the case of Brown vs. Brown, above rendered; the Court then rendered its third decision in the case of Brown vs. Brown, reported in 106 N. C. R., pages 451 etc., modifying its second decison rendered in this case, and holding for reasons therein stated, that Grant No. 251 to David Allison was good up to and east of the Meigs and Freeman line, but not west of it, and the effect of which decision was to hold that Grants No. 226 and No. 225 to William Cathcart, and Grant No. 253 to John Gray Blount were good up to and east of the Meigs and Freeman line, but not west of it.

I have heretofore called attention to the conflict of opinion between the Supreme Court of the United States in the case of Latimer vs. Poteet, above cited, and the decision of our Supreme Court in the case of Brown vs. Brown, reported last in 106 N. C. R., pages 451 etc., in that the Supreme Court of the United States held in the case of Latimer vs. Poteet, that all of Grant No. 226, issued by the State to William Cathcart on the 20th of July, 1796, calling to contain 49,920 acres of land, was void for the reason that the same lay west of the Holston Treaty line, and that the fifth section of the Act of 1783 was in full force and effect, and that all of Grant No. 226 was void; while our Supreme Court in the case of Brown vs. Brown, reported in 106 N. C. R., pages 451 etc., held that so much of Grant No. 251 to David Allison that lay east of the Meigs and Freeman line was valid, but not west of it; and as before stated, the effect of this decision was to hold that so much of Grants No. 226 and No. 225 to William Cathcart and Grant No. 252 to John Gray Blount, that lay east of the Meigs and Freeman line were valid grants.

I will here state that such title as David Allison acquired by Grant No. 251 and John Gray Blount acquired byGrants No. 252 and No. 253 passed by mesne conveyances, tax titles, court proceedings, wills, etc., to Robert Love and J. R. Love during the year 1834. See deed made by Thomas H. Blount and Wm. A. Blount, executors of John Gray Blount, deceased, to Robert Love and Jas. R. Love, bearing date of December 10, 1834, recorded in Book D, page 308, record of deeds of Haywood County, N. C. While some few citizens of Haywood County succeeded to the title and occupied land that was excepted in Grant No. 251 to David Allison and Grant No. 252 to John Gray Blount as previously appropriated, about one-half the citizens of Haywood County, and a considerable number in Jackson County, acquired title to the land that they occupied and claimed through the executors of J. R. Love and trustees of the Love Estate.

I have heretofore called attention to the first decision of our Supreme Court in this State, bearing on the title to land that lay inside the boundary reserved to the Cherokee Indians by the fifth section of the Act of 1783, in the case of Avery vs. Strother, reported in 1st N. C. R., page 560, involving the title to a 640-acre tract of land that lay immediately on the west side of Pigeon River opposite what was known as the "Flowery Gardens," in which the Court held that the grant under which the plaintiff, Avery, claimed was void for two reasons:

First, that at the time of taking out of the grant by plaintiff, the same was not in any county in the State at that time;

And second, that the same lay inside the boundary reserved to the Cherokee Indians by the fifth section of the Act of 1783, and the same was void for the reason that the entry and grant of the same was prohibited by the sixth section of the Act of 1783, which was then in full force and effect, and my comment on the same.

This decision was rendered at June Term, 1802.

This tract of land lies about two miles above the Town of Canton, and was later known as the Chambers' Farm, and formerly belonged to Mrs. M. E. Hilliard of Asheville, N. C., and was later purchased from Mrs. Hilliard or the Hilliard Estate by Charlie Wells, and this tract of land now belongs to the Estate of Charlie Wells.

The next decision rendered by our Supreme Court, affecting the title to land within the boundary of land reserved to the Cherokee Indians by the fifth section of the Act of 1783, was the case of Strother vs. Cathey, reported in 5th N. C. R., star page 162, which involved the title to a 640-acre tract of land which lay on the west side of Pigeon Riven, within the boundary reserved to the Cherokees by the fifth section of the Act of 1783. This decision was rendered during July Term, 1807.

The plaintiff, Strother, claimed title to this tract through a grant issued by the State of North Carolina to John Carson on May 19, 1803, upon an entry made during the year 1791, and after the title of the Cherokees was extinguished to the same by the Treaty of Holston of July 2, 1791; while the defendant, Cathey, claimed title to the same tract through a grant issued by the State to him on December 8, 1787, before the title of the Cherokees was extinguished by the Treaty of Holston of July 2, 1791. The plaintiff, Strother, insisted that the grant to Carson was a valid grant as the entry was made and the grant issued thereon to Carson after the title of the Cherokees had been extinguished by the Treaty of Holston of July 2, 1791.

The defendant, Cathey, contended as follows:

First, that by the Treaty of Holston of July 2, 1791, the Cherokees relinquished their claim of title to the area between Pigeon River and the Holston Treaty line to the United States, and that the United States was the owner of this area.

Second, that if his grant was void for the reason that the sixth section of the Act of 1783, prohibiting the entry and grant of land reserved to the Cherokees by the fifth section of the Act of 1783, was in full force and effect, that the plaintiff's grant was void for the same reason, and the plaintiff had to recover upon the strength of his title, and not on the weakness of the defendant's title.

Third, that his grant could not be attacked collaterally by the plaintiff, but only by a direct proceedings for that purpose.

The Court, however, refused to sustain the contention of the defendant, and held that while the states surrendered their power to make treaties with the Indian tribes upon the adoption of the Constitution of the United States, that the State of North Carolina made the United States its agent to negotiate treaties with the Indian tribes within its border; but the State of North Carolina and the other States, following the policy of the European countries, never recognized any title in the Indian tribes, except the right of occupancy, and when the title of the Cherokees was extinguished by the Holston Treaty, the land was relieved of the encumbrance of the Cherokees and the title reinvested in the State of North Carolina. And the Court held that the defendant's grant was absolutely void for the reason that at the time of the entry and grant, the title of the Cherokees had not been extinguished, and the sixth section of the Act of 1783 was in full force and effect, and that the officers of the State had no authority to issue the grant to the defendant and his grant was void; and this fact could be shown on the trial of the case. The Court also refused to sustain the contention of the defendant in every particular.

The Court also refused to sustain the contention of the defendant that the plaintiff's grant was void, for the reason that the fifth section of the Act of 1783 aforesaid had not been expressly repealed, and was in full force and effect, but the Court held that the prohibition of the entry and grant of the land reserved to the Cherokees by the fifth section of the Act of 1783 was to cultivate peace and friendship with the Cherokees, and while the fifth section of the Act was not expressly repealed, after the title of the Cherokees was extinguished to the land in controversy by the Treaty of Holston of July 2, 1791, the sixth section of the Act of 1783 was effectually and substantially repealed, as the Cherokees had no further interest in the matter, and held that the grant under which the plaintiff, Strother, claimed title was a valid grant.

The position taken by the Court in this case that the right of the Cherokees to the land reserved to them by the fifth section of the Act of 1783 was only a right of occupancy and that the fee to this land remained in the State of North Carolina was fully sustained by the decision of the Supreme Court of the United States rendered more than thirty years later in the case of Latimer vs. Poteet, supra, reported in 14th Pet., page 4, (39 U. S. R.).

It will be observed that this decision affected the title to land to which the Cherokees had relinquished their claim of title by the Treaty of Holston of July 2, 1791, and this decision was rendered during the year 1807, about nine years after the title of the Cherokees had been extinguished to the land lying in between the Holston Treaty line and the Meigs and Freeman line by the Treaty of Tellico of October 2, 1798, and upon the principle enunciated in the case of Strother vs. Cathey, supra, after the Treaty of Tellico of October 2, 1798, the land that lay between the Holston Treaty line and the Meigs and Freeman line was also subject to entry and grant under the general entry and grant laws of the State.

The effect of the decision in the case of Strother vs. Cathey, supra, was to validate the title to Grant No. 251 to David Allison, Cathcart Grants No. 226 and No. 225, and Blount Grant No. 252 up to and east of the Holston Treaty line of July 2, 1791; and on account of the Holston Treaty line not having been run from the Hawkins and Meigs post on top of the Smoky Mountains through North Carolina to the South Carolina Indian boundary line, the citizens, or at least a part of the citizens, in that section of country were under the impression, after the Meigs and Freeman line was run in 1802, that the Meigs and Freeman line was the Holston Treaty line; and after the decision was rendered by the Court in the case of Strother vs. Cathey, the same was accepted as the law of the State and acted upon as such in the transfer of title to real estate in both Haywood and Jackson Counties, until the decision was rendered by the Supreme Court in the case of Brown vs. Brown, reported in 103 N. C. R., page 213, in which the Court held that that part of Grant No. 251 to David Allison that lay within the boundary of land reserved to the Cherokee Indians by the fifth section of the Act of 1783 was void under the sixth section of that Act, which as before stated upset the title to about half the land in Haywood County, and about 50,000 acres in Jackson County. A great many of the citizens in both Jackson and Haywood Counties who had acquired title through the Love Estate had been in possession of the same under deeds as color of title for a sufficient length of time to ripen the title to the same, but a great many people had purchased timber tracts from the Loves, boundaries containing from 1,000 to 2,500 acres, and the Love Estate still retained title to from 75,000 to 100,000 acres in Haywood County and about 35,000 acres in Jackson County, on which there had been no possession, except ranging of stock by the claimants, so it can be seen how the decision of the Supreme Court in the case of Brown vs. Brown, supra, (reported in 103 N. C. R., page 213), aforesaid, upset titles in Haywood and Jackson Counties.

After the trial of the case of Brown vs. Brown in the Superior Court of Jackson County by Judge Graves, who held that that part of Grant No. 251 to David Allison that lay inside the boundary reserved to the Cherokees by the Act of 1783 was void, when this decision became known, the citizens of both the counties of Jackson and Haywood rushed to the office of the entry taker and laid entries covering the area in the two counties affected by the decision. The entry takers in the two counties were kept busy day and a good part of the night for weeks.

Immediately after the first decision was rendered by the Supreme Court in the case of Brown vs. Brown, supra, (reported in 103 N. C. R., page 213), the J. R. Love Estate, on behalf of the plaintiff, W. A.

Brown, filed a petition for a rehearing of the case and immediately after this decision was rendered, the representatives of the Love Estate and the citizens of Haywood and Jackson Counties who had acquired title through the Love Estate did not think under the circumstances that it was at all improper for them to approach and lay their grievances before the members of the Supreme Court, and commenced bombarding the Honorable A. S. Merrimon, Associate Justice of the Supreme Court who delivered the opinion, and other members of the Supreme Court, with letters calling the attention of the members of the Supreme Court to how the decision had upset titles in Haywood and Jackson Counties and rendered some people homeless. About the same time, parties who had laid entries on land in Haywood and Jackson Counties commenced bombarding members of the Supreme Court with letters insisting that the decision of the Court was proper and should not be reversed, and a number of the judges were approached personally in reference to the matter.

During the session of the General Assembly of 1889 and before the Supreme Court reversed its decision by the second decision rendered in the case of Brown vs. Brown, an act was passed, Chapter 284, Public Laws of 1889, entitled, "An act to validate certain state grants in the counties of Haywood, Jackson, and Swain," which validated the title to all grants issued by the State to parties between the years 1791 and January 1, 1887, for lands lying in Haywood, Jackson, and Swain Counties, N. C., east of the Meigs and Freeman line, which act contained a proviso in words as follows:

"That wherever within said territory and within said dates any such grants may conflict or lap, the junior grants shall be given force and effect. Which act was ratified the 7th day of March, 1889.

When this act was introduced, the same was referred to the House Judiciary Committee, of which Hon. W. A. Hoke of Lincoln County was the chairman, and the writer was present at the hearing of the same. Judge Hoke announced on behalf of the Committee that the Committee was disposed to validate the old grants up to the Meigs and Freeman line affected by the decision of the Supreme Court in the case of Brown vs. Brown, first reported, but the Committee had their doubts as to whether or not this could be done so as to divest the title of the parties who had laid entries on the land during the years 1886-87, and for that reason the proviso was inserted in the act, giving the junior grantees preference.

Judge Hoke later became Associate Justice and Chief Justice of the Supreme Court and was one of the ablest lawyers in the State.

After this act was passed, the Supreme Court reversed its first decision by the second decision in the case of Brown vs. Brown, reported in 103 N. C. R., page 221, and later modified its second decision in the case of Brown vs. Brown, holding Grant No. 251 to David Allison good up to the Meigs and Freeman line, but not west of it, after which the parties who had laid entries and obtained grants on land in 1886-87 abandoned their claims of title to the same.

The Supreme Court in rendering its second decision in the case of Brown vs. Brown, in reversing its first decision, based its reversal on a four- line statute, referred to and set out in its decision, which it found was not discovered when it rendered its first decision. This certainly was an emergency decision, and the Court made use of this statute in an honest effort to prevent upsetting of titles to land; and by reference thereto it will be seen that this four-line statute was never intended to authorize the entry and grant of any lands, but only prescribed the manner in which a party who had laid a large number of entries might include the same in one survey and one grant. The four-line statute referred to was passed in 1794 as an amendment to an act of 1784.

At the date of the passage of the Act of 1784 it appears that one person could lay any number of entries, but no one entry could exceed 640 acres, and the Act of 1784 was passed to permit a party who had laid a large number of entries in swamp land in eastern North Carolina to include all the entries in one survey and one grant; and the Act of 1794 as an amendatory to the Act of 1784 was passed to apply to lands in other parts of the State.

The four-line statute referred to was Act of 1794, set out in 1st Pot. Rev. Chapter 423, amendatory of the statute (Acts 1784, 1st Pot. Rev. Chapter 202).

In a brief filed by the law firm of Merrimon, Adams and Johnson, the writer and E. C. Ward, attorneys for the defendants in the case of W. Vance Brown et al vs. Geo. H. Smathers et al, in commenting on this four-line statute use the following language.

"At first impression we thought the sentence, 'That all the lands in this state, lying to the eastward of the line of the ceded territory,' etc., might with the same reason be applied to the line of the territory ceded by this State to the Cherokee Indians by the Act of 1783 above described; but we find that the act has been construed to mean east of the Tennessee line in the case of Mendenhall vs. Gassells, 3 Dev. & Bat. Law, page 49, but applied there for the purpose which we insist the statute was intended to serve, to-wit, to allow a person who had made a large number of entries in 640 acre tracts, as prescribed in the third section of the Act of 1777, Chapter 114, 1st Pot. Rev., page 275, to embrace all such entries in one survey and grant. (See also Polk, Lessee, vs. Wendell and others, 9th Cranch, page 87). So when we consider the four-line statute in connection with the entry laws of 1777, and the subsequent entry laws prior to its enactment, it would seem that it was not intended to open up any lands to entry and grant, but only to regulate the manner in which lands already entered, or which thereafter might be entered as prescribed by law, should be surveyed and granted."

The writer fully concurs in the views expressed by the attorneys for the defendant in this case.

I am informed that after the Act of 1794 aforesaid, all the large grants taken out in the State, and especially the Allison, Blount, and other large grants, during the year 1796 were granted on numerous 640 acre entries, all of which were included in one survey and one grant.

The writer further concurs in the opinion expressed by the writer and the other attorneys for the defendant in their brief filed in the case of Brown vs. Smathers, above cited, in words as follows:

"Before leaving this branch of the subject, we wish to state that in our opinion the first decision of this Court rendered by Judge Merrimon in the case of Brown vs. Brown, reported in 103 N. C. R., pages 213, etc., was legally sound and if it had been rendered before the decision was rendered in the case of Strother vs. Cathey during the year 1807, it would not have been disturbed. Judge Merrimon, in delivering the opinion of the Court in that case, held that as the sixth section of the Act of 1783 prohibited the entry and grant of the boundary of land set apart to the Cherokee Indians by the fifth section of said act, the land in controversy in that action was not subject to entry and grant on the date of the issuing of the Allison grant on the 29th of November, 1796, without regard to the question as to whether the Indian title had been extinguished or not. We think this opinion was in accordance with the intention of the Legislature at the time the act was passed in 1783, as the object of the act was twofold:

1st. To cultivate peace and friendship with the Indians;

2nd. Not to allow the better lands inside this boundary to be entered and granted under the general entry and grant laws of the State, as this boundary of land included some of the finest valley lands on the west side of Pigeon River and the valleys of Tuckaseegee, Tennessee and Hiawassee Rivers in Western North Carolina, and a good part of the land was of a superior quality to other lands embraced under the general entry and grant laws of the State. This policy of not allowing these lands to be entered and granted under the general entry and grant laws of the state was manifested by subsequent acts of the legislature as the Indian title was extinguished from time to time west of the Meigs and Freeman line, in the manner hereinbefore set out.

By reference to the opinion of the Supreme Court in the case of Strother vs. Cathey, 1st Mur. N. C. R., pages 162, it will be seen that in that case the Court held that as the plaintiff claimed title to land in controversy in that action under grant from the State that was issued to him after the Treaty of Holston of July 2, 1791, and west of the Holston Treaty line, the Court held in that case that the object of the Legislature of North Carolina by the enactment of the sixth section of the Act of 1783 in prohibiting the entry and grant of any lands in the boundary reserved to the Indians by the fifth section of said act was to cultivate peace and friendship with the Cherokees and that the extinguishment of the Indian title substantially and effectually repealed the statute, and held the plaintiffs' title good. This decision was accepted by the legal profession as being the law from the date of the rendering of the opinion of the Supreme Court (in the case of Strother vs. Cathey, supra, in 1807), up to the time of the rendering of the first opinion by the Supreme Court in the case of Brown vs. Brown in 1889. By reference to the decision of this Court rendered by Judge Merrimon on the first hearing in the case of Brown vs. Brown, reported in 103 N. C. R., pages 213, etc., it will be seen that the opinion in the case of Strother vs. Cathey was over-ruled, and it does seem to us that when the Court decided to reverse its decision in the case of Brown vs. Brown as first rendered, it should not have resorted to the four-line statute aforesaid, but should have reaffirmed the opinion in the case of Strother vs. Cathey, supra. For even if the decision of the Court in this case was not sound, the same had stood from the year 1808 up to the time of the rendering of the first decision in the case of Brown vs. Brown in 1890, and people had acquired title to a good part of the land in Haywood County and a considerable portion in Jackson County between Pigeon River and the Meigs and Freeman line through this decision, and this decision should not have been disturbed under the doctrine of "Stare Decisis". For a full discussion of the doctrine of Stare Decisis see this subject discussed on pages 158 to pages 195 in 26th Vol. Amer. and Eng. Enc. of Law, Second Edition, entitled "Stare Decisis".

I deem it proper here to call attention to questions that I have heard were formerly raised by parties to the title of the State to the land embraced within the boundary reserved to the Cherokees by the fifth section of the Act of 1783, that is, that by the numerous treaties made and entered into between the commissioners of the United States and the chiefs and head men of the Cherokee Nation the title to the land relinquished by the Cherokees by the several treaties, vested in the United States.

By reference to the Treaty of Tellico of October 2, 1798, and subsequent treaties, it will be seen that the language used in these treaties is that the Cherokees relinquish and cede to the United States the title to the land extinguished by the treaty, and by reference to the decision of our Supreme Court in the case of Strother vs. Cathey, supra, it will be seen that the defendant, Cathey, insisted that when the Treaty of Holston was entered into between the United States and the Cherokees, the title of the Cherokees extinguished by this treaty vested in the United States. The Court, however, refused to sustain the contention of the defendant, and held that while the states surrendered their power to make treaties with the Indian tribes upon the adoption of the Constitution of the United States, the State of North Carolina made the United States its agent to negotiate treaties with the Indian tribes within its border; but the State of North Carolina and the other states, following the policy of the European countries, never recognized any title in the Indian tribes, except the right of occupancy, and when the title of the Cherokees was extinguished by the Holston Treaty, the land was relieved of the encumbrance of the Cherokees and the title reinvested in the State of North Carolina.

But notwithstanding this decision, this question was continued to be raised and many insisted that as the title of the Cherokees was extinguished by the treaties aforesaid, the title vested in the United States, until the decision was rendered by the Supreme Court of the United States in the case of Latimer vs. Poteet, reported in 14th Pet., page 4 (39 U. S. R.), when the Court held in that case that the State of North Carolina could grant the fee in the land in controversy in that action, subject to the Indian right of occupancy, but held in that case that as the tract in controversy, being Grant No. 226 to William Cathcart that lay inside the boundary reserved to the Cherokees by the fifth section of the Act of 1783, lay west of the Holston Treaty line, and the title of the Cherokees had not been extinguished, the sixth section of the Act of 1783 was in full force and effect, and that all of this grant was void. This opinion, together with the opinion of the Supreme Court in the case of Strother vs. Cathey, supra, settled the matter that the right of the Indians was only a right of occupancy, and when this right was extinguished by the treaties, any interest the Indians had in the land ceased.

When the writer was a law student at the Dick and Dillard School at Greensboro, N. C., during the year 1880, in a talk he had with Hon. Robert R. King, then an attorney at Greensboro who had been a law student of Chief Justice Pearson, Mr. King advised the writer that Judge Pearson in his law lectures at his law school at Richmond Hill, in referring to the Act of 1783, granting to the Cherokees the boundary of land set out in the fifth section of the Act of 1783, said that this was one of the few cases of a base or qualified fee in North Carolina.

A base or qualified fee, as I understand it, as defined by Sir William Blackstone, was a grant by the Crown of Great Britain to a party and his heirs to real estate so long as they should remain on and occupy the same, but when they ceased to occupy the same, the land reverted to the Crown. Anderson's Dictionary of Law defines a base or qualified fee "as a grant 'to A and his heirs, tenants of the manor of Dale,' that is, as long as they continue tenants. This estate is a fee, because it may endure forever, yet the duration depends upon a circumstance, and this debases the purity of the donation." See second Volume B 1. Com. 109.

I have heretofore called attention to the fact that the Supreme

Court of our State in the case of Strother vs. Cathey and the decision of the Supreme Court of the United States in the case of Latimer vs. Poteet, before cited, held that the boundary of land reserved and granted to the Cherokees by the fifth section of th Act of 1783 was not a fee simple title, but the Cherokees only had a right of occupancy to this boundary; and when the Indians abandoned their possession by treaty or otherwise, that their rights ceased therein.

But notwithstanding the decision of the Supreme Court of this State in the case of Strother vs. Cathey and the decision of the Supreme Court of the United States in the case of Latimer vs. Poteet, above cited, holding that the State of North Carolina could grant the fee in the land subject to the right of occupancy of the Cherokees, I remember about thirty years ago an article appeared in some paper in Chattanooga or Nashville, Tennessee, in which it was stated that some title examiner in the Forest Service, in examining the treaties made and entered into between the United States and the Cherokees, gave it as his opinion that on account of the language used in these treaties, that is "the Cherokees relinquish and cede to the United States" the land referred to in the treaties, the title to all the land in Western North Carolina within the boundary reserved to the Cherokees by the fifth section of the Act of 1783, vested in the United States, and that the possession had by parties claiming title to the land under the State would not protect them as the statute would not run against the United States, and this attorney recommended to Hon. Gifford Pinchot, then United States Forester who was endeavoring to corral all the land he could as a part of the Forest Reserve, to take action to recover all the lands in Western North Carolina reserved to the Cherokees by the fifth section of the Act of 1783; but evidently Mr. Pinchot did not think much of the recommendation of this attorney, as no action was ever taken in the matter by the United States.

Another question that was raised as to the title to the land reserved to the Cherokees by the fifth section of the Act of 1783 was that the title by this act vested in fee in the Cherokees as tenants in common, and the writer remembers that one, James Taylor, Sr., who died about ten years ago, and who from soon after the Civil War up to the time of his death, figured extensively in the affairs of the Eastern Band of Cherokees, and the Cherokee Nation formerly in Indian territory, now Oklahoma, consulted a number of attorneys about filing petitions in the different counties inside the boundary reserved to the Cherokees in Western North Carolina for partition and sale of the land on behalf of the Cherokees, but Mr. Taylor never succeeded in getting any attorney to think much of his position in the matter. It would certainly have been a job to have ascertained the heirs of the Cherokees who lived at that date, in fact it would have been impracticable to do this; in fact, the only way to have handled the matter would have been to declare all the Cherokees in the east and west as the heirs of the Cherokees in 1783.

I will here call attention to an effort of the Interior Department of Washington, D. C., to take the census of such of the Cherokee Indians as were heirs of the Cherokees who were entitled to participate in the per capita and subsistence fund under the Treaty of 1835 in the last payment made to the Cherokees in a suit authorized by Congress that was first brought in the Court of Claims at Washington, D. C., and later went to the Supreme Court of the United States, some ten or fifteen years ago, in which the Court held that the Cherokees were entitled to this per capita and subsistence fund and directed payment to be made to the Cherokee Indians entitled thereto, being the last payment made to the Cherokees.

The Court in its decree in that case directed that this fund should be distributed "per stirpes," that is to the heirs of the Indians who were entitled to the same under the Treaty of 1835, and prior treaties. It appears that under the Treaty of 1819, the Cherokees relinquished their claim to about one-third of the land east of the Mississippi River in accordance with the estimated number of about one-third of the Cherokees who emigrated to the Indian Territory under that treaty, and the Cherokees who emigrated under the Treaty of 1819 were afterwards known as the "old settlers," or the "Western Cherokees," and in a suit formerly brought by the old settlers against the United States, their per capita and subsistence fund under the Treaty of 1835 and prior treaties had been paid to them, and only the Eastern Cherokees, those who emigrated to the Indian territory under the Treaty of 1835, and the Eastern Band of Cherokees were entitled to participate in the fund in the last suit, and the Secretary of the Interior, in accordance with the decree of the Court entered in that suit, endeavored to take a census of the heirs of the Eastern Cherokees, that is those who emigrated to the Indian territory under the Treaty of 1835, and the Eastern Band of Cherokees, and in the effort, found that the intermarriages between the Old Settlers and the Eastern Cherokees were mixed up, and found that there were eighty-two Indians in the former Indian territory, now Oklahoma, named "John," who had no other name, and these Indians did not know whether they were descendants of the Old Settlers or the so-called Eastern Cherokees, and found that it was totally impracticable to distinguish the desendants of the Eastern Cherokees from those of the Old Settlers, and the Court finally had to revise its decree and direct the payment per capita to all the Cherokees in Oklahoma, and the Eastern Band of Cherokee Indians.

The writer remembers James Taylor, Sr., quite well. Mr. Taylor claimed to be part Indian, but he had no appearance of an Indian and was generally referred to by the Eastern Band of Cherokees as a "white Indian," and an Indian for the purpose of participating in the enjoyment of the lands and funds of the Eastern Band of Cherokees, and the Western Cherokees.

Mr. Taylor left a son by the name of James Taylor, who is still living, and now claims to be a resident of Cherokee County, who is continuously seeking conferences with attorneys in Asheville and elsewhere in Western North Carolina, claiming to represent individual Indians of the Eastern Band of Cherokees in an effort to recover funds due to the Indians by the United States, and raising the same question as raised by his father, that by the Act of 1783 the title to the land reserved to the Cherokee Indians by the fifth section of the Act of 1783 vested in fee in the Cherokees as tenants in common; but so far as I have been able to learn, the attorneys whom James Taylor, Jr., has consulted do not seem to think much of his scheme.

I will add that I think the United States has paid to both the Eastern Band of Cherokees and the Cherokees in Oklahoma all the funds to which they are entitled under any and all treaties entered into between the United States and the Cherokees under and prior to the Treaty of New Echota, Georgia, December 29, 1835.

This concludes my history of the title to lands lying east of the Meigs and Freeman line back to the top of the Blue Ridge.

I will now take up and discuss how the title was acquired to lands west of the Meigs and Freeman line in this state, under the Cherokee land laws and the general entry and grant laws of this State.

As before stated, the lands lying west of Pigeon River in this State, reserved to the Cherokees by the fifth section of the Act of 1783, were formerly known and now often referred to as the "Chrokee Country," but the Cherokee Land Laws only relate to the land lying west of the Meigs and Freeman line in this State.

The title to all the lands lying in between Pigeon River and the Meigs and Freeman line was acquired under the general entry and grant laws of this State and the title to a part of the lands lying in between the Meigs andFreeman line and Tennessee River was acquired under Commissioners' Sale under the Act of 1819 and acts amendatory thereof, and a part under the general entry and grant laws under the Act of 1835 and acts amendatory thereof until the same were repealed by the Cherokee Land Laws of 1852; and a part under the Cherokee Land Laws of 1852 and acts amendatory thereof; and a part of the lands lying west of Tennessee River in this state was acquired by Commissioners' Sale under the Acts of 1836 and acts amendatory thereof, and a part under the Cherokee Land Laws under the Act of 1852 and acts amendatory thereof, until the same were repealed by the Act of 1883, before cited, after which time all the lands in the Cherokee Country were made subject to entry and grant under the general entry and grant laws of this State.

By the Treaty entered into between the United States and the

Cherokees of 1819, the Cherokees relinquished their claim of title to all the land lying between the Meigs and Freeman line and Tennessee River, and at the next session of the General Assembly of North Carolina following this treaty, an Act was passed in 1819 prohibiting the entry and grant of the land within this area, and providing the manner in which the lands acquired by the Treaty were to be disposed of by the State.

The first, second, third, fourth, fifth, seventh, eighth and tenth sections of said act are as follows:

"1. That as soon as may be convenient after the passage of this act, the Governor shall appoint two commissioners whose duty it shall be to superintend and direct the manner in which the said lands shall be surveyed and laid off into sections containing from fifty to three hundred acres of land; that they shall further cause the principal surveyor to note down in each of said sections the quality of the land contained therein, stating that it is of the first, second or third quality; and in all cases where it can be done with convenience, or the situation of the land will admit of it, such portion of the adjoining mountainous lands shall be included in each section as may be deemed sufficient for buildings, fences, fuel and other necessary improvements.

"2. That one principal surveyor of skill and integrity, shall be appointed by the Governor, with full power and authority to appoint as many deputy surveyors, chain carriers and markers, and to employ as many pack horses as may be thought necessary to complete the said survey in the most speedy and effectual manner; for whose conduct the said principal surveyor shall give bond and security in the sum of ten thousand dollars, payable to the Governor for the time being, for the faithful discharge of the several duties imposed by this act. It shall further be the duty of the said principal surveyor, under the directions of the commissioners aforesaid, to cause each section by him surveyed to be measured and marked, and the corners to be clearly designated on trees, or otherwise, with the number of each section.

"3. That each surveyor shall note in his field book the true situation of all mines, springs, mill seats and water courses, over which the lines he runs shall pass, and those continguous thereto; that the said field book shall be returned to the commissioners, who shall cause their principal surveyor therefrom to make a description of the whole land surveyed, in three connected plats, one of which, when completed, shall be transmitted to his Excellency, the Governor, one to the secretary's office, and the other lodged and recorded in the clerk's office of the County of Haywood.

"4. That it shall be further the duty of the said commissioners to ascertain and fix upon some central and eligible spot for the erection of the necessary public buildings, whenever that section of the State may be erected into a separate county, and that four hundred acres surrounding said site shall be reserved for the future disposition of the legislature.

"5. That no portion of said lands shall be surveyed and laid off into sections, except so much thereof as in the estimation of said commissioners will sell for fifty cents per acres; and that the residue of said lands shall be reserved for the future disposition of the legislature, and that no part or portion thereof shall be liable to be entered in the entry taker's books for the County of Haywood, or elsewhere, until provision be made by law for the disposal thereof; and entries heretofore made, or grants obtained or which may be hereafter made, otherwise than as provided by this act, be and the same are hereby declared to be utterly void and of none effect.

"6. That the Governor, on receipt of the plats and drafts heretofore provided for in this act, shall give notice by proclamation in all the newspapers published in the city of Raleigh and in such other papers in the adjoining states of South Carolina, Georgia, Virginia, and Tennessee, of the time and place of sale, as he may deem advisable which in no case shall be less than two months from the date of the notice, that the said lands shall be exposed at public sale to the highest bidder at Waynesville, in the County of Haywood, under the superintendence of the said commissioners; and the sale shall be kept open for the space of two weeks and no longer.

"7. That the said commissioners shall require of each and every purchaser to pay down, at the time of sale, one-eighth part of the purchase money, and shall take bond and security for the payment of the balance in the following instalments, viz: The balance of one-fourth at the expiration of twelve months, one-fourth at the expiration of two years, one other fourth at the end of three years and the remaining fourth at the end of four years; in no instance shall a grant or grants issue to the purchaser, until the whole of the purchase money be paid in full; and in case of failure to pay the whole when due, and the money cannot be obtained by a judgment on their bond, then and in that case, the land shall revert to the State, and be liable again to be sold for the use and benefit of the State.

"8. That if during the time of said sale, any section of land noted to be of first quality, shall not command in the market the sum of four dollars per acre, the said commissioners shall postpone the sale of such section until further directed by the legislature; and in like manner lands of the second quality not commanding three dollars, and lands of the third quality not commanding two dollars, shall be postponed as aforesaid, and report thereof made to the Governor.

"10. That the said commissioners shall give to each purchaser a certificate describing the land by him purchased with a plat of the lot and number of the section conformable to the plan returned to the secretary's office; upon the production of which proof of the payment of the purchase money made to the secretary by the treasurer's receipt, it shall be the duty of said secretary to issue a grant to the purchaser for the said lot of land in the usual and common form."

In pursuance to the Act of 1819 the Governor appointed Commissioners, who employed surveyors to survey out such of the lands lying in between the Meigs and Freeman line and the Tennessee River as would sell for 50 cents per acre and above at that time and classify the same in accordance with said Act and the Commissioners in pursuance to said Act and Acts amendatory thereof proceeded with their work in the surveying and selling of said land until the year 1835, when it was apparent that all the land had been surveyed that would sell for a price greater than the other vacant lands of the State, subject to entry and grant under the general entry and grant laws of the State, and there was no reason why the unsurveyed lands lying in between the Meigs and Freeman line and Tennessee River should not be made subject to entry and grant as other vacant lands within the State, and an Act was passed by the General Assembly of North Carolina, Chapter 6, Public Laws of 1835, page 7, which reads as follows:

"An Act authorizing the entering of the unsurveyed lands acquired by treaty from the Cherokee Indians, A. D., one thousand, eight hundred and seventeen and one thousand eight hundred and nineteen, in the Counties of Haywood and Macon."

"Be it enacted by the General Assembly of the State of North Carolina, and it is hereby enacted by the authority of the same, that from and after the first day of May next, it shall and may be lawful for any person or persons to enter any vacant and unsurveyed lands that have been acquired by treaty from the Cherokee Indians, in the year of one thousand eight hundred and seventeen, and one thousand eight hundred and nineteen, under the same rules, regulations and restrictions that are already provided by law for entering vacant lands in this State, and all laws and clauses of laws coming within the meaning and purview of this act, be and the same are hereby repealed."

The Act of 1835, which opened up the land lying in between the Meigs and Freeman line and the Tennessee River to entry and grant under the general entry and grant laws of the State was amended by Chapter 7, page 29, Public Laws of 1836 and 37, ratified on the 10th day of January, 1837, entitled "Cherokee Lands."

The language used in the amended act is in words and figures as follows:

"Be it enacted by the General Assembly of the State of North Carolina, and it is hereby enacted by the authority of the same, That nothing in the aforesaid act contained shall be so construed as to authorize or allow the entry of any portion of the said lands, which were reserved or alloted to any Indian or Indians under said treaties, which the State has since acquired by purchase; and that the Secretary of State be, and he is hereby directed to issue no grant for any portion of the lands of the latter description, until the General Assembly shall otherwise order and direct."

The lands referred to in this act are those reserved to individual Indians by the second and third sections or articles of the Treaty of 1819 and purchased by the State from said Indians as shown by the act of the General Assembly of North Carolina, in the years 1823-24 aforesaid.

A number of individual Indians to whom reservations were made by the Treaty of 1819 conveyed their reservations to white persons which sales were ratified by the General Assembly in 1821. (See ratification Act set out on pages 71 and 72 of the Second Volume of the Code of 1883 of North Carolina under Chapter 11, entitled "Cherokee Lands.")

Most of the other Indians who secured reservations under the Treaty of 1819 conveyed their reservations to the State of North Carolina. (See individual Indians who sold their reservations to the State set out in Section 2380 on page 75 of the Code of 1883 of North Carolina.)

It appears that the State of North Carolina protested against the action of the United States in allowing reservations to be made to the individual Indians within the boundary relinquished by the Cherokees under the Treaty of 1819 and included a number of these reservations in sales made by the commissioners under the Act of 1819, and that the matter of protest of the State against the action of the United States in making reservations to the individual Cherokees was finally adjusted by the United States refunding to the State of North Carolina the amount paid by the State in extinguishing the title of the individual Indians.

The Act of 1819 and the Acts amendatory thereof, relating to the disposition of the Cherokees' lands up to the year 1835 are set out on pages 188 to 214 inclusive in the Second Volume of the Revised Statutes of 1836 of North Carolina entitled "Cherokee Lands," and the Acts relating to the Cherokee Lands from the year 1819 up to the time the Act was repealed in 1883 is set out on pages 65 to 109 inclusive of the Second Volume of the Code of 1883 of North Carolina under Chapter 11, entitled "Cherokee Lands."

After the time of the passage of the Act, chapter 6, Public Laws of 1835, making the land lying in between the Meigs and Freeman line and the Tennessee River subject to entry and grant under the general entry and grant laws of the State; a part of these lands then lay in Haywood and a part in Macon Counties, as there were only two counties at that time in Western North Carolina west of Buncombe County, and they were Haywood and Macon Counties. A part of this area lay in what is now Swain and Jackson Counties, and a part in Macon County.

Under the provisions of this Act a part of the land lying in between the Meigs and Freeman line and the Tennessee River was entered and granted to various persons, and this Act continued in force, until repealed in 1852, when all the vacant and unsurveyed lands lying west of Meigs and Freeman line in this State were made subject to entry and grant under the Cherokee Land Laws hereinafter referred to and set out, and a part of the lands lying in between the Meigs and Freeman line and the Tennessee River were disposed of and sold by Commissioners' Sale under the Act of 1819, and a part entered and granted under the Act of 1835, and a part entered and granted under the Cherokee Land Laws of 1852, and Acts amendatory thereof, hereinafter referred to and set out, and some of it entered and granted to parties after the Cherokee Land Laws were repealed under the Act of 1883, hereinbefore, and hereinafter referred to and set out.

Buncombe County was created from territory taken from Burke and Rutherford Counties during the year 1792 and formerly included all of the land west of the Blue Ridge in North Carolina. See the Act creating Buncombe County giving the boundary lines, set out on pages 107 and 108 Second Volume of Revised Statutes of 1836 of North Carolina.

Haywood County was created from territory taken from Buncombe County during the year 1808 and which at that time included all the territory in western North Carolina, west of the present Buncombe County. See the Act creating Haywood County giving the boundary lines set out on pages 134 etc., Second Volume of the Revised Statutes of 1836 of North Carolina.

Macon County was created during the year 1828 out of territory taken from Haywood County and at that time included all the territory in western North Carolina, west of Haywood County. The Act creating Macon County giving the boundary lines is set out on pages 144-5 Second Volume of Revised Statutes of 1836 of North Carolina.

Cherokee County was created by Public Laws of 1839 from territory taken from the western part of Macon County and at that time included all of what is now Cherokee, Clay and Graham Counties.

As before stated, the title of the Cherokees to all lands occupied by them east of the Mississippi River was extinguished by the Treaty of New Echotah of December 25, 1835, and at the next session of the General Assembly of this State following the ratification of the Treaty of 1835, an Act was passed, Chapter Public Laws of 1836 of North Carolina, providing the manner in which the lands acquired by the Treaty of 1835 should be disposed of, which Act provided among other things that the land so acquired by the Treaty of 1835 should not be subject to entry and grant, but so much of the land as would sell for 25 cents per acre and above that price should be surveyed out and classified in five sections. The land of the first class to be sold for a sum not less than $4.00 per acre; the second class for a sum not less than

$2.00 per acre; the third class for a sum not less than $1.00 per acre; the fourth class for a sum not less than 50 cents per acre; and the fifth class for a sum not less than 25 cents per acre; and after the land was surveyed out and classified as above stated, it was to be exposed to sale by commissioners at public auction to the highest bidder, and if the land failed to bring the price fixed by the commissioners, the same was to be bid in by the commissioners for the future disposition of the General Assembly of this State.

This Act appears to have been patterned after the Act of 1819. (See this Act set out on pages 209 to 214 inclusive of the Second Volume of the Revised Statutes of 1836 of North Carolina; also on pages 80 to 85 inclusive of Sections 2396 to 2412 inclusive in the Second Volume of the Code of 1883 of North Carolina, under the head of "Cherokee Lands.")

Maps were prepared by the surveyors who surveyed out the Cherokee lands in pursuance to the Acts of 1819 and 1836 and Acts amendatory thereof, numbering the tracts by sections and showing the districts in which the same were located in the several counties, and one copy of each map was deposited with the secretary of state and one copy was deposited with the commissioners at Franklin, and it is my information that copies of these maps can be found in the office of the secretary of state and office of the register of deeds at Franklin. This work was the only survey that approximates a system of surveys in North Carolina, as most of the land entered under the general entry and grant laws of this State and in pursuance to the Cherokee Land Laws of 1852 were surveyed as desired by the persons who entered the land.

The Act of 1836 was amended from time to time and continued in force and effect and the lands acquired by the Treaty of 1835 continued to be surveyed and sold by the commissioners until a preemption right was given to poor and needy persons to enter and grant not to exceed 100 acres of land by Chapter 25, Public Laws of 1850-51. This pre-emption right applied first to lands in Macon County and later to lands in Cherokee County. See these pre-emption rights set out in the Act of 1850-51 on pages 101 to 105 inclusive in the Second Volume of the Code of 1883 of North Carolina. This pre-emption right was extended to both residents and occupants in Macon and Cherokee Counties, N. C. The pre-emption right extended to residents of Cherokee County by the Act of 1850-51 was embodied in Sections 2458 to 2462 inclusive of the Second Volume of the Code of 1883 of North Carolina, and reads as follows:

"SEC 2458. Extends the pre-emption right to residents in Cherokee. 1850-51, c. 25, s. 7.

"And whereas, many poor persons, being destitute of homes, have also settled upon the unsurveyed lands in the County of Cherokee, which lands were not surveyed under the Act of one thousand eight hundred and thirty-six, because they were not considered worth twenty cents per acre; all persons, who, prior, to the first day of January, one thousand eight hundred and fifty-one, resided on any of said lands, or had made any improvements thereon which add value to the land, shall be entitled to a pre-emption privilege to one hundred acres, to include their improvements, at twenty cents per acre; and upon making satisfactory proof to the agent of Cherokee bonds that he or she is entitled to the pre-emption privilege within the meaning of this section, it shall be his duty to issue a certificate to such person claiming the pre-emption privilege, setting forth the location of the one hundred acres claimed; and upon such certificate it shall be competent for the persons entitled to the pre-emption privilege to have the said lands surveyed, at his or her own expense, in a square or oblong square, to include his or her improvements; and duplicate copies of such survey shall be made, one to be forwarded to the secretary of state; and the other to be presented, with the original certificate of occupancy, to the agent; and upon payment being made to him, of one fourth of the price of said land, and upon the purchasers entering into bonds with two or more securities, to be approved by the agent, payable to the state in three annual installments, for the remaining three-fourths, he shall issue to said purchaser certificates of purchase, setting forth the number of the tract, the district in which situated, the number of acres and the price sold for.

"SEC. 2459. Certificates. 1850-51. c. 25, s. 8.

"The certificates issued to the purchasers under this chapter, shall entitle them to all rights and privileges the holders of certificates were entitled to under the Act of one thousand eight hundred and thirty-six.

"SEC. 2460. Advance payments. 1850-51, c. 25, s. 9.

"All persons who make advance payments under this chapter, shall be entitled to the same discounts as provided for under the twelfth section of the Act of one thousand eight hundred and thirty-six, prescribing the mode of selling Cherokee lands.

"SEC. 2461. Two occupants. 1850-51, c. 25, s. 10.

"In all cases where two occupants occupy the same lands, or live near each other, unless otherwise agreed upon between themselves, the line shall be run so as to divide the distance equally between their dwelling houses; and in case two persons claim the same improvements and the occupant right thereto, the person having the prior right, unless he has conveyed his claim to the subsequent settlers, shall have the right of pre-emption.

"SEC. 2462. Time of privilege limited. 1850-51, c. 25, s. 11.

"The rights of pre-emption hereby granted to persons residing on, or who own improvements on the surveyed lands in the Countis of Macon and Cherokee, and also upon the vacant lands in the last named county, provided for in the Act of eighteen hundred and fifty and fifty-one, chapter twenty-five, shall have until the first day of October, one thousand eight hundred and fifty-one to avail themselves of the pre-emption privilege and to give bonds as required by this chapter."

These pre-emption tracts are generally known as Pre-emption or Old Occupant Tracts.

The Act of 1836 was amended from time to time and the lands were surveyed and disposed of by commissioners' sale until the same were laid open to entry and grant to old and needy persons under the Pre-emption Acts aforesaid, and the remainder of the unsurveyed and unsold land lying west of the Meigs and Freeman line was made subject to entry and grant under the Cherokee Land Laws, Chapter 119, Public Laws of 1852.

Sections 1 to 6 inclusive of Chepter 119, Public Laws of 1852, read as follows:

"SEC. 2464. Office of entry taker established in Cheroke 1852. c. 119, s. 1.

"An entry taker's office shall be opened in the County of Cherokee, for the entry of vacant lands in said county, and an entry taker shall be elected as is required in other counties of this State, and until such election shall be made, the governor shall have the power to appoint some suitable person, resident in said county, to discharge the duties of said office as hereinafter directed.

"SEC. 2465. When, how and at what price lands may be entered. 1852. C. 119, s. 2.

"From the first day of February, one thousand eight hundred and fifty-three, till the first day of June thereafter, any one may enter any of the unsold lands in said county at the rate of fifty cents per acre, and thereafter any land remaining may be entered at the rate of twenty cents per acre for the next three months from the first day of June, and thereafter all of said unsold lands that may be unentered may be entered at ten cents per acre for twelve months, and thereafter at the same rates of other vacant lands in this State.

"SEC. 2466. Persons entering lands to file their bonds with the entry-taker, etc., 1852. c. 119, s. 3.

It shall be lawful for all persons entering vacant lands in said County of Cherokee to file their bonds, with approved security, with the entry-taker, payable to the State in four equal annual installment, which shall, when paid, be in full of the purchase money for the tract or tracts so entered, and upon proof of such payment as herein provided, the secretary of state shall issue the grant or grants according to the entry and survey thereon, and in case the land shall have been surveyed by authority of the State, the grant shall issue according to the survey so made, and not otherwise, and no portion of any tract so surveyed shall be granted without the whole.

"SEC. 2467. What grants governor may sign. 1852, c .119, s 4.

"The governor shall sign no grants on entries and surveys made under this chapter, unless as much as fifty acres shall be included in each survey, and unless such survey shall be a square rectangle not more than twice as long as wide.

"SEC. 2468. Vacant lands in Macon and Haywood may be entered. 1852, c. 119, s. 5.

"All the vacant lands in the Counties of Macon and Haywood may be entered under this chapter at the legal rates; and all the land in said counties heretofore entered and not paid for, may be paid for, as herein provided for the lands lying in Cherokee County, and all the money and lands that may be received by the entry-taker of either of the said Counties of Cherokee, Macon, and Haywood, shall be paid to contractors for making the said Western Turnpike Road, on the certificate of the agent for making said road, until the same is completed.

"SEC. 2469. Surveyor for Cherokee elected. 1852, c. 119, s. 6.

"A surveyor shall be elected for the County of Cherokee, under the same rules and regulations, and shall perform all the duties and be under all the penalties, as other county surveyors, in this state." See these sections set out on pages 104 and 105 of Second Volume of the Code of 1893 of North Carolina, under head of "Cherokee Lands."

The effect of the above Acts was to repeal the Act of 1835 opening up the land between the Meigs and Freeman line and the Tennessee River to entry and grant under the general entry and grant laws of the State and making this area subject to entry and grant under the Cherokee Land Laws of 1852 above cited.

The Act of 1852 was amended from time to time but the Cherokee lands continued to be entered and granted under the provisions of the Act of 1852 and Acts amendatory thereof until the same was repealed by the Act of 1883, since which time all the unsurveyed and vacant lands within the Cherokee country have been entered and granted under the general entry and grant laws of the State. (See Page 108, Section 2478, Second Volume of the Code of 1883 of North Carolina.)

In my preparing abstracts of title for the Champion Fibre Company for what is known as the Whiting Lands in Graham and Cherokee Counties, N. C., Mr. W. J. Damtoft turned over to me a typewritten copy of an abstract of title prepared by Hon. Duff Merrick for the Kanawha Hardwood Company, for what is known as the Snowbird Lands, and which constituted a part of the Whiting Lands, purchased by the Champion Fibre Company; and I found that this abstract, as well as other work done by Mr. Merrick in that section of country, contained a lot of information pertaining to the Cherokee Land Laws, which was valuable to me in my work.

I find that Mr. Merrick, in the preface of this abstract, calls attention to the fact that these lands were entered and granted under the Cherokee Land Laws and the difficulties he encountered in the investigation of the title to the same, which is in words as follows:

"Preface"

"The lands discussed in this abstract very largely lie in what is now Graham County. Until 1872, Graham County was a part of Cherokee County, which accounts for the fact that in the various grants the lands are described as being in Cherokee County as they were all entered prior to 1872, although in a number of instances the grants were not issued until some years later. They are a part of the lands formerly belonging to the Cherokee Indians. After having been acquired by treaty they were from time to time thrown open to entry by the State under special statutes, the provisions of which differed very materially from the laws relating to the granting of other public lands. For instance, the lands were sold on credit of one, two, three, and four years, and the purchaser gave notes with approved security. When the last of these notes were paid, he received a certificate of final payment, and, upon the presentation of this certificate to the secretary of state, the purchaser was entitled to a grant. These certificates, as well as entries, could be transferred by assignment, which explains the frequency with which it occurs that grants were issued to persons other than the original enterers. Among other provisions was one providing that where the sureties paid the notes they were entitled to have the grants issued to them. Naturally this method of doing business led to many complications and furnished abundant opportunity for fraud, and it has sometime happened that as many as three grants have been issued upon the same entry. But the confusion thus arising has practically all been cleared away by operation of the statutes of limitation and the decision of the Supreme Court of the State.

"A more serious matter is the lapping of grants one upon another. There was no division of these lands by the State into sections and quarter sections, nor any attempt to keep such a record as they were granted as would prevent the same land from being granted more than once. Laps are numerous and there are instances where lands are covered by three or four grants. Care is required therefore, to see that there are no grants of older date covering the lands under investigation, and generally the assistance of a surveyor is needed. We have been familiar with these particular lands for a number of years, first having examined the titles of most of them in 1901, and we believe we have discovered and noted all grants of older title overlapping any of the lands covered by this abstract."

I fully concur in the views expressed by Mr. Merrick above set out.

I will now set out the difference between lands entered and granted under the General Entry and Grant Laws of this State and the lands entered and granted under the Cherokee Land Laws above cited.

1st: Under the General Entry and Grant Laws of the State, only citizens of the State were permitted to enter and grant the same, but if a grant was issued to an alien or a non-resident, the same could not be attacked collaterally, but could only be set aside by a suit instituted by the Attorney General of the State. (See case of Johnson vs. Lumber Company, reported in 144th N. C. R., pages 717 etc.). While under the Cherokee Land Laws under the Act of 1852 and Acts amendatory thereof, anyone could enter and grant the Cherokee Lands and without any limitation as to quantity, except the Pre-emption or Occupant tracts, which were limited to 100 acres and less, and which could only be entered and granted by residents of the State.

As to the necessity of a party being a resident and making improvement on the land entered and granted under the Pre-emption Acts of 1850-51, see case of Barnett vs. Woods, reported in 50th N. C. R., page 428 etc. The Court used the following language in the opinion in that case:

"CHEROKEE LANDS—ACTS OF 1850—NECESSITY OF RESIDENCE.

"Under the Act of 1850, relating to preemptions, a citizen of a contiguous state who had made an improvement on Cherokee lands, but never resided thereon, is not entitled to a preemptoin right."

As before stated, there was no restriction as to the number of acres of land that could be entered and granted under the Cherokee Land Laws, except as to the pre-emption and occupant tracts, which were limited to 100 acres. Most of the entries made in what is now Cherokee, Graham, and Clay Counties were for 640 acre tracts and less, but a great many tracts were entered in these counties all the way from one thousand to fifteen thousand acres, and a great many tracts were entered in what is now Swain and Jackson Counties west of the Meigs and Freeman line under the Cherokee Land Laws, of from five to ten thousand acres and in some cases more; and one tract known as the Whittier Boundary was entered and granted by Welsh, Battle, and Love, calling to contain 50,000 acres, when as a matter of fact the same surveyed out more than 75,000 acres.

The State had a two-fold object in permitting anyone whether residents of this State or not to enter and grant Cherokee lands under the Act of 1852, and Acts amendatory thereof.

1st: To induce persons to settle on the Cherokee lands in order to make the same more valuable; but the main object at that time appeared to be to raise money to complete the Western Turnpike Road from Salisbury to Ducktown, Tennessee, and to build roads generally throughout the Cherokee country and reimburse the State for the money paid out in the survey of the Western North Carolina Railroad as evidenced by several of the numerous acts of legislation relating to the Cherokee lands.

Another difference between the lands entered under the General Entry and Grant Laws of the State and the entering and granting under the Cherokee Land Laws was that if a grant was taken out on the Cherokee lands in violation of the statute, it was not necessary to institute a direct proceedings to set such grant aside, but such grant could be attacked collaterally on the trial or hearing of the cause, and if such grant was shown to be taken out in violation of the statute, the same would be declared void by the Court. (See case of Stanmire vs. Powell, reported in 35 N. C. R., page 312 etc.; also Brown vs Brown, reported in 103 N. C. R., pages 213 etc.; see also case of Harshaw vs. Taylor, reported in 48 N. C. R., pages 513 etc.)

Another difference between the General Entry and Grant Laws and Cherokee Land Laws was that a party who entered under the General Entry and Grant Laws of this State, could, if he so desired, abandon his claim under the entry without liability to the State at any time. The enterer under the General Entry and Grant Laws acquired a mere option to buy. (See Frazier vs. Gibson, 140th N. C. R., pages 272 etc.) Under the Cherokee Land Laws, a party who entered land and filed his bonds for the purchase price was bound to carry out his contract. Such an entry and purchase amounted to a contract between the State and the enterer. (See case of Higdon vs. Rice, reported in 119 N. C. R., pages 623 etc.; also Frasier vs. Gibson, reported in 140 N. C. R., pages 272 etc.; also Kimsey vs. Munday, reported in 112 N. C. R., pages 816 etc.)

Our Supreme Court in the case of Ritchie vs. Fowler, reported in 132 N. C. R., pages 788 etc., held where a party obtains a grant from the State for land that had been previously entered and the senior enterer later obtained a grant for the same land, and the grant of the senior grantee had been on record for more than 10 years, and no action had been taken by the senior enterer and junior grantee to declare the senior grantee trustee for his benefit, where neither party was in possession of the land, that the junior grantee was barred by the ten year Statute of Limitations, then Code Section 158. This decision has been affirmed by our Supreme Court in several subsequent decisions as follows: McAden vs. Palmer, 140 N. C. R., pages 258 etc.; also Frasier vs. Gibson, 140 N. C. R., pages 279 etc.; also Frasier vs. Cherokee Indians, 146 N. C. R., pages 477 etc.; and other later decisions cited in Allen's Digest on page 829; but our Supreme Court held in the case of Anderson vs. Meadows, reported in 159 N. C. R., pages 405 etc., that this rule applied only where the land was subject to entry and grant. The facts set out in the opinion of the Court in this case are as follows:

The plaintiff, Anderson, acquired title to the land by an entry made in pursuance to the Cherokee Land Laws under the Act of 1852, and the defendant acquired title to the land by a sale made by commissioners under the Act of 1819, chapter 97. The court held in that case from the foregoing facts that only the vacant and unsurveyed lands were made subject to entry and grant under the Cherokee Land Laws of 1852, and as the land claimed by the defendant had been surveyed and the party from whom he derived title had purchased the land at commissioner's sale under the Act of 1819, the same was not subject to entry and grant under the Act of 1852, and the fact that the grant under which the plaintiff claimed title had been on record for more than 10 years before the grant was issued to the party from whom the defendant claimed title, would not protect the plaintiff in his claim of title, as the grant under which the plaintiff claimed was void under the Act of 1852 and the Court so declared.

Referring again to the decision in the case of Ritchie vs. Fowler, reported in 132 N. C. R., pages 788 etc., this decision will also apply to grants issued under the General Entry and Grant Laws of the State.

A party who enters land either under the General Entry and Grant Laws of this State or the Cherokee Land Laws in order to protect himself against subsequent enterers, in required to set out in his entry such a description of the lands as will give notice to everybody of the lands intended to be entered, or in case the entry is vague and uncertain, reduce the same to certainty by a survey. (See case of Johnson vs. Shelton, 39 N. C. R., page 85; also Fisher vs. Owen, 144 N. C. R., page 649; and numerous other cases bearing on his point cited under section 12 on pages 578, 579, and 580, set out in Volume 10 of Enc. Dig. of N. C. Reports.)

Abstracts Of Grants

I deem it proper before concluding my history on the Cherokee Land Laws, to call attention to the difference between the recording of grants and abstracts of grants in the County where the land lies.

I will first call attention to the difference between the contents of a complete grant and an abstract of a grant. A complete copy of the grant contains the grant number, the warrant or entry number upon which the same was issue, recites the consideration or price per acre for the land, contains a description of the same, and testimonial clause gives the date of the issuing of the grant and contains the Great Seal of State and is signed by the Governor and countersigned by the Secretary of State, and there is attached to the grant a certificate of the surveyor who surveyed the land with plat attached thereto and made a part of the grant.

The abstract of the grant only contains the grant number, a description of the land conveyed, date of the issuing of the grant and in some cases the name of the Governor and Secretary of State appears signed to the abstract, but in many cases the name of the Governor and Secretary of State is not given.

A complete copy of the grant is not recorded in the office of the Secretary of State, but only a synopsis or abstract of the grant is recorded in what is known as the "Abstract Book."

The grant usually recited that the grantee is required to record the same in the County where the land lay within twelve months or the same would be void, but the General Assembly from time to time extended the time for recording grants. See Janney vs. Blackwell, reported in 138 N. C. R., page 437. When the grantee had the grant recorded in the County where the land lay, as a general rule only the grant was recorded, but in some cases the certificate of survey with the plat attached thereto and made a part thereof was also recorded.

Prior to the Act of our General Assembly, Public Laws of 1915, Chapter 249, Section 1, abstracts of grants recorded in the County where the land lay, not signed by the Governor, were not sufficient to pass title to the grantee for the land therein granted..

See case of McLellan vs. Chishold, reported in 64 N. C. R., pages 323, etc.

Also Beam et al, vs. R. B. Jennings, reported in 96 N. C. R., page 82.

Also Marshall vs. Corbitt, reported in 137 N. C. R., page 555.

As I understand the opinions of the Court in the above cases, unless an abstract of a grant was signed by the Governor and counter-signed by the Secretary of State, the recording of the same in the County where the land lay would not be valid, or pass title to the land, prior to the Act of 1915 referred to, but under the Act of 1915 which has been brought forward and incorporated in Section 1752 of the Code of 1927 of North Carolina under head of "Evidence," abstract of grants recorded in the County where the land lay with or without the signature of the Governor and the Great Seal of the State is sufficient to pass title to the grantee therein named. Section 1752 is in words and figures as follows:

"Certified copies of grants and abstracts—For the purpose of show-ing title from the State of North Carolina to the grantee or grantees therein named and for the lands therein described, duly certified copies of all grants and of all memoranda and abstracts of grants on record in the office of the secretary of state, given in abstract or in full, and with or without the signature of the governor and the great seal of the state appearing upon such record, shall be competent evidence in the courts of this state or of the United States or of any territory of the United States, and in the absence of the production of the original grant shall be conclusive evidence of a grant from the state to the grantees named and for the lands described therein."

This section has been held constitutional by our Supreme Court. See case of Howell vs. Hurley, reported in 170 N. C. R., page 401. Sections 1753 and 1754 bearing on this point read as follows:

1753: "Certified copies of grants and abstracts recorded—Duly certified copies of such grants and of such memoranda and abstracts of grants may be recorded in the county where the lands therein described are situated, and the records thereof in such counties, or certified copies thereof, shall likewise be competent evidence for the purpose of showing title from the state of North Carolina to the grantee or grantees named and for the lands described therein."

1754: "Copies of grants certified by clerk of secretary of state validated—All copies of grants heretofore issued from the office of the secretary of state, duly certified under the great seal of the state, and to which the name of the secretary has been written or affixed by the clerk of the said secretary of state, are hereby ratified and approved and declared to be good and valid copies of the original grants and admissible in evidence in all court of this state when duly registered in the counties in which the land lies; all such copies heretofore registered in said counties are hereby declared to be lawful and regular in all respects as if the same had been signed by the secretary of state in person and duly registered.

"Editor's Note. Prior to the enactment of this section it was consistently held that the clerk of the secretary had no power to certify and affix the great seal of the state to copies of grants and other papers from the secretary of state's office. Beam vs. Jennings, 96 N. C. 82, 2 S. E. 245, but such acts on the part of the clerk are now validated by the provisions of this section."

In the course of my investigation of title and preparation of abstracts of title for the land of the Champion Fibre Company in Cherokee, Graham, and Clay Counties, N. C., I found that not only the Champion Fibre Company but also a great many other people had to rely on recorded abstracts of grants to show title out of the State. Grants were issued by the State to one, W. H. Herbert, for several hundred tracts of land in Cherokee County during the year 1860 and prior and subsequent thereto. A part of these tracts lies in what is now Clay and Graham Counties, N. C., and a great many of these grants were lost or misplaced without being recorded, and the same condition existed as to other claimants, and no doubt the same condition exists throughout the State, and the Champion Fibre Company et al became purchasers of the same; and it became necessary to secure certified copies of the abstricts of these grants from the Secretary of State and have the same recorded in Clay, Cherokee, and Graham Counties, N. C., in order to show title out of the State by the claimants under these grants; and I found that some of these recorded abstracts contained the name of the Governor and Secretary of State, and some only the name of the Governor, and some did not contain either the signature of the Governor or the Secretary of State, but these abstracts were made competent evidence on the trial or hearing of any cause by reason of the above quoted acts of the Code of 1927 of North Carolina, which were held to be valid in the case of Howell vs. Hurley, above quoted.

In the course of my investigation of the title to land of the Champion Fibre Company and the William M. Ritter Lumber Company for lands west of the Meigs and Freeman line and especially in what are now

Clay, Cherokee, and Graham Counties, N. C., I found that a considerable part of the land in Clay, Cherokee, and Graham Counties was entered and granted by non-residents, mostly upon entries made in Cherokee County.

There were ninety-six of what was known as the Peet and Gilbert grants taken out in Cherokee County, some of which now lie in Cherokee and some in Clay and Graham Counties. Most of these grants were taken out during the year 1860. W. H. Peet, at the time of the granting of these lands, was a resident of New Orleans, Louisiana, and Lyman W. Gilbert, at the time of the granting of these lands, was a resident of New York City. Most of these grants contained 640 acres and less; some of the grants for land that now lies in Graham County were for 5,000, 10,000, and 15,000 acres.

I also found that the title to the Peet interest in the Peet and Gilbert tracts was made to purchasers by non-residents who came to this state and qualified as administrators before the Probate Judge and the Clerk of the Superior Court in Cherokee and other counties and sold the same under court proceedings, and that a great many natives took out grants junior to the Peet and Gilbert grants, and other grants were issued by the State to non-residents, and that these junior grantees insisted that the senior grants issued to Peet and Gilbert and other non-resident grantees were void on account of their being non-residents, and that the transfer deeds made by non-residents who came to this State and qualified as administrators and sold the land under court proceedings, were void for the reason that only residents of the State could qualify as administrators. As these objections have continuously been made by the junior grantees and may arise hereafter, I deem it proper here to show that such objections are unfounded.

GRANTS TAKEN OUT BY NON-RESIDENTS FOR LAND WEST OF THE MEIGS AND FREEMAN LINE UNDER THE CHEROKEE LAND LAWS

I will now take up and discuss the question of the validity of grants taken out by non-residents for lands lying west of the Meigs and Freeman line under the Cherokee Land Laws.

By reference to the Act of 1852, Section 2465, of the Second Volume of the Code of 1853, hereinbefore set out, it will be seen that anyone could enter and grant the unsold Cherokee lands; but notwithstanding the language used in this Act, a number of junior grantees had continuously insisted that the senior grants taken out by non-residents were void for the reason that only residents of the State under the General Entry and Grant Laws of the State could enter and grant land, and that the Cherokee Land Laws only authorized the entry and grant in subordination to the General Entry and Grant Laws of the State, and it appears that these junior grantees who had taken out junior grants that lay inside and lapped on the Peet and Gilbert grants, induced the Attorney-General of the State to bring a suit to vacate the Peet and Gilbert grants, which suit was brought by the Attorney-General against Belding et al, who had purchased the Peet and Gilbert grants.

This suit was brought during the year 1890 in the Superior Court of Graham County to vacate the Peet and Gilbert grants on the grounds that Peete and Gilbert were non-residents, which suit was entitled:

"The State of North Carolina ex rel
Attorney General, Plaintiff
vs.
D. W. Belding, D. W. Strickland,
M. M. Belding, A. N. Belding,
Henry Stix, Nathan Stix, Louis
Krohn, D. M. Hyman, Nathaniel
Newburg, and J. W. Cooper"

and after the Attorney General brought the suit, it appears upon investigation of the matter that he decided that the action could not be sustained and took a non-suit in the case, but notwithstanding the fact that the Attorney General took a non-suit in this case, a number of the junior grantees continued to deny the validity of the Peet and Gilbert grants taken out by other non-residents within the Cherokee country, and claimed that the grants were void for reasons above stated, until this question was finally settled by a decision of our Supreme Court in a case I appeared in for the plaintiff, entitled Johnson vs. Lumber Company, reported in 144 N. C. R., pages 717 etc. My client, the plaintiff, in the suit, derived title to the lands in controversy by and through grants issued to John T. Foster, who was an alien, and the defendant contended that the grants under which my client, the plaintiff, claimed title, were void for the reason that John T. Foster was an alien, but the Court below in the trial of the suit in Swain County, held otherwise, and the defendant carried the case on appeal to the Supreme Court and the judgment of the Court below was affirmed.

Chief Justice Clark in delivering the opinion of the Court in this case on page 720 used the following language:

"If, as the defendant contends, Foster was an alien, the law at that time applicable to Cherokee lands (which this was) did not debar aliens (Laws 1852-53, ch. 169). The general land law did not apply to these lands, as was expressly provided by section 18, chapter 31, Laws 1854-55. But even if an alien was prohibited from entering the lands, the State could only divest his title, for "an alien has capacity to take but not capacity to hold lands; .... he cannot hold it against the sovereign, should the sovereign choose to assert his claim thereto, as forfeited, but against all the rest of the world the alien has full capacity to hold, and he can hold even against the sovereign until the estate of the alien be divested by an office found or some other equally solemn sovereign act."

"Rouch vs. Williamson, 25 N. C., 146; Wilson vs. Land Co, 77 N. C., 457."

By reference to the opinion of the Court above, you will see that the Court held that Foster obtained the grants for the land in controversy under the Cherokee Land Laws, under the Act of 1852, and Acts amendatory thereof, and that Foster, who was an alien, could enter and grant the same, and this decision stands as the law of the State, so you will see that this matter has been finally settled.

SECOND

ACT OF NON-RESIDENTS COMING TO THIS STATE AND QUALIFYING AS ADMINISTRATOR OR ADMINISTRATRIX BEFORE THE PROPER OFFICERS OF THE COUNTY AND FILING BOND AND OBTAINING LICENSE TO SELL LAND BY PROPER PROCEEDINGS AND MAKE TITLE TO LAND HELD TO BE VALID BY OUR SUPREME COURT.

I will now take up and discuss claims made by parties in the past and that will probably be made in the future that a non-resident can not come to this State and qualify as administrator or administratrix on the estate of deceased parties, and title acquired by parties under such non-resident administrator or administratrix is void.

In my work in the investigation of title to lands of the Champion Fibre Company in Graham County, I found that the Company acquired title to the Peet interest in the ninety-six Peet and Gilbert grants through William Bartlett, who qualified as adminisrator of W. H. Peet, and who was a non-resident, and remembering that our statute provided that a non-resident could not qualify as an administrator and administer on the estate of deceased persons in this State, I decided the first thing to do was to look up the law on this subject and see what our Supreme Court had decided on such matters; and I found that our Supreme Court had held that where a non-resident qualified as an administrator and made bond, that he was not disqualified to act as such administrator, and I made a report to the Company accordingly. The following contains the statute and authorities cited by me on this subject.

Section 8, Chapter 1, entitled "Administration," set out on page 3 of Code of 1927 of North Carolina, is in words as follows:

"DISQUALIFICATIONS ENUMERATED.—The clerk shall not issue letters of administration or letters testamentary to any person who, at the time appearing to qualify—

"1. Is under the age of twenty-one years.

"2. Is a non-resident of this state; but a non-resident may qualify as executor.

"3. Has been convicted of a felony.

"4. Is adjudged by the clerk incompetent to execute the duties of such trust by reason of drunkenness, improvidence or want of understanding.

"5. Fails to take the oath or give the bond required by law.

"6. Has renounced his rights to qualify."

There are numerous decisions cited under the above subsections rendered by our Supreme Court, but I will only refer to certain ones that have a bearing on the case in point.

The above sections were provided for by our statute of 1868.

Now it would appear from sub-section 2 of Section 8 above quoted that a non-resident could not qualify as administrator before the clerk in this state, but our Supreme Court has held to the contrary.

Our Supreme Court in the case of Moore vs. Eure, reported in 101 N. C. R., on page 16, uses the following language:

"The Administrator is appointed by the Court, and is required to take an oath and give the bond required by law, and a non-resident who does this is not included in the disqualifications of The Code s 1377. Administrators, whether resident or non-resident, are required to give bond, and so are executors who reside out of the state—THE CODE s 1515 etc."

The following are opinions of our Supreme Court affirming the decision of the Court in the case of Moore vs Eura, supra, to wit:

Fann vs. R. R. 155 N. C. R., page 136.

Bachelor vs Overton 158 N. C. R., page 397 etc.

Marshall vs. Kemp 190 N. C. R., page 491.

The following is the language used by the Court in the case of Fann vs. R. R., above quoted:

"It appearing that Administrator of decedent has been appointed by the clerk, objection cannot be taken to the legality of his appointment upon the question of residence of such administrator, etc. (Revisal Section 16) in an action for damages for his negligent killing, for the error, if any committed, must be corrected by proceedings instituted directly for the purpose."

The Supreme Court of our State later on made practically the same ruling in the case of Bachelor vs. Overton 158 N. C. R., page 397 etc. The Court in this case held in effect that although it was made to appear that the party applying for letters of adminisration in this State was formerly a non-resident of this State, that it would be presumed that the applicant furnished evidence satisfactory to the Court at the time of his appointment, that he intended in good faith to become a resident of the State, that the action of the Court in making the appointment could not be attacked collaterally, or at least this is the way I construe the two decisions of our Supreme Court last above quoted. That is, the Court would not go back of the decision of the clerk in matters of this kind.

When I first read the decision of our Supreme Court in the case of Hall vs. Southern R. R. Co., reported in 146 N. C. R., page 345, etc., it appeared to me that there was a conflict in the opinion of the Court in this case and in the cases of:

Fann vs. R. R., 155 N. C. R., page 136.

Bachelor vs. Overton, 148 N. C. R., page 397.

but upon a more careful reading of the case of Hall vs. Southern R. R. Co., I am of the opinion there does not appear to be any conflict. The second syllabus in the opinion of our Supreme Court in the case of Hall vs. Southern R. R. Co., supra, is in words as follows:

"2. SAME—NON-RESIDENTS—STATE COURTS.

"A non-resident cannot be appointed as administrator, under the laws of our State (Revisal, Sec. 5, subsec. 2); and a non-resident administrator appointed in the State of his intestates residence and domicile cannot, as such, sue in the Courts of our State, under the provisions of Revisal, sec. 59."

By careful examination of the facts in this case it will be seen that the plaintiff in this suit had not qualified as administrator of his intestate in this State, and the opinion of the Court in this case is based solely on the grounds that the plaintiff had been appointed administrator of his intestate by the Courts of Virginia, and attempting to sustain his action in the Courts of this State under the provisions of the Revisal Sec. 59. Hence the language used in this syllabus of the case in words as follows:

"A non-resident cannot be appointed as administrator, under the laws of our State (Revisal, sec. 5, subsec. 2), is misleading in that the plaintiff in that case had not qualified as administrator of his intestate in this State, and had nothing to do with the case, and all the Court held in that case was that a foreign administrator could not, under our statute, sustain an action as such against anyone in this State."

When I first read the decision of the Supreme Court in this case, it appeared to me that the title to a considerable part of the Gennett lands might be affected by the decision for the reason that the Gennetts had derived title to a considerable part of their land by and through administrators who, according to the report made by Mr. Taylor, appeared to be non-residents, and who had qualified before the clerks of Superior Courts of Cherokee and Graham Counties, N. C., as administrators, and had petitioned and secured orders from the Court to sell lands in order to pay the debts of said estates and made deeds accordingly; but upon a careful examination of the decisions of the Supreme Court, above quoted, I feel sure that there is no question about the validity of these sales on this ground.

I will add that the decision of our Supreme Court in the case of Moore vs. Eure was rendered in 1888, about 20 years after Section 8, Chapter 1, became a law, and the decision of our Supreme Court in the case of Fann vs. R. R. Co. was rendered in 1911, and the case of Bachelor vs. Overton in 1912, and both of the two later decisions were rendered after the decision of our Supreme Court in the case of Hall vs. R. R. Co. in 1907.

This completes my report on how title was acquired to land west of the Blue Ridge in this State, but I think it proper to call attention to certain statutes that affect the title to land in the Cherokee country and which also affect the title to land generally in this State, namely:

FIRST

Registration Act and Probate and Registration of Deeds and Conveyances for Land.

SECOND

Heirship.

THIRD

Actions for the Recovery and Quieting of the Title to Land.

I will first take up and discuss the effect that the Registration Act of 1885 has on titles derived before and since the passage of this Act.

The Connor Registration Act was passed by the General Assembly of North Carolina during the year 1885, being Chapter 147, Section 1, of the Public Laws of 1885. This Act was brought forward and incorporated in Section 3309 under head of "Probate and Registration," on page 1059 of the Revised Code of 1927 or North Carolina.

The following is the full text of this Act:

"S. 3309. Conveyances, contracts to convey, and leases of land.— No conveyance of land, or contract to convey, or lease of land for more than three years shall be valid to pass any property, as against creditors or purchasers for a valuable consideration, from the donor, bargainor or lessor, but from the registration thereof within the county where the land lies: Provided, the provisions of this section shall not apply to contracts, leases or deeds executed prior to March first, one thousand eight hundred and eighty-five, until the first day of January, one thousand eight hundred and eighty-six; and no purchaser from any such donor, bargainor or lessor shall avail or pass title as against any unregistered deed executed prior to the first day of December, one thousand eight hundred and eighty-five when the person holding or claiming under such unregistered deed shall be in the actual possession and enjoyment of such land, either in person or by his tenant, at the time of the execution of such second deed, or when the person claiming under or taking such second deed had at the time of taking or purchasing under such deed actual or constructive notice of such unregistered deed, or the claim of the person holding or claiming thereunder. (Rev. s. 980; Code, s. 1245; 1885, c. 147, s. 1.)."

By reference thereto it will be seen that the provisions of this Act should not apply to anyone taking under a second deed from the same grantor who had actual or constructive notice of such first unregistered deed, etc.

Prior to the passage of the Connor Act in 1885 where a grantor conveyed land by deed and later conveyed the same land to another party, who had his deed recorded first, the later would take no title as against the first purchaser from the grantor even though he had no notice of the first deed.

See case of Phifer vs. Barnhart, reported in 88 N. C. R., pages 333 etc., and numerous cases cited thereunder. The following is the second and third sections of the syllabus set out in the opinion of the Supreme Court in this case:

"INJUNCTION—UNREGISTERED DEED, WHAT IT CONVEYS.

"2. The bargainee in an unregistered deed has a legal title, which, though incomplete, cannot be defeated by the mere act of the bargainor in executing another deed to a third party, without notice, and whose deed is registered.

"3. Although such deed cannot be given in evidence until registered, and does not therefore convey a perfect title, yet, when registered, it relates to the time of its execuion, and the title becomes complete."

By reference to the decision of the Court in this case it will be seen that a party taking a second deed from the grantor or a sale made under execution against the grantor even without notice would take no title to the land, and although the party taking under the first deed would be required to have the deed recorded before offering the same in evidence, when so recorded, the deed would relate back to the time of the execution and delivery of the deed. However, it was otherwise where the party acquired title through a mortgage deed that was not recorded as the mortgage deed would have to be recorded in order to protect the purchaser against purchasers and creditors for value from the grantor.

See case of Robinson vs. Willoughby, reported in 70th N. C. R., page 358, and cases cited thereunder. The following is the language of the Court used in this case:

"Since the statute of 1829, deeds in trust and mortgages, are of no validity whatever, as against purchasers for value and creditors, until they are registered; and they take effect only from and after registration.

"No notice, however full and formal, will supply the place of registration."

The Connor Act does not apply to registration of grants. Nearly all the grants issued by the State to grantees under registration acts of the State provided that the grants should be registered in the County where the land lies within one or two years, or the same would be void; but nearly every session of the Legislature of our States passed acts extending the time for registration of grants, as will be seen by reference to the decision of our Supreme Court in the case of Janney vs.

Blackwell, reported in 138 N. C. R., page 437.

PROBATE AND REGISTRATION

Now it is not my purpose to go into a general discussion of all the statutes bearing on the probate and registration of deeds and conveyance for land in this State and decisions of our Supreme Court rendered thereunder bearing on the probate and registration of deeds and conveyances for land in this State, as this would take a volume and would not serve any useful purpose, but only to call attention to the material provisions of the probate and registration laws of this State and the decisions of our Supreme Court thereunder, affecting the title to land, that I think will be beneficial to the legal profession.

Now, as to the probate and registration of deeds and conveyances for land, it appears to me that North Carolina by its statutes and decisions of the Supreme Court rendered thereunder, has been more exacting in its requirements as to the acknowledgements of the execution of deeds and conveyances for land and probate and registration of the same, than any other State in the Union, which has resulted in nearly every session of our Legislature since the passage of the first acts requiring registration of deeds and conveyances for land, passing acts curing the defective probate and registration of deeds, some of which will be hereinafter referred to and set out.

I am advised that the statutes of Alabama and certain of the other states provide that when the execution of a deed is acknowledged by grantor before any officer of the State authorized to take probate of deeds and conveyances and is certified to under his or her official seal, that this is sufficient to authorize the registration of the same in the County where the land lies without any officer passing on the certificate of such officers, and when so recorded, is prima facie evidence of the execution of the deed by the grantor to the grantee for the land therein described, but the same could be impeached for fraud or mistake; and that such deed, when so recorded in the County where the land lies, would be admissible as testimony in the trial or hearing of a cause involving the title of said land, but such probate would not be sufficient in this State under our statutes, to authorize the registration of such deed, as I will presently show.

To commence with, a deed is good as between the parties without registration. Under a former statute, it was held that registration of a deed between the parties was necessary in the case of White vs. Holly, reported in 91 N. C. R., page 67; but under a later statute it was held by our Suprme Court that registration of the instrument was not necessary between the parties. See decisions of our Supreme Court bearing on this point, set out under Section 3309 in the Code of 1927 of North Carolina, under Chapter 65, entitled "Probate and Registration," in words and figures as follows:

"AT PRESENT INSTRUMENT GOOD BETWEEN PARTIES WITHOUT REGISTRATION.—A deed is good and valid between the parties thereto without registration, and may be proved on the trial as at common law. Warren vs. Williford, 148 N. C. 474; Weston vs. Roper Lumber Co., 160 N. C. 263, 266, 75 S. E. 800.

"Contracts to convey land, as between the parties thereto, may be read in evidence without being registered. Hargrove vs. Adcock, 111 N. C. 166, 16 S. E. 16."

"SAME—DEED EFFECTIVE UNDER STATUTE OF USES.— Under this section registration is not necessary to the validity of a deed for valuable consideration, effective under the Statute of Uses, as between the parties. In cases where livery of seisin was formerly required registration still supplies the place of that ceremony. Hinton vs. Moore, 139 N. C. 44, 46, 51 S. E. 787."

"SAME—REGISTRATION AFTER COMMENCEMENT OF ACTION.—As between the parties, there being no question of title arising from prior registration of junior deeds, a deed registered after the commencement of an action is admissible in evidence. Hudson vs. Jordan, 108 N. C. 10, 12 S. E. 1029."

"SAME—ANALOGY WITH SECTION 3311.—The Connor Act (the amendment to this section) has substantially the same legal effect upon deeeds that the Act of 1819 had upon mortgages and deeds in trust (Robinson vs. Willoughby, 70 N. C. 358, 362), leaving them, although unregistered, valid as between the parties and as to all others except purchasers for value, and creditors. King vs. McRackan, 168 N. C. 621, 624, 84 S. E. 1027."

The principal object, however, in the probate and registration of deeds is to protect the grantee as against purchasers and creditors of the grantor, and especially so since the Connor Act of 1885. See Connor Act and decisions of our Supreme Court bearing on this point set out in Section 3309, in Code of 1927 of North Carolina, under head of "Probate and Registration."

The officials of this State who are authorized to take probate of deeds and conveyances for land in this State are enumerated and set out in Section 3293 under Chapter 65, entitled "Probate and Registration," in the Code of 1927 of North Carolina, in words and figures as follows:

OFFICIAL OF STATE AUTHORIZED TO TAKE PROBATE.— "The execution of all deeds of conveyance, contracts to buy, sell or convey lands, mortgages, deeds of trust, assignments, powers of attorney, covenants to stand seized to the use of another, leases for more than three years, releases and any and all instruments and writings of whatsoever nature and kind which are required or allowed by law to be registered in the office of the register of deeds or which may hereafter be required or allowed by law to be so registered, may be proved or acknowledged before any one of the following officials of this state: the several justices of the supreme court, commissioners of affidavits appointed by the governor of this state, the clerk of the supreme court, the several clerks of the superior court, the several clerks of the criminal courts, notaries public, and the several justices of the peace. (Rev. s. 989; Code, S. 1246; 1899, c. 161, ss. 1, 3; 1897, c. 87.)

SECTION 3294, "OFFICIALS OF THE UNITED STATES, FOREIGN COUNTRIES, AND SISTER STATES," ON PAGE 1054 UNDER CHAPTER 65, ENTITLED, "PROBATE AND REGISTRATION."

The officials of the United States, foreign countries and sister states who are authorized to take probate of deeds and conveyances for land in this State are enumerated and set out in Section 3294 of same chapter, which is in words and figures as follows:

OFFICIALS OF THE UNITED STATES, FOREIGN COUNTRIES, AND SISTER STATES.—"The execution of all such instruments and writings as are permitted or required by law to be registered may be proved or acknowledged before any one of the following officials of the United States, of the District of Columbia, of the several states and territories of the United States, of countries under the dominion of the United States, and of foreign countries: Any judge of a court of record, any clerk of a court of record, any notary public, any commissioner of deeds, any mayor or chief magistrate of an incorporated town or city, any ambassador, minister, consul, vice consul, consul general, vice consul general, or commercial agent of the United States, any justice of the peace of any state or territory of the United States. If the proof or acknowledgment of the execution of an instrument is had before a justice of the peace of any state of the United States other than this state or of any territory of the United States, the certificate of such justice of the peace shall be accompanied by a certificate of the clerk of some court of record of the county in which such justice of the peace resides, which certificate of the clerk shall be under his hand and official seal, to the effect that such justice of the peace was at the time the certificate of such justice bears date an acting justice of the peace of such county and state or territory and that the genuine signature of such justice of the peace is set to such certificate." (Rev., s. 990; 1899, c. 235, s. 6; 1905, c. 451; 1913, c. 39, s. 1; Ex. Sess. 1913, c. 72, s. 1.)

See decisions of our Supreme Court bearing on the probate of deeds and conveyances for land set out under the above sections

Section 3297 of the Code of 1927 of North Carolina, provides, "WHEN SEAL OF OFFICER NECESSARY TO PROBATE," which is in words and figures as follows:

"When proof or acknowledgment of the execution of any instrument by any maker of such instrument, whether a married woman or other person or corporation, is had before any official authorized by law to take such proof and acknowledgment, and such official has an official seal, he shall set his official seal to his certificate. If the official before whom the instrument is proved or acknowledged has no official seal he shall certify under his hand, and his private seal shall not be essential. When the instrument is proved or acknowledged before the clerk or deputy clerk of the superior court of the county in which the instrument is to be registered, the official seal shall not be necessary." (Rev., s. 993; 1899, c. 235, s. 8.)

See decisions of our Supreme Court in this State cited under the above section on page 1055 under chapter 65, entitled, "Probate and Registration."

The seal is not required to be affixed to a certificate of acknowledgment, unless the same was required by statute at that date. See case of Westfelt vs. Adams, reported in 131 N. C. R., page 379. The Court held in that case as follows: "NO SEAL WHEN NOT REQUIRED BY STATUTE"—The certificate of probate to a deed need not have a seal if not required by statute at the date of the execution."

In the case of Johnson vs. Eversole Lumber Company, before cited, the Court held as follows: "WHEN TAKEN IN OTHER STATE.— Under Rev. Code, c. 21, PP. 2, a commissioner of deeds for North Carolina, residing in another state, is not required to affix his seal to the certificate of acknowledgment of a deed conveying real estate in North Carolina."

The following are what I understand to be some of the requirements of the statutes of this State for a valid probate and registration of deeds and conveyances for land:

First, if the execution of a deed is acknowledged by the grantor before a Justice of the Peace in the county where the land lies and the deed is to be recorded and the same is certified to by the J. P. under his hand and private seal, and the certificate of the J. P. is in proper form and the Clerk of the Superior Court or other officer of the County authorized to take probate of deeds shall so adjudge, and the certificates are in proper form and the deed is ordered to be recorded together with the certificates, and the deed is so recorded, this constitutes a valid registration.

Second, if, however, the execution of the deed or conveyance for land is acknowledged by the grantor before a Justice of the Peace and the certificate of the J. P. is certified to by the Clerk of the Superior Court or other officer authorized to take probate of deeds and conveyances for land other than that of the County where the land lies, before the deed can be recorded in the County where the land lies, the Clerk of the Superior Court in the County where the deed was acknowledged must certify to the same in accordance with the provisions of Section 3296, under chapter 65, entitled "Probate and Registration," in the Code of 1927 of North Carolina, which is in words and figures as follows:

"BY JUSTICE OF PEACE OF OTHER THAN REGISTERING COUNTY."—

"If the proof of acknowledgment of any instrument is had before a justice of the peace of any county other than the county in which such instrument is offered for registration, the certificate of proof or acknowledgment made by such justice of the peace shall be accompanied by the certificate of the clerk of the superior court of the county in which said justice of the peace resides, that such justice of the peace was at the time his certificate bears date an acting justice of the peace of such county, and that such justice's genuine signature is set to his certificate. The certificate of the clerk of the superior court herein provided for shall be under his hand and official seal." (Rev., s. 992; 1899, c. 235, s. 4.) And when so certified, the Clerk of the Superior Court or other probating officer in the County where the land lies and the deed is to be recorded shall pass on both the certificate of the J. P. and that of the Clerk of the Superior Court, and if the same appear to be in proper form of law and sufficient, so adjudge, and order the deed or conveyance together with the certificates to be recorded, and when so recorded, the same will constitute a valid registration.

The failure of parties to follow the requirement of our statute where the grantor acknowledged the execution of a deed or conveyance for land before a Justice of the Peace and certified to by the Clerk of the Superior Court or other probating officer in a County other than in the County in which the land lies and the deed is to be recorded, has resulted in a great deal of litigation and many curative acts of our Legislature.

Third, if the execution of a deed is acknowledged by the grantor before a probate judge of a County other than that of the registration of a deed, and the same is recorded without being passed upon by the Judge of the County of the registration, it is directory only, and failure to comply therewith does not avoid the probate.

See case of Holmes vs. Marshall, reported in 72 N. C. R., page 37.

See case of Young vs. Jackson, reported in 92 N. C. R., page 144.

See also case of Darden vs. Neuse, etc., Steamboat Company, Supra, reported in 107 N. C. R., page 437.

In the case of Holmes vs. Marshall, Supra, the Court held "According to the requirement of Acts 1868-69, c. 64, that the certificate of the probate judge of a county other than that of the registration of a deed shall be passed on by the judge of the county of the registration, is directory only, and failure to comply therewith does not avoid the probate."

In the case of Darden vs. Neuse, the Court held that "Where the acknowledgment or proof of execution of a deed or other paper required to be registered is taken by any officer outside of the county where the land lies, it may be registered without any adjudication or order of registration by the clerk of the superior court of the latter county added to the certificate of the officer taking the acknowledgment, as Code, PP. 1246, subsec. 2, providing that the clerk of the superior court where the land lies shall pass upon the acknowledgments taken before other officers, is merely directory."

I do not think, however, that where the execution of a deed is acknowledged by the grantor before a Notary Public when certified to under his notarial seal, even in the County where the land lies, if recorded without the certificate of the Notary Public being passed upon by the Clerk of the Superior Court or other probating officer of the County where the land lies would be a valid registration, for the reason that while a Notary Public is authorized under the statutes of this State to take the acknowledgments of grantors in the execution of deeds a Notary Public has no such probating powers under the statute as would authorize him or her to direct the recording of such instruments. But his or her certificate could only be used as a basis upon which the proper officer of the County could pass on the sufficiency of the certificate and order the instrument to be recorded, under Section 3305 of the Code of 1927 of North Carolina, under Chapter 65, entitled "Probate and Registration"; and even in the County where the land lies the same would have to be passed upon by the Clerk of the Superior Court or other probating officer of the County and adjudged to be in due form of law and sufficient, and ordered to be registered, before the same would constitute a valid registration.

See case of White vs. Connelly reported in 105 N. C. R., page 65.

Where a deed or conveyance for land is acknowledged by the grantor before the Clerk of the Superior Court or proven by a witness before the Clerk in the County where the land lies and the deed is to be recorded, or acknowledged before a Justice of Peace in the County where the land lies and the deed is to be recorded, certified to by the Clerk, it is not necessary for the Clerk or the probating officer to affix his official seal to the certificate but only date and sign the same in his official capacity. But in cases where the deed or conveyance for land is to be recorded in a County other than that in which the acknowledgment was taken, it is necessary for the Clerk to certify to the same under his official seal as well also as where he certifies to a copy of a deed or contract to convey land that is to be recorded in the County where the land lies.

Where a deed is executed by a corporation and the deed recites that the corporate seal of the Company is affixed thereto, and the deed is recorded in the County where the land lies but the record where the deed is recorded fails to indicate the seal of the corporation by scroll, it will be presumed that the Register of Deeds by oversight failed to indicate the seal by scroll on the record, although the seal of the corporation may not have been affixed to the deed.

Or where the execution of a deeed or conveyance for land is acknowledged before a Notary Public, Clerk of the Superior Court, or other officials who are authorized to take probate of deeds, recites that the same was certified under their seals and the seal or scroll is not indicated on the record where such deed or conveyance is recorded, it will be presumed that the seal was affixed to the certificate by the Register of Deeds, but the Register of Deeds, by oversight, failed to indicate the same by scroll on the record, although as a matter of fact the seal of the official may not have beeen affixed to the instrument.

See case of Heath vs. Cotton Mills, reported in 115 N. C. R., page 204.

See case of Johnson vs. Eversole Lumber Company, reported in 147 N. C. R., pages 249 etc.

A deed, although signed by the grantor without the seal or scroll affixed to the signature of the grantor, although good as a contract to convey, is not good as a deed. A deed is definedby 2nd Blk. Com. star page 395 as an instrument of "writing signed, sealed, and delivered."

See case of Strain vs. Fitzgerald, reported in 128 N. C. R., pages 396, etc.

While our Supreme Court in this State has held that if the execution of a deed is acknowledged by the grantor before a probate judge of a County other than that of the registration of a deed, and the same is recorded without being passed upon by the Judge of the County of the registration, it is directory only and not mandatory, and failure to comply therewith does not avoid the probate as shown by the decisions of our Supreme Court in the cases of Holmes vs. Marshall, Young vs. Jackson, and Darden vs. Neuse, above cited, I find, however, that in all cases where the execution of deeds or contracts to convey land was acknowledged before non-resident officials authorized to take probate of deeds and conveyances for land in pursuance to Section 3294 of the Code of 1927 of North Carolina, above cited, that our Supreme Court has uniformly held that the certificates of such non-resident officials should be passed upon by the Clerk of the Superior Court or other official authorized to pass on the same in the County where the land lies and the deed is to be recorded, and the same adjudged to be in due form and according to law and sufficient before the same would constitute a valid registration, and deeds so recorded without the same being passed on by the Clerk of the Superior Court or other official authorized to pass on the same would be utterly void.

I find, however, conflicting opinions between the Supreme Court of our State and the Supreme Court of the United States in cases where the execution of a deed for land in this State was acknowledged by the grantor prior to the adoption of our Code of Civil Procedure of 1868 before a Commissioner of Deeds for North Carolina, resident in the District of Columbia or elsewhere in other states and recorded in the County where the land lies upon the certificate of such Commissioner of Deeds without the certificate of such Commissioner of Deeds being passed upon and adjudged to be in due form and sufficient by the proper officer in the County where the land lay and the deed was to be recorded.

The Supreme Court of the United States during the year 1915 in the case of the United States vs. The Hiawassee Lumber Company, reported in 238 U. S. R., pages 553, etc., held that in a controversy affecting the title to a 5,000 acre boundary of land in Clay County, N. C., where the execution of a deed was acknowledged on February 7, 1868, before John S. Hollingshead, a Commissioner of Deeds for North Carolina, resident in the District of Columbia, and recorded in the Office of the Register of Deeds of Clay County, N. C., on February 23, 1869, without the certificate of such Commissioner of Deeds being passed upon by the proper official of Clay County, N. C., at that time, was a valid registration under the statutes and decisions of the Supreme Court of North Carolina, cited in the opinion of the Court in that case; while the Supreme Court of North Carolina during the year 1922 in the case of Fibre Company vs. Cozad, reported in 183 N. C. R., page 600, held that the probate of a mortgage deed executed by W. H. Herbert to W. E. Snoddy on December 8, 1866, for twelve tracts of land in Cherokee County, N. C., acknowledged before Isaac H. Hall, a Commissioner of Deeds for North Carolina, resident in the City of New York, on the 24th of December, 1866, and recorded in the Office of the Register of Deeds of Cherokee County, N. C., in Book K, page 221, on October 23, 1867, in almost the exact words of the probate of the deed taken before J. S. Hollingshead, Commissioner of Deeds, above cited, was void for the reason that the deed was recorded upon the certificate of Isaac H. Hall, Commissioner of Deeds for North Carolina, resident in the City of New York, on December 24, 1866, without the certificate of the Commissioner of Deeds being passed upon by the proper officer of Cherokee County, N. C.

By reference to the decision of our Supreme Court in the case of Fibre Company vs. Cozad, supra, it will be seen that Chief Justice Clark dissented from the opinion of the majority of the Court for reasons set out in his dissenting opinion.

By reference to the decision of the Court in the case of the United States vs. Hiawassee Lumber Company, Supra, it will be seen that the plaintiff, the United States, claimed title to the 5,000 acre tract of land in Clay County in controversy in that suit by and through a deed made and executed by Edwin B. Olmsted and wife of the City of Washington, D. C., to Levi Stevens of the same City, bearing date February 7, 1868, and the execution of the deed was acknowledged by the grantors and the privy examination of the wife taken before John S. Hollingshead, a Commissioner of Deeds for North Carolina, resident in the City of Washington, D. C., on the same date, and which Commissioner certified to the acknowledgment of the deed by the grantors in proper form and ordered the deed to be recorded, and the deed was so recorded in the Office of the Register of Deeds of Clay County,N. C., on February 23, 1869, without the certificate of such Commissioner of Deeds being passed upon by the official authorized to take probate of deeds in Clay County, N. C. While the defendant, the Hiawassee Lumber Company, claimed title to the same land, first through a decree of the Superior Court of Macon County, N. C., in an equity action brought by one, Swepson, against Olmsted in the year 1882, which resulted in a deed of conveyance made pursuant to the decree and order of the Court by Kope Elias, Commissioner, to A. Rosenthal, dated October 28, 1882, and duly registered in Clay County, N. C., on October 17, 1890.

Second, through a quitclaim deed by Edwin B. Olmsted and wife to Rosenthal, dated October 31, 1882, registered in Clay County, N. C., on November 12, 1906, quitclaiming all interest of the grantors in the land described in the Kope Elias deed.

As above stated, the plaintiff, the United States, held in the suit of the United States vs. the Hiawassee Lumber Company, Supra, that the registration of the deed from Olmstead and wife to Stevens was a valid registration under the statutes and decisions of the Supreme Court of North Carolina, and especially so under an Act of the Legislature of North Carolina, passed and ratified during the year 1868, adopting the Code of Civil Procedure, which Act ratified and confirmed deeds recorded upon like certificates of Commissioners of Deeds prior to the adoption of the Code of Civil Procedure in 1868, and the Court held in that case that the plaintiff, the United States, was entitled to recover the 5,000 acre tract of land in Clay County, N. C., in controversy in that suit .

While the Supreme Court of North Carolina held in the case of Fibre Company vs. Cozad, Supra, that where a mortgage deed was executed by W. H. Herbert to W. E. Snoddy, bearing date December 8, 1866, through and under which the plaintiff, the Champion Fibre Company, claimed title to the twelve tracts of land in controversy in that case, the execution of which mortgage deeed was acknowledged before Isaac H. Hall, Commissioner of Deeds for the State of North Carolina, resident in the City of New York, on December 24, 1866, and which deed was recorded upon such certificate by the Register of Deeds of Cherokee County, N. C., in Book K, page 221, on October 23, 1867, without the certificate of the Commissioner of Deeds being passed upon by the proper official or probating officer of Cherokee County, N. C., and the Court held such registration to be void, which in effect reversed the decision of the Supreme Court in the case of the United States vs. the Hiawassee Lumber Company, Supra.

I take it that under the rules laid down by the Supreme Court of the United States, that in case a like controversy should arise in the future in either the State or United States Courts, under like acknowledgment of deeds taken before a Commissioner of Deeds for North Carolina, resident in the District of Columbia or elsewhere in other states, that the Courts would follow the decision of our Supreme Court in the case of Fibre Company vs. Cozad, above cited.

In the course of my work in the investigation of the title and in the preparation of abstracts of title for the Champion Fibre Company and others for lands in Cherokee, Clay and Graham Counties, N. C., I found that a number of deeds were executed by non-residents to parties in these three counties, and the execution thereof acknowledged before a Commissioner of Deeds in the District of Columbia and in other states, were recorded in the County where the land lay without the certificate of such Commissioner of Deeds being passed upon by the probate judge or proper official of the County authorized to pass on the same, which resulted in a lot of litigation. I found in a number of cases that acts of our Legislature had been passed curing such defective probates. I found in some cases that the vendors, and especially W. H. Herbert, had conveyed the same land twice, and I found in some cases that the parties had produced the original deeds and had the same re-probated and re-recorded; but in all cases where the parties had conveyed the second time before the curative acts were passed, our Supreme Court held that the second purchaser from the vendor for value had acquired a good title to the land.

By reference to the decision of our Supreme Court in the case of Fibre Company vs. Cozad, supra, it will be seen that the Court referred to an act passed by the General Assembly of North Carolina during the year 1913, curing the defective probate of deeds acknowledged before a Commissioner of Deeds in other states, but held that in as much as Cozad acquired title to the land in controversy through W. H. Herbert and the deed from Herbert was recorded before the curative act of 1913 was passed, that Cozad acquired a good title to the tract of land in controversy in that suit.

As before stated, our Legislature from time to time has passed acts curing defective probate and registration of deeds and conveyances for land, which acts as between parties have been held valid by our Supreme Court, but void as to creditors and purchasers for value from the donor or bargainer before such curative acts were passed and ratified, as held by our Supreme Court in the case of Fibre Company vs. Cozad, above cited, and cases cited under the decision of the Court in that case.

See numerous curative acts set out in Sections 3366(a) to 3366(o) of the Code of 1927 of North Carolina, under Chapter 65, entitled "Probate and Registration."

Among other validating acts above referred to, see Section 3366(i) and Section 3366(j) and decision of the Supreme Court cited under Section 3366(i), which is in words and figures is as follows:

Section 3366(i)—"VALIDATION OF INSTRUMENTS REGISTERED WITHOUT PROBATE.—In every case where it shall appear from the records in the office of the register of deeds of any county in the state that any instrument of writing required or allowed by law to be registered prior to January first, eighteen hundred and sixty-nine, without any acknowledgment, proof, privy examination, or probate, or upon a defective acknowledgment, proof, privy examination, or probate, the record of such instrument may notwithstanding, be read in evidence in any of the courts of this state, if otherwise competent. This section shall not apply to suits pending March 6, 1923, or affect any vested rights." (1923, c. 215, s .1.)

EDITOR'S NOTE.—"It is suggested in 1 N. C. Law Rev. 302, where this section is summarized, that it probably means that the registration must have been made prior to 1869, and that this and the following section should be considered as amendments or additional sections to ch. 35 Art. 2, secs. 1751-1788, and ch. 65, Art. 4, secs. 3329-3366."

Section (j)—"REGISTRATION ON DEFECTIVE PROBATES BEYOND STATE.—In every case where it shall appear from the records in the office of the register of deeds of any county in this state that any instrument required or allowed by law to be registered, bearing date prior to the year one thousand eight hundred and thirty-five, executed by any person or persons residing in any of the United States, other than this state, or in any of the territories of the United States, or in the District of Columbia, has been proven or acknowledged, or the privy examination of any feme covert taken thereto, before any officer or person authorized by any of the laws of this state in force prior to the said year one thousand eight hundred and thirty-five to take such proofs, privy examinations and acknowledgments, and the said instrument has been registered in the proper county without the certificate of the governor of the state or territory in which such proofs, acknowledgments or privy examinations were taken, or of the secretary of state of the United States, when such certificate or certificates were required, as to the official character of the person taking such acknowledgment, proof or privy examination, as aforesaid, and without an order of registration made by a court or judge in this state having jurisdiction to make such order, then and in all such cases such proofs, privy examinations, acknowledgments and registrations are hereby in all respects fully validated and confirmed and declared to be sufficient in law, and such instruments so registered may be read in evidence in any of the courts of this state. This section shall not apply to suits pending March 6, 1923, or affect any vested rights." (1923, c. 215, ss. 2, 3.)

By reference to these sections it will be seeen that the same only validated probates up to the year 1869.

During the session of our General Assembly in 1935 an act was passed and ratified on the 14th day of March, 1935, amending Section 3366(i), being Chapter 92, entitled: "AN ACT TO AMEND SECTION THEE THOUSAND THREE HUNDRED SIXTY-SIX (i) OF THE CONSOLIDATED STATUTES, RELATIVE TO DEFECTIVE PROBATE OF INSTRUMENTS OF WRITING," which is in words and figures as follows:

THE GENERAL ASSEMBLY OF NORTH CAROLINA DO ENACT:

"SECTION 1. That section three thousand three hundred sixty-six (i) of the Consolidated Statutes be and the same is hereby amended by striking out all of said section and inserting in lieu thereof the following:

" 'Three thousand three hundred sixty-six (i) VALIDATION OF INSTRUMENTS REGISTERED WITHOUT PROBATE. In every case where it shall appear from the records in the Office of the Register of Deeds of any County in the State that any instrument of writing required or allowed by law to be registered has been registered, prior to January first, nineteen hundred and twenty, without any acknowledgment, proof, privy examination, probate, adjudication and order of registration, or upon a defective acknowledgment, proof, privy examination, probate, adjudication and order of registration, the record of such instrument may, notwithstanding, be read in evidence in any of the Courts of this State, if otherwise competent. This Act shall not apply to creditors and purchasers for value, or to pending suits. This Act shall apply to the Counties of Graham and Cherokee only.'

SEC. 2. "That all laws and clauses of laws in conflict with the provisions of this Act are hereby repealed.

SEC. 3. "That this Act shall be in force and effect from and after its ratification.

"Ratified this the 14th day of March, A. D. 1935."

This Act validated certain probate and registration up to January 1, 1920.

By reference to this Act it will be seen that the same only applies to Cherokee and Graham Counties, N. C.

By reference to the foregoing curative acts it will be seen that the same only cure defective probate and registration of deeds up to the time limited therein. The last above cited curative act cures defective probates therein referred to up to January 1, 1920, since which time the acknowledgment of the execution of deeds for land in this State and the probating and recording of the same in the County where the land lies must be done in accordance with the existing statutes on the date of the execution of the deeds, or such registration will be void. This concludes my report on the probate and registration of deeds.

Heirship

I have heretofore called attention to the fact that a good part of the land in what are now Graham, Cherokee, and Clay Counties, N. C., was entered and granted by non-residents of this State, and the title to a good part of the land in these three counties was acquired by parties who were non-residents who came to this State and qualified as administrators on estates of deceased parties, who as such administrators instituted acts before the proper officer in the County where the land lay, making the heirs of such parties, parties defendant in the suit for the purpose of obtaining assets to pay the indebtedness of the Estate, and upon orders made by the Court, the land was sold for such purpose and the same purchased by parties and report made by the administrators of such sale, and the sale was confirmed by the Court, and the non-residents who entered and granted the land, and the purchasers of the land through such non-resident administrators who came to this State and qualified and made bond were valid, notwithstanding objections that had been made in the past and that might be made in the future to title to land thus acquired.

I find, however, that the title to a good part of the land in these three counties was derived through heirs of non-residents of this State, and in case of litigation over the land, in deraigning title to the land derived through the heirs of such non-residents, it will become necessary for the party claiming title to the land derived through the heirs of non-residents or residents of this State to show by proper evidence the heirs of such deceased party.

I will now give what I understand to be necessary to establish heirship.

I find some authorities cited in the 22nd Volume of the Amer. & Eng. Enc. of Law, 2nd Edition, set out on pages 640 et seq, that have an important bearing on heirship, and by reference to page 644 it will be seen that only slight evidence is required to establish heirship, and the sufficiency of the evidence for this purpose is left largely to the discretion of the judge.

The two clauses bearing on this point set out on page 644 are in words as follows:

"DEGREES OF RELATIONSHIP: Nor is it necessary that the degree of relationship between the declarant and the person in question should be made out. It is enough if some relationship is shown.

"QUESTION FOR JUDGE: It is a question for the judge to decide whether the relationship has been sufficiently established to admit the evidence."

By reference to page 653 of the above volume, it will be seen that recitals in deeds and recitals of pedigree in bills and answers in chancery are held to be sufficient evidence to establish heirship in certain cases. The two clauses bearing upon this point set out on page 653 are in words as follows:

"RECITALS: Recitals in deeds, wills, and marriage settlements have been held to be admissible in proof of pedigree, subject to the qualifications noted in the preceding sections of this title."

"PLEADINGS, RECORDS, ETC.: In regard to recitals of pedigree in bills and answers in chancery, a distinction has been taken between those facts which are not in dispute and those which are in controversy, the former being admitted, and the latter excluded."

I find that recitals in a deed are only binding upon parties to the deed. See case of Gaylord vs. Respass, reported in 92 N. C. R., pages 553, et seq.

Now it would appear from the authorities above cited as to recitals of pedigree in bills and answers in chancery, when the same are not disputed they would be sufficient evidence to establish heirship.

Under our constitution of 1868 the distinction between law and equity was abolished, and partition proceedings are classed as special proceedings, and are the same as proceedings in chancery under the old practice.

In cases where the heirs of deceased parties reside in the County where the litigation is pending, or in the locality of the same, heirship could be established by some relative or someone who lived in the locality of the family and was familiar with the members of the family; but where it becomes necessary to show heirship by parties outside of the State, then it would be necessary to take the deposition of some relative of the family or someone well acquainted with the members of the family, in order to show the relationship.

I will here state that the first step to take in reference to heirship is to first satisfy myself as to who are the heirs of such deceased non-resident, and then go to the party representing the opposing side, or his or their attorney, and assure him of the fact that I have made a thorough investigation of the matter and have become fully convinced as to who the heirs of the deceased party are and furnishing him with the names of the same, calling attention to the fact that admission of heirship would save a lot of trouble and cost and expense to both sides; and in numerous cases I have had, I have never failed in getting the other side to admit the heirship in writing, and thereby save the trouble and the cost and expense of taking the deposition of witnesses as to such heirship.

I find that the title to the major portion of the timber tracts in Graham County and a portion in what are now Cherokee and Clay Counties, N. C., now held by persons, corporations, and some by the United States Forest Service, was acquired by and through deeds and conveyances made by the heirs and administrators of deceased non-residents; and where the deeds were executed by heirs of deceased non-residents, most of these deeds contained recitals that they were the only heirs of the deceased party, and this being so, our Legislature passed and ratified an act on March 7, 1931, being Chapter 159, Public Local Laws of 1931, entitled, "AN ACT TO MAKE RECITALS IN CERTAIN INSTRUMENTS PRIMA FACIE EVIDENCE OF HEIRSHIP IN GRAHAM COUNTY," making the recitals contained in deeds and judgments and decrees of the Court executed more than thirty-five years prior to the passage and ratification of the Act, prima facie evidence of such heirship, which act is in words and figures as follows:

Preamble: Grant of lands in Graham County to non-residents.

"Whereas, seventy-five per cent of the lands in Graham County are wild, unimproved and unoccupied mountain land, and,

Whereas, a large portion of said lands were granted to non-residents of North Carolina who are now dead and who left heirs whose residence are unknown to the present owners of such lands, and,

Heirs have re-conveyed lands.

"Whereas, said heirs have, in many instances, conveyed said land by deed reciting said heir-ship, and,

Difficulty of establishing heirship.

"Whereas, in introducing said titles in evidence it causes great and unnecessary expense, trouble and inconvenienve to prove said heir-ship: Now therefore,

"THE GENERAL ASSEMBLY OF NORTH CAROLINA DO ENACT:

Recitals of heir-ship in deeds prima facie evidence of such heir-ship where deeds are more than 30 years old.

"Section 1. That the recitals of any deed which has been registered in the office of Register of Deeds of Graham County for a period of thirty years or more, reciting that the grantors or any of them is or are the heir or heirs of any person therein named, shall be prima facie evidence of the heirship of such party or parties, when said deed is introduced as a link in the chain of title.

Same provision as to old judgments.

"Sec. 2. That where a judgment has been entered in the office of the Clerk of the Superior Court of Graham County for thirty years or more, in which the recitals in either the pleadings or judgment recites that certain party or parties therein named is or are the heir or heirs of a certain person or persons therein named, said recitals therein shall be prima facie evidence of such heirship upon the introduction of said record in evidence where same is a link in the chain of title.

Application of act.
"Sec. 3. That this act shall only apply where the parties to an action claim title under and through separate and distinct chains of title.

Pending litigation uneffected.
"Sec. 4. That this act shall not effect pending litigation.

Applicable only to Graham County.
"Sec. 5. That this act shall apply to Graham County only.

Conflicting laws repealed.
"Sec. 6. That all laws and clauses of laws in conflict with the provisions of this act are hereby repealed.

"Sec. 7. That this act shall take effect from and after its ratification.

"Ratified this the 7th of March, A. D. 1931."

When I first read this act I was in doubt as to whether or not a deed or judgment would have to be on record for thirty years previous to the ratification of the act on the 7th of March, 1931, but upon further consideration of the matter I am of the opinion that if a deed or judgment has been on record for thirty years prior to the time same is offered in evidence, the statute will apply.

In this connection I will call attention to the fact that our Supreme Court has held that one of several heirs or tenants in common can maintain and defend an action on behalf of himself and his co-tenants for the benefit of all.

See: Moody vs. Johnson—112 N. C. R., page 798.

This concludes my report on Heirship.

ACTIONS TO RECOVER AND QUIET TITLE TO LAND

Our Legislature, during the year 1893, passed and ratified an Act, being Chapter 6 of the Public Laws of 1893, entitled: "AN ACT TO DETERMINE CONFLICTING CLAIMS TO REAL PROPERTY," which is in words and figures as follows:

"THE GENERAL ASSEMBLY OF NORTH CAROLINA DO ENACT:

"SECTION 1. That an action may be brought by any person against another who claims an estate or interest in real property adverse to him, for the purpose of determining such adverse claims.

"SECTION 2. That if the defendant in such action disclaim in his answer any interest or estate in the property, or suffer judgment to be taken against him without answer, the plaintiff cannot recover costs.

"SECTION 3. That this act shall be in force from and after its ratification.

"Ratified the 31st day of January, A. D., 1893."

See this act brought forward and incorporated in Section 1743 on page 644 of the Code of 1927 of North Carolina, under Chapter 34, entitled "Estates."

Prior to the passage of this Act there were two methods open to the plaintiff to establish title to land.

1. One was an action of ejectment, where the defendant was in possession.

2. The other was where the plaintiff was in possession of land, to bring suit against the defendant to remove the claim of title of the defendant as a cloud upon the planitiff's title, and this continued to be the practice both in the State and United States Courts up until the passage of the Act of 1893 of the General Assembly permitting a party to bring an action, although not in possession of the land, against the defendant to remove the claim of the defendant as a cloud upon his title.

Our Supreme Court has held in numerous cases that the Act of 1893 was valid and that a plaintiff could sustain an action against a defendant under the Act to remove the defendant's claim as a cloud upon the plaintiff's title without the plaintiff being in possession of the land.

See decisions of our Supreme Court bearing on this point set out under Section 1743 of the Code of 1927 of North Carolina, above cited.

Upon the adoption of our Code of Civil Procedure in 1868-69 by our Legislature, separate actions of law and equity were abolished, and if a plaintiff in an action alleged facts that would entitle him to recover in an action at law under former practice or a suit in equity under former practice, he would be entitled to recover in one action.

Section 133, set out in Clark's Code of Civil Procedure, Annotated, reads as follows:

"FORMS OF CIVIL ACTIONS; DISTINCTION BETWEEN ACTIONS AT LAW AND SUITS IN EQUITY ABOLISHED. C. C. P., S. 12. CONST., ART. IV, s. 1."

"The distinction between actions at law and suits in equity, and the forms of all such actions and suits heretofore existing, are abolished, and there shall be hereafter but one form of action for the enforcement or protection of private rights, and the redress of private wrongs, which shall be denominated a civil action."

See decisions of our Supreme Court set out thereunder, bearing on this point.

But by reference to the decision of Judge Parker of the United States Circuit Court of Appeals, rendered in the case of Arthur A.

Wood, Forest Supervisor, vs. R. L. Phillips et al, rendered on June 17, 1931, it will be seen that Judge Parker held that in that case under the equity practice of the United States Court, a plaintiff cannot sustain an action against a defendant to remove a cloud upon his title under the Act of 1893 of North Carolina, unless the plaintiff is in possession of the land, which to my minds is a case in which the United States refuses to follow the decisions of the State courts on land matters, and it appears to me also that the decison of Judge Parker in this case on the question of possession is contrary to the decisions of the Supreme Court of North Carolina. And while, as above stated, the general rule is that the United States Court will follow the decisions of the State Courts in cases involving the title to land within the states, this will depend very largely upon whether the United States Courts want to follow the decisions of the State Court, and if they don't want to follow the same, they will find some excuse for not doing so.

In addition to the remedy open to the plaintiff for the recovery of land under an action of ejectment and to remove a cloud upon title under Section 1743 of the Code of 1927 of North Carolina, above cited, the plaintiff can bring suit under what is known as the Torrens Act, set out as chapter 47, pages 813 etc., of the Code of 1927 of North Carolina, under the head of "Land Registration."

By reference to the Torrens Act it will be seen that an action can be maintained by the plaintiff against all parties claiming title to an interest in the land adversely to the plaintiff, whether under the same or different claims, in one suit.

As the sections contained in the Torrens Act are very numerous and the provisions of the Act somewhat complicated, I will only set out and comment on what I understand to be the material provisions of the Act, which are as follows:

First, the plaintiff files his petition, setting up his claim of title to the land, making such parties as are known to him who claim an interest in the land adversely to the plaintiff as well as any and all other parties who might assert a claim of title to the same adversely to the plaintiff, parties defendant, and then proceeds to have notice of the action served on the parties in accordance with the provisions of the Act; and after the notice of the action is served on the parties and some of the defendants have filed answers to the petition, and the time has elapsed for filing an answer by other defendants, whether answer is filed or not, the Judge appoints an attorney as Title Examiner, who is in effect a referee, who proceeds to a hearing of the cause, and the plaintiff can then proceed to offer his chain of title in evidence, and his testimony in support of the same; and the defendants who have answered can do the same; but no judgment can be taken against the defendants who have failed to answer by default. And the Title Examiner will then pass on the title of both the plaintiff and the defendants, just as a referee would do; and after the Title Examiner completes the hearing and passes on the testimony offered by both sides, he makes his report to the Court, and if the referee reports the title of the plaintiff good, and the claim of title of the defendants unfounded, and if no exception is filed thereto, or if exceptions are filed and overruled by the Court, and the report of the Title Examiner is confirmed by the Judge and judgment rendered accordingly in favor of the plaintiff, and the judgment and decree of the Court is certified to and recorded in the office of the Register of Deeds in the County where the land lies in accordance with the provisions of the Act, all parties who were made defendants in the suit and answered, as well as those who failed to answer, and all parties who were served with notice of the action in the manner prescribed by the Act, including infants and persons under disabilities, would be barred from ever thenafter asserting any claim of title or interest in the land, set out in the petition and judgment and decree of the Court.

While an action to clear up the title to land would be pretty expensive under the Torrens Act, it appears to me that in a case where the party is owner of a large boundary of very valuable land that is claimed by parties not in possession of the same, and the plaintiff is not fully advised as to parties who may assert a claim of title to the same adversely to the plaintiff, it would be desirable to clear up the title under the provisions of the Torrens Act, for as I understand it where the plaintiff is not sure as to all the parties who might assert a claim of title to the same, when notice of the action is given by a summons headed, "To all whom it may concern," that even if the parties are not named as defendants, when this notice is published for the period required by the statute, it will be a sufficient notice to all parties who might assert a claim of title to the land, including infants and persons under disabilities; and if they fail to assert and set up a claim of title to the land, any interest that they may have in the land would be barred thereafter by the judgment and decree of the Court entered in the suit.

Another advantage in clearing up a title under the Torrens Act is that the action can be sustained against all parties claiming title to the land adversely to the plaintiff, whether under the same or different claims, without the action being multifarious, but no judgment can be taken in an action under the Torrens Act against defendants failing to answer by default, as the plaintiff is required to show title to the land before recovering judgment as against defendants failing to answer; while in an action instituted by the plaintiff against adverse claimants under Section 1743 of the Code of 1927 of North Carolina, where the plaintiff alleges in his complaint facts that would entitle him to recover, and the complaint is verified, and the defendant fails to answer, the plaintiff would be entitled to a judgment against the defendant by default. But on account of the expense of prosecuting an action under the Torrens Act, unless the title is involved to a large and valuable boundary of land, I think it would be preferable to clear up the title under Section 1743, above cited; but the plaintiff in an action under Code Section 1743 could not join in the same action, defendants claiming under different sources of title, as such action would be multifarious and this could only be done under the Torrens Act.

If, however, a party is the owner of a tract or boundary of land and a number of parties are in possesion of the same, claiming title to the same adversely to the plaintiff under different claims of title, then the action of ejectment is preferable to either an action under the Torrns Act or Code Section 1743, as the plaintiff would be entitled to recover judgment as against all the defendants in possession, where he showed a superior title to the land.

But in cases where the plaintiff is the owner of land and a party that is not in possession of the land is claiming title to the same adversely to the plaintiff, then the remedy of the plaintiff for clearing up the title to the land is either under Code Section 1743 or under the Torrns Act.

So it will be seen that there are now three methods open to the plaintiff to recover and quiet the title to land:

FIRST

By an action of Ejectment, where the defendant is in possession of the land.

SECOND

Under Code Section 1743 of 1927 of North Carolina, where the defendant is not in possession of the land, and is claiming title to the land adversely to the plaintiff, and the plaintiff desires to remove the claim of title of the defendant as a cloud upon his title.

THIRD

Under the Torrens Act, to quiet title as against adverse claimants in one suit.

This concludes my report on acts to recover and quiet the title to land.

There are four subjects bearing on the title to land that I have not so far discussed, namely:

COLOR OF TITLE
FEE SIMPLE TITLE
STATUTE OF PRESUMPTIONS,
STATUTE OF LIMITATIONS,
and
TITLE BY PRESCRIPTION OR POSSESSION

COLOR OF TITLE

In defining color of title in the case of Smith vs. Proctor, reported in 139 N. C. R., p. ₃s 314 etc., Chief Justice Hoke in delivering the opinion of the Court held in that case, that "color of title is a paper writing (usually a deed) which professes and appears to pass a title, but fails to do so." This appears to me to the best and clearest definition of what it takes to constitute color of title that I have found anywhere.

See also case of Seals vs. Seals, reported in 165 N. C. R., page 409. See also other cases cited on pages 249-250 of First Vol. Enc. Dig. of North Carolina Reports, under head of "Adverse Possession."

Formerly, a grant issue by the State to a party for land that had already been granted was color of title, but by Chapter 490, Public Laws of 1893, ratified the Sixth of March, 1893, a grant issued by the State to a party for land previously granted is absolutely void and not even color of title.

See Chapter 490, Public Laws of 1893 of North Carolina, page 455.

See this act brought forward and incorporated in Sec. 7545, Chapter 126, Code of 1927 of North Carolina, entitled "State Lands," and decisions of our Supreme Court cited thereunder.

Fee Simple Title

At common law, in order to pass a fee simple title, after giving the name of the grantee, the words "his heirs and assigns," or if to a corporation, the words "its successors and assigns," were required to be added in order to pass a fee simple title to the land; but under Chapter 19, entitled "Conveyances," Art. I, "Construction and Sufficiency," of the Code of 1927 of North Carolina, fee is presumed, though the word "heirs" is omitted, unless it appears in the deed that the grantee meant to convey a less estate.

Section 991, above quoted, reads as follows:

"When real estate is conveyed to any person, the same shall be held and construed to be a conveyance in fee, whether the word "heir" is used or not, unless such conveyance in plain and express words shows, or it is plainly intended by the conveyance or some part thereof, that the grantor meant to convey an estate of less dignity."

Statute Of Presumptions And Statute Of Limitations And Title By Prescription Or Possession

Prior to the adoption by North Carolina of the new constitution in 1868 and the adoption of the Code of Civil Procedure during the General Assembly of North Carolina of 1868-69 there were no Statutes of Limitations, but only Statutes of Presumptions; but Statutes of Limitations in both real and personal actions were enacted by the General Assembly of North Carolina of 1868-69 and incorporated in the Code of Civil Procedure.

I give below the sections of the Code of Civil Procedure that provided when and how the State would be barred from an action for the recovery of real estate.

Sec. 139. "The State will not sue any person for, or in respect of, any real property, or the issues or profits thereof, by reason of the right or title of the State to the same.

"(1) When the person in possession thereof, or those under whom he claims, shall have been in the adverse possession thereof for thirty years, such possession having been ascertained and identified under known and visible lines or boundaries, shall give a title in fee to the possessor.

"(2) When the person in possession thereof, or those under whom he claims, shall have been in possession under colorable title for twenty-one years, such possession having been ascertained and identified under known and visible lines or boundaries.

"Sec. 140. All such possession as is described in the preceding section, under such title as is therein described, is hereby ratified and confirmed, and declared to be a good and legal bar against the entry suit of any person, under the right or claim of the State."

See these sections set out on pages 24, 26, and 27 in Clark's Code of Civil Procedure, annotated, third edition.

As above stated, these same sections were adopted by the General Assembly of North Carolina at its session in 1868-69 when the Code of Civil Procedure was adopted, and the same have been brought forward, subject to slight modifications, and incorporated in the revisal of all the laws of this state from the adoption of the Code of Civil Procedure up to the present time, and these Statutes of Limitations have continued in full force and effect from the year 1869 up to the present time.

See these sections set out as sections 425, subsections one and two and section 427 on pages 113 and 114 at bottom, of North Carolina Revised Code of 1927, under head of article four "Limitations Real Property." See also section 426 set out on page 114 of Revised Code of North Carolina of 1927, which reads as follows:

"Possession presumed out of state.—In all actions involving the title to real property title is conclusively deemed to be out of the state unless it is a party to the action, but this section does not apply to the trials of protested entries laid for the purpose of obtaining grants, nor to actions instituted prior to May 1, 1917." (1917, c. 195.)

See also cases of Supreme Court of North Carolina cited under section 425 aforesaid.

In the case of Melvin vs. Waddell, 75 N. C. R., page 361, in passing on the sections above cited, the court held:

"The question of the presumption of a grant from adverse possession has never been regarded as one to be decided upon natural presumptions as to facts, but upon a statutory or arbitrary rule established by the Legislature, or by the Courts, to prevent the uncertainty of titles which would arise if the question in each case were to be determined by a jury, on their belief of the fact, derived from a consideration of all the circumstances in evidence."

In the case of Price vs. Jackson, 91st N. C. R., 11, 14, in passing upon the statutes above quoted, the court held as follows:

"But the law is now changed, and the thirty years' adverse possession which was formerly held to be a presumption of a grant, is now by statute made, under certain circumstances, an absolute bar against the State."

In the case of Brown vs. Spivey, 109 N. C. R., page 57, and Alexander vs. Gibbon, 118 N. C. R., page 797, the court held that "the law presumes possession unexplained to be an adverse possession."

The above decisions appear to be overruled or at least rendered inoperative by reason of the provisions of Section 386, First Vol. of Pell's Revisal of 1908, as held by a later decision of our Supreme Court in the case of Bland et al vs. Beasley et al, reported 145 N. C. R., pages 168, etc.

The Court held in the latter case as follows:

"There is no presumption that the possession of real estate is adverse." "MONK vs. WILMINGTON, 137 N. C., 322. Revisal sec. 386, provides that possession by another shall be deemed 'to have been under and in subordination to the legal title,' unless such possession is shown to have been adverse."

In the case of Walden vs. Ray, 121 N. C. R., page 237, the Court held:

"Thirty years' adverse possession of land will bar an action by the State, and such possession need not be absolutely continuous nor need there be any connection between the tenants."

In the case of Price vs. Jackson, 91st N. C. R., page 11, and Phipps vs. Pierce, 94 N. C. R., page 514, the Court held:

"Thirty years' adverse possession, which was formerly held to be a presumption of a grant, is now by statute an absolute bar against the State. But in such case the plaintiff must now show that the possession was held up to known and visible boundaries."

Under the head of PRESCRIPTION, set out under Section 2 on pages 1216, etc., of 22nd Volume Amer. and Eng. Enc. of Law, the writer uses the following language:

"Validity of rights acquired by prescription are in all respects as perfect and absolute as those acquired by grant."

In the next section the writer uses the following language:

"Thus it is held that the user of an easement grant by prescription may be proved by parole, but clear and convincing proof is required to establish the claim."

The following are decisions of the Supreme Court of North Carolina and the United States bearing on the location and title to land:

"The Court will presume that all the necessary parties were before the court in the case—from the recitals—"

See Sutton vs. Jenkins, 147 N. C. R., page 11.

See also Hare vs. Holloman, 94 N. C. R., page 14.

See also Morris vs. Jentry, 89 N. C. R., page 248.

See McNeely vs. Laxton, 149 N. C. R., 237, 63 S. E. 278.

See also cases cited in 2nd Vol. Enc. Digest of North Carolina Reports under the head of "Boundaries," on pages 616, etc.

In the case of Hare vs. Holloman the Court uses this language:

"The judgment roll of the foreclosure proceedings is not before us, and the action referred to only by its title. Under the maxim, 'Omnia Presumuntur Rite Esse Acta', we must take the proceedings to be regular until it is shown to the contrary. In addition to the fact that the names of all the parties to an action are not generally set out in the title, there is a general presumption that legal proceedings are regular and that all necessary parties have been made."

REGULARITY OF JUDGMENT:—

A judgment, in the absence of proper proof of fraud, must be presumed to have been fairly and regularly taken.

Wiseman vs. Penland, 79 N. C. R., 197.

"The recitals of decrees in registered conveyances by an officer of the Court were prima facie evidence of such decrees, though the decrees themselves not registered."

"Riley & Co. vs. Carter, 165 N. C. R., 334. 81 S. E., 414.

McKee vs. Lineberger, 87 N. C. R., 181.

Carolina Iron Co. vs. Abernathy, 94 N. C. R., 545."

"The recitals in a deed of a commissioner appointed by the Court to sell lands are prima facie sufficient to show his authority to do so. (Irvin vs. Clark, 98 N. C. R., 437, 4 S. E. 30), and the proceedings wherein it was made may not be attacked collaterally for irregularity, but only by motion in the cause to have the judgment therein set aside. (Rackley vs. Roberts, 147 N. C. R., 201, 60 S. E. 975) cited and approved. Baggett vs Lanier, 178 N. C. R., 129, 100 S. E. 254."

An administrator is an officer of the court, and stands on the same footing as a commissioner of the court.

A party who claims title by possession either under deeds as color of title or under known and visible boundary lines, without color, must show the possession to be adverse during the statutory period, otherwise the possession will be presumed to be under the true owner of the land.

See case of Bland vs. Beasley, reported in 145 N. C. R., pages 168 etc., in which the following language is used by the Court in the third section of the syllabus of that case:

"3. Same—Adverse Possession—Legal Title—Color—Presumption.

"There is no presumption that the possession of one under and in subordination to the legal title is adverse, and when the title is thus claimed by adverse possession, or for seven years under color, the burden is upon him who relies thereon to show such possession to have been continuous, uninterrupted, and manifested by distinct and unequivocal acts of ownership."

Our Supreme Court takes judicial notice of the fact that all the earlier surveys of this state were often if not always inaccurate. See case of Duncan vs. Hall, 117 N. C. R., pages 443, etc.

Our Supreme Court also takes judicial notice that all the earlier surveys of this State were made by surface measurement and not by level measurement. See case of Duncan vs. Hall, 117 N. C. R., pages 443, etc. Also case of Stack vs. Pepper, 119 N. C. R., pages 438, etc.

Our Supreme Court, however, later on held that the only accurate way in order to determine the acreage in a tract of land was by level or horizontal measurement. See case of Gilmer vs. Young, 122 N. C. R., pages 806, etc.

By reference to the decision of the Supreme Court in this case it will be seen that there was a majority opinion and that two of the Judges, Douglas and Furches, dissented, but I think there will not be any question but what in a controversy as to the location of any tracts of land that if it was an old survey, it would be competent to show that the earlier measurements were made by surface and not by level measurement.

As a general rule the line of another tract, which is called for, controls courses and distances, being considered the more certain description, and it makes no difference whether it is a marked, or an unmarked, or a mathematical line.

See Slade vs. Cherry, 7 N. C. R., pages 69 etc.

See Corn vs. McGary, 48 N. C. R., pages 496 etc.

See Hill vs. Dalton, 140 N. C. R., page 9.

See Whitticker vs. Cover, 140 N. C. R., pages 380 etc.

See Moore vs. McClain, 141 N. C. R., pages 473 etc.

There are numerous decisions of our Supreme Court bearing on this point cited in 2nd and 13th Volumes of Enc. Dig. of N. C. R., under head of "Boundaries." One of the earliest decisions of our Supreme Court on this point is the case of Sandifer vs. Foster, 2nd N. C. R., page 237.

In the case of Sasser vs. Alford, 3rd N. C. R., page 148, the Court held as follows:

"The natural boundary described in a deed is to be followed if it can be ascertained; but if the jury doubt which is the natural boundary, and are satisfied from the evidence that the artificial boundary was considered by the proprietor as the true one, they may establish it by their verdict."

There are, however, exceptions to the general rule, that the line of another tract called for when well established will prevail as against a call for course and distance; in the case of Bowen vs. Roper Lumber Co., 153 N. C. R., page 366, the court uses the following language bearing on this point:

"Natural objects called for in a patent or deed, sufficiently placed or identified, as a rule, control course and distance, and this last rule very generally obtains unless the facts and accompanying data clearly shows that its application would lead to an erroneous conclusion. Bowen vs. Roper Lumber Co., 153 N. C. R., 366; 69 S. E., 258; Tucker vs. Satterthwaite, 123 N. C. R., 511; 31 S. E., 722."

In the case of the Ritter Lumber Company vs. Montvale Lumber Co., reported in 169 N. C. R., page 80, the Court uses the following language:

"As a general rule, monuments, natural or artificial, referred to in a deed control its construction, rather than courses and distances; but this rule is not inflexible; it yields whenever, taking all the particulars of the deed together, it would be absurd to apply it."

So it will be seen that even when a line or corner of another tract is called for that is well established in the grant or deed, if the same is unreasonable and inconsistent with other calls and data in the grant or deed, and will result in an erroneous conclusion, the same will not prevail against course and distance called for in the instrument.

The line of another tract called for is the line that was recognized as such at the date of the issuing of the grant, although it may not be the correct line.

See case of Redmond vs. Stepp, reported in 100 N. C. R., pages 213, etc.

Our courts in the location of lands embraced in grants and deeds always endeavor to get at the intention of the parties from the instrument, regardless of technical rules. See case of Elliott vs. Jefferson, 133rd N. C. R., page 207. The rule laid down by the court in this case is as follows:

"Delvin on Deeds No. 835 says: 'But it is doubtful how far arbitrary rules can be of service where the only object is to determine the intention of the parties. In fact, the truth was well expressed by Mr. Justice Sanderson (Walsh vs. Hill, 38 Cal. 481, 487), who said that "in the construction of written instruments we have never derived much aid from the technical rules of the books. The only rule of much value is to place ourselves as near as possible in the seats which were occupied by the parties at the time the written instrument was executed, then taking it by its four corners, read it." This is the main object of all constructions. When the intention of the parties can be ascertained, nothing remains but to effectuate that intention.'"

See case of Ayers vs. Watson, reported in 137 U. S. R., page 584, in which the Court held as follows:

"The beginning corner of a survey does not control more than any other corner actually ascertained; and it is not necessary to follow the calls of the grant in the order they stand in the field notes, but they may be reversed and the lines traced the other way whenever by so doing the land embraced will more nearly harmonize all the calls and objects of the grant; but where to reverse the calls would not have that effect, courses and distances of the survey should be followed."

The boundary lines in a junior grant are no evidence as to the true lines of a senior grant.

See Sasser vs. Herring, 14 N. C. R., pages 340, etc.

See Euliss vs. Joseph McAdems, 108 N. C. R., pages 507, etc.

See Hill vs. Dalton, 136 N. C. R., pages 339, etc.

See Hill vs. Dalton, 140 N. C. R., page 9, and cases cited.

ORIGIN OF TITLE OF LANDS NOW OWNED BY CHEROKEE INDIANS IN NORTH CAROLINA

Before completing this history, I deem it proper to call attention to an erroneous impression that prevails with many people that the land now owned and occupied by the Eastern Band of Cherokees and individual Indians of the Band in Jackson and Swain Counties, N. C., including the Qualla Boundary, was reserved to the Cherokees by treaties made and entered into by and between the United States and the Cherokees between the year 1790 and 1799; and will here state that Col. William H. Thomas is in part responsible for this erroneous impression by reason of a letter written by him to the Hon. James Graham, then member of Congress from this district, on October 16, 1838. The following is a copy of this letter, which is to be found on pages 205, etc., of Wheeler's "History of North Carolina."

To The Hon. James Graham.

Haywood County, North Carolina, October 15th, 1838.

"Sir—I perceive in your speech, delivered in the House of Representatives, in May, 1838, on the Bill making appropriations for preventing and suppressing Indian hostilities, you make mention of Cherokee Indians forming a settlement in the District you represent, as being TEMPERATE, ORDERLY, INDUSTRIOUS and PEACEABLE. I have been acquainted with those Indians since the formation of the settement referred to, and know your statement as above mentioned to be correct. But as you may be unacquainted with the circumstances attending the formation of that settlement, and with the cause of their becoming temperate, I hope the following statement in relation thereto may not be unacceptable to you, as the Representative of the District in which they reside.

"So early as the year 1806, two Deputations attended Washington City from the Cherokee natives; one from the lower towns, to make known to the President their desire to remove West of the Mississippi, and pursue the hunter's life; the other Deputation, representing, in part, the Cherokees belonging to the above settlement, to make known to the President their desire to remain on the lands of their fathers, and become cultivators of the soil. The President answered their petitions as follows: 'The United States, my children, are the friends of both parties. As far as can be reasonably asked, they are willing to satisfy the wishes of both. Those who remain may be assured of our patronage, our aid, and good neighborhood.' The Treaties made between the United States and the Cherokee Nation, in the years 1817 and 1819, made provision for those desiring to remain, agreeable to the promise of the President; and they were made citizens of the United States, and each family was allowed a reservation of six hundred and forty acres of land. The whites claimed the same lands, under a purchase made of the State. Suits were instituted in favor of the Indians, and by our Courts, were decided in their favor, and possession was surrendered to them by the whites. Afterwards they were induced to sell their reservations to the Commissioners of the State, and to purchase lands in the white settlement, where they now reside, in the neighborhood of the hunting ground reserved to the Cherokee hunters by the Treaties concluded with the Cherokee nation between the years 1790 and 1799; which privilege, as a part of the Cherokee nation, they continue to enjoy.

"Until the year 1830 they were as intemperate as any other Indians on our frontier. About that time the principal chief of the above settlement, by the name of Drowning Bear (or, You-Na-Guska), becoming convinced that intemperance would destroy himself and people, determined to live temperate, and persuade his people to follow his example. I was present when he assembled them. On that occasion he informed his people that he had been considering and devising ways to promote their happiness in future. He said he had become convinced that intemperance was the cause of the extermination of the Indian tribes situated in the neighborhood of the whites: referring them to the present and previous situation of the Catawba (or Inctahquo) Indians, with whom they were acquainted, as an evidence of the injurious effects of intemperance. He directed his clerk to write in the Indian language as follows: 'The undersigned Cherokees, belonging to the town of Qualla, agree to abandon the use of spiritous liquors.' It was immediately signed by the old chief, who was followed by the whole town.

"He then told them that he had served them upwards of forty years, without any pecuniary consideration whatever, his entire object being to promote their interest. He was pleased to see that they yet had confidence in him. He would advise them to remain where they were, in the State of North Carolina; a State, he considered, better and more friendly disposed to the Red man than any other. That should they remove west, they would there be, also, in a short time, surrounded by the settlements of the whites, and probably be included in a State disposed to oppress them.

"To the above cause (temperance) is to be attributed their present state of improvement. The time previously spent in scenes of dissipation is now spent in useful employment. Each family is now capable of reading the Scriptures in their own language, manufacturing their own clothing, and understand farming and the mechanical arts as well as their white neighbors, to whom they are indebted for kind treatment, and a friendly disposition in advancing them in improvement.

"It is to be hoped that, by a continuance of that kind guardianship exercised over them by the State of North Carolina, they will ere long become a civilized community of Indians, and furnish an example of the benevolent policy of the State towards the few of those unfortunate people who have taken shelter under the protction of her law."

"Very respectfully,   "Your obedient servant,
                                          "WILLIAM H. THOMAS."

I especially call attention here to the following language used by Col. Thomas in the letter to Mr. Graham:

"The Treaties made between the United States and the Cherokee Nation, in the years 1817 and 1819, made provision for those desiring to remain, agreeable to the promise of the President; and they were made citizens of the United States, and each family was allowed a reservation of six hundred and forty acres of land. The whites claimed the same lands, under a purchase made of the State. Suits were instituted in favor of the Indians, and by our Courts, were decided in their favor, and possession was surrendered to them by the whites. Afterwards they were induced to sell their reservations to the Commissioners of the State, and to purchase lands in the white settlement, where they now reside, in the neighborhood of the hunting ground reserved to the Cherokee hunters by the Treaties concluded with the Cherokee nation between the years 1790 and 1799; which privilege, as a part of the Cherokee nation, they continue to enjoy."

Now the only treaties made and entered into between the Commissioners appointed on behalf of the United States and the Cherokees between the years 1790 and 1799 were the Treaty of Holston of July 2, 1791, and the Treaty of Tellico of October 2, 1798, and by reference to these treaties it will be seen that not a foot of land was reserved to the Cherokees by either of these treaties, but by the Treaty of Holston of July 2, 1791, the title of the Indians was extinguished to all of the land lying east of the Holston Treaty Line, which is the Hawkins Line shown on the Royce and Moffett maps, and by the Treaty of Tellico of October 2, 1798, the title of the Cherokees was extinguished up to the Meigs and Freeman line, shown on Royce and Moffett maps.

Now, what I think Col. Thomas intended to say was this: that the lands occupied by the Eastern Band of Cherokee Indians were in the locality and lay inside the lands to which the title of the Cherokees was extinguished by the Treaties of 1791 and 1798 aforesaid, and not that they acquired title to land by virtue of these treaties. I will here state that about thirty years ago I was employed by the United States to investigate the title to the Cherokee Training School property at Cherokee, N. C., and accordingly did this work and prepared an abstract of title to the same, and in the course of my work I found that the Meigs and Freeman line, run in pursuance to the Tellico Treaty of October 2, 1798, ran right through the Cherokee Training School property and part of the property lay to the east of this line and part lay to the west of it.

Now, it is true, as stated by Col. Thomas in his letter to Mr. Graham, that certain reservations were made to individual Indians, then resident in the states of Georgia, North Carolina, and Tennessee, by the Treaty of 1819, and among others a reservation was made to an Indian named "Bear" or Yonah, known as the "Bear Tract," which covers a part of what is now Bryson City, and was formerly owned by Hon. T. D. Bryson, the father of Judge T. D. Bryson, now Professor of Law at Duke University, Durham, N. C. Like reservations were made to individual Indians by the Treaty of December 25, 1835, of New Echota, Ga., but the United States Senate refused to ratify the same, and this provision in the Treaty was stricken out, which was a breach of good faith on the part of the United States.

I will here state that in the course of my employment as special Assistant United States Attorney in charge of the litigation prosecuted by the United States in behalf of the Eastern Band of Cherokee Indians in the two old suits of the Eastern Band of Cherokee Indians vs. William H. Thomas, William Johnston, et al, and the United States vs. William H. Thomas, William Johnston, et al, pending in the United States Court for the Western District of North Carolina, which former suit by consent of parties was referred to Messrs. Barringer, Dillard, and Ruffin for arbitration, and who after hearing the testimony made an award, which was made the judgment and decree of the Court at November Term 1874 of said Court, I had occasion to look into and run down the title of the Indians to all of the land awarded and decreed by the Court to the Indians as aforesaid, namely, the Qualla Boundary and the sixty-eight scattered tracts conveyed in what was known as the Sibbald deed, executed by William Johnston and others to the Commissioner of Indian Affairs at Washington, D. C., in trust for the use and benefit of the Eastern Band of Cherokee Indians, situate, lying, and being in Jackson, Swain, Cherokee, and Graham Counties, N. C.; and know the fact to be that the Indians derived title to the Qualla Boundary and all other tracts by and through grants issued by the State of North Carolina to William H. Thomas and others, as will be seen by reference to the award of the arbitrators and the decree of the Court aforesaid.

SUPPLEMENT

INCE preparing the foregoing work, several attorneys in the counties west of Haywood have suggested that in as much as I had set out in my history copies of the acts of the Legislature creating the counties of Burke, Rutherford, Buncombe, and Haywood, it would be desirable for me also to set out copies of the acts creating the other counties west of the Blue Ridge, and I have accordingly set out copies of the acts creating the counties of Cherokee, Clay, Graham, Henderson, Jackson, Macon, Madison, Swain, Transylvania, and Yancey, in the following pages:

CHEROKEE COUNTY

Cherokee County was cut off from Macon County during the years 1838-39.

The following is copy of the Act of the General Assembly of North Carolina creating the County of Cherokee, being Chapter 10, Public Laws of 1838-9, Page 18, the Preamble and the Act reads as follows:

"An Act to erect the territory of this State lately acquired by treaty from the Cherokee Indians, into a separate and distinct County, by the name of Cherokee.

"Be it enacted by the General Assembly of the State of North Carolina, and it is hereby enacted by the authority of the same, That all that part of Macon County bounded as follows, viz: beginning at the junction of the Tennessee and Tuckaseegee rivers; thence down the main channel of the Tennessee river to the State line of Tennessee; thence with said Tennessee line, to where it intersects the Georgia line; thence with the line dividing this State from Georgia, eastwardly, to the mountain dividing the waters of Hiwassee and Valley rivers, from those of the Nantahala river; thence along with the highest summit, and various courses of the said mountain to the point of beginning, be, and the same is hereby erected into a separate and distinct County, by the name of Cherokee, with all the rights, privileges and immunities of other Counties of this State." The next Chapter, 11, of the same session of the General Assembly entitled, "An Act supplemental to the Act erecting the County of Cherokee, provided for the organization of said County."

The 5th Section of this latter Act reads as follows:

"V: Be it further enacted, That the justices of the peace of the County of Cherokee, at their first court, shall proceed to appoint a Clerk, Sheriff, and other county officers (entry taker excepted), in the same manner, and under the same rules as are prescribed by law for other counties of this State."

The boundary lines of the County of Cherokee, as created by the act aforesaid, include all the territory or section of country acquired by treaty from the Cherokee Indians in 1835, except the watershed of Nantahala River, which latter section of the country was retained as a part of the County of Macon.

CLAY COUNTY

Clay County was cut off from Cherokee County in the year 1861.

The following is copy of Act creating Clay County:

"An Act to Lay Off and Establish a New County by the Name of Clay. Public Laws of 1860-61, Chapter 6, Page 8.

"Section 1. Be it enacted by the General Assembly of the State of North Carolina, and it is hereby enacted by the authority of the same, that a new County is hereby laid off and established, to be formed out of a portion of Cherokee County, bounded as follows:

"BEGINNING at the Southeast corner of Cherokee County on the Georgia line, thence to run in a northern direction along the top of the Chunckey Gal Mountain with the Main line, between Shooting Creek and Nantahala River to the top of the highest mountain, between Fiars Creek and Valley River; thence in a south-west direction along the top of the highest mountain, between Fiars Creek and Peachtree to the Hiawassee River, thence in a southward direction, so as to strike the point of a ridge that divides the waters of little Brasstown Creek and big Brasstown Creek, then southward to the point of the ridge, thence along the highest point of the ridge between the little Brasstown and Pine Log to the Georgia line, thence east with the Georgia line to the BEGINNING.

"Section 2. Be it further enacted, that the said County of Clay be and is hereby invested with all the rights and immunities of the other counties in this State, except a member in the House of Commons, which is not to be allowed until the next apportionment in the year 1872.

"Section 3. Be it further enacted, That the citizens included in the proposed new county shall pay their proportionable part of the debt now contracted, and owing by the County of Cherokee.

"Section 4. Be it further enacted, That all the moneys hereafter due to Cherokee County for common school purposes shall, after the organization of Clay County, be divided between the counties of Clay and Cherokee, according to the federal population in each county, any law to the contrary notwithstanding.

"(Ratified the 20th day of February, 1861.)"

GRAHAM COUNTY

Graham County was cut off from Cherokee County in the year 1872. The following is copy of the Act creating Graham County:

"Laws of North Carolina (Public) 1871-1872, Chapter LXXVII.

Proviso. "Section 1. THE GENERAL ASSEMBLY OF NORTH CAROLINA DO ENACT, That all that part of Cherokee county included within the following bounds, to wit: Beginning at a stake at the mouth of Slick Rock Creek on the lines of North Carolina and Tennessee, and running with said line to the top of Unacoee Mountain, thence to the Laurel-top, thence with divide mountain between Beaver Dam, Hanging Dog and Snowbird creeks, to the top of the mountain between Snowbird creek and Valley river and Cheoee; thence east, with the meanders of the mountain to the top of the same, to the line of Cherokee and Macon counties; thence northward with that line to the bank of Tennessee river, thence with the meanders of the bank of said river to the beginning; be and is hereby created into a separate and distinct county, by the name of Graham, with all the rights, privileges and immunities incident and belonging to the other counties in this state: Provided, Said county shall not be entitled to a representative under the apportionment made by this general assembly.

When act to be in force. "Section 2. This act shall be in force from and after its ratification.

"Ratified the 30th day of January, A. D., 1872."

HENDERSON COUNTY

Henderson County was cut off from the southern part of Buncombe County in the years 1838 and 1839.

The following is copy of the Act creating Henderson County:

Laws of North Carolina—1838-1839:

"An Act to lay off and establish a county by the name of Henderson.

"Be it enacted by the General Assembly of the State of North Carolina, and it is hereby enacted by the authority of the same, that all the Southern portion of Buncombe County, beginning on the top of Pisgah Mountain, on the Haywood line, and from thence taking the dividing ridge between Hominy Creek and Mills River to the dividing ridge between Mill's River and Avery's Creek; from thence keeping said ridge to the head of Isreal's Branch; from thence taking down said Branch, to French Broad River; from thence, up said River opposite the mouth of Cane Creek; from thence, taking up Cane Creek, to the Buncombe Turnpike Road; from thence, taking said road, to the top of the ridge between Cane Creek and Mud Creek; from thence, taking the main dividing ridge, between Cane Creek and Clear Creek waters, to the top of Bearwallow Mountain, on the Rutherford line; from thence, with the Rutherford line, to the South Carolina line; from thence, with the South Carolina line, to the Macon line; from thence, with the Macon line, to the Haywood line; from thence, with the Haywood line, to Pisgah, the beginning, be, and the same is hereby erected into a separate and distinct County, by the name of Henderson.

Be it further enacted, that this act shall be in full force from and after its passage. Ratified 13th December, 1838."

JACKSON COUNTY

Jackson County was cut off from part of Haywood and part of Macon Counties in the year 1851.

The following is copy of the Act creating Jackson County:

"An Act to Establish a New County by the Name of Jackson. Laws of North Carolina, Session 1850-51.

"Chapter XXXVIII.

"Section 1. Be it enacted by the General Assembly of the State of North Carolina, and it is hereby enacted by the authority of the same, That all that part of the counties of Haywood and Macon included within the following bounds, to wit:

"BEGINNING on the extreme height of the Scott's Creek mountains, where the State road crosses; thence with the top of that mountain, which divides the waters of Pigeon river from the waters of Tuckasege, near to the line that divides the counties of Henderson and Haywood; thence with said line to the line which divides the States of North and South Carolina; thence with a line to be run from said line to the top of the Fodderstack mountain, so as to include Wm. Barns' plantation within the new county; thence with the top of said mountain to the Whiteside mountain; thence to the top of Cowee Mountain, to where the State road crosses it; thence with the top of said mountain, which divides the waters of Tuckasege river from the waters of the Tennessee river to the top of the mountain at the head of Alarka Creek; thence along the top of said mountain, and the ridge that divides the waters of Alarka Creek from those of Tuckasege river to the Tuckasege river opposite the mouth of Forney's Creek; thence with the top of the first ridge below said creek to the top of the Smokey mountain; on the Tennessee line; thence with said line and the top of said mountain to where the Oconalufta Turnpike road crosses it; thence with the top of said mountain to the Bald mountain, that divides the waters of Oconalufta from the waters of Cattaloocha Creek; thence along the dividing ridge to where the Soco and Jonathan Creek road crosses; thence on the top of the Balsam mountain that divides the waters of Richland Creek from the waters of Tuckasegee river to the BEGINNING, at the State road; BE, and the same is HEREBY erected into a separate and distinct county by the name of Jackson, with all the rights, privileges and immunities that other counties in this State have and enjoy.

"(Ratified 29th January, 1851)."

MACON COUNTY

Macon County was cut off from Haywood County in the year 1828.

The County of Haywood, when created in 1808, embraced within its bounds all the Indian reservation of 1783, in North Carolina, and some territory east of said reservation.

The County of Macon was taken from the territory of the western part of Haywood County and created by Chapter 50, Private Laws of 1828, page 27, of the book containing laws of North Carolina, from 1828 to 1831. The title of the act and the act reads as follows, to wit:

"An act to erect that section of country commonly called the Cherokee Purchase into a separate county."

"Be it enacted by the General Assembly of the State of North Carolina, and it is hereby enacted by the authority of the same, that all that part of Haywood County bounded as follows (viz.): beginning on the Tennessee line, on the extreme height of the Great Smoky Mountain; thence along the main summit of a ridge that divides the waters of the Oconaluftee River from those of Deep Creek to the head of Newton's Mill Creek; thence down the said creek to the Tuckasega river; thence up the main channel of the river to the first main fork above the mouth of Caney Fork of said river; thence along the ridge dividing the forks of said river to the top of the main Blue Ridge, which divides the eastern from the western waters; thence eastwardly along the various courses of the said Blue Ridge to the South Carolina line; thence with said line to Ellicott's rock on the east bank of the Chattouga river; thence with the line dividing this State from Georgia to the line of Tennessee; thence along with the Tennessee line to the extreme height of the Great Smoky Mountain, to the point of the beginning, be, and the same is hereby erected into a separate and distinct county, by the name of Macon, with all the rights, privileges and immunities of the other counties of this State.

II. And be it further enacted, That all lands within the county hereby created, which have been or may be purchased from the State but not granted, shall be deemed liable to taxation in the same manner as lands entered, but not granted, are by the laws of the State."

See: Also Act set out on pages 144 and 145 of the 2nd Vol. of the Rev. Stat. of North Carolina.

See: Supplemental Act, Chap. 51, p. 30, passed at the same session of the General Assembly of North Carolina, providing for the organization of the said County of Macon.

By reference to the boundary lines called for in the above entitled act, it will be seen that the entire county, as created by the act, lay west of the Meigs and Freeman line.

MADISON COUNTY

Madison County was cut off from parts of Buncombe and Yancey Counties in the year 1851.

The following is copy of the Act creating Madison County:

"Laws of North Carolina, 1850-51. Page 91.

"Counties—Chapter XXXVI—1850-'51.

An Act to lay off and establish a County by the name of Madison.

"Section 1. To be established out of portions of Buncombe and Yancey.

"Section 1. Be It Enacted by the General Assembly of the State of North Carolina, and it is Hereby Enacted by the Authority of the Same, That a county by the name of Madison shall be, and the same is hereby laid off and established out of portions of Buncombe and Yancey counties, in the following bounds: Beginning on the Paint Rock on the Tennessee line, and running with that line East to the top of the ridge that divides the waters of Ivy and Laurel from the waters of Caney River; then, with the top of said ridge, by way of Ivy Gap and Point Gap, and passing the same to a ridge that divides the waters of Big Ivy from those of Little Ivy; thence a direct course to the mouth of Sandymush Creek; thence up said creek to the forks thereof; thence with the top of the ridge that divides the waters of Big and Little Sandymush Creeks, to the Haywood line; thence with said line to the line of the State of Tennessee and with the same to the beginning; and the said county shall be, and is hereby invested with all the rights, privileges and immunities of the other counties in this State.

"(Ratified 27th January, 1851.)"

Following above is Chapter XXXVII, pages 92 to 97 inclusive, showing a supplimental act directing a survey of the boundaries between the counties effected, but making no changes in their lines, and directing the political division of the counties, etc.

SWAIN COUNTY

Swain County was cut off from part of Jackson and part of Macon Counties in the year 1871.

The following is copy of the Act creating Swain County:

"Public Laws of North Carolina 1870-1871, Chapter XCIV.

"An Act to Establish a New County by the Name of Swain.

New county created.

"Section 1. The General Assembly of North Carolina Do Enact, That all that part of the counties of Jackson and Macon, included within the following bounds, to wit: beginning on the line of the State of Tennessee, where the Tennessee river crosses said line; thence up said river to where the Cherokee county line leaves the same; thence with the line of said county to the point at which the road leading from the waters of Nantahala river to the waters of Cheowee river crosses said line; thence with said road to within one-fourth mile of Captain N. S. Jarrett's mill nearest his present residence; thence crossing Nantahala river on a straight line to the Shallow ford on Tennessee river; thence crossing the said river last named and running with the dividing ridge to the Jackson county line on the top of Cowee mountain, so as to include the waters of Tabors creek and Alarka creek in the new county hereby created; thence with the line of the said county of Jackson to a spur of the said Cowee mountain and running thence with said spur to the Tuckasegee river so as to include the waters of Conley's creek in the county created by this act; thence crossing said river on a direct line, and running thence on the same to the Oconeelufty river to a point opposite the mouth of Adam's creek; thence up the last named river to the mouth of Soco creek; thence with the dividing ridge between said Oconeelufty river and Soco creek and following said main dividing ridge to the Tennessee line to the beginning; be and the same is hereby created into a separate and distinct county, by the name of Swain, with all the rights, privileges and immunities incident and belonging to the other counties in this state.

When act to be in force.

"Sec. 2. This act shall be in force from and after its ratification.

"Ratified the 24th day of February, A. D. 1871."

TRANSYLVANIA COUNTY

Transylvania County was cut off from Henderson and Jackson Counties in the year 1861.

The following is copy of the Act creating Transylvania County:

"Public Laws of North Carolina, Session of 1860-1861, Chapter 10, Page 19.

"Section 1. Be it enacted by the General Assembly of the State of North Carolina, and it is hereby enacted by the authority of the same, That a county by the name of Transylvania be laid off and established out of the counties of Henderson and Jackson with the following boundary, to wit: beginning at the standing stone, on the South Carolina line, near the head waters of Green river and Little river, and runs with the Blue Ridge to Green river gap, thence a straight line to the top of Hickory mountain, thence a straight line to the top of the mountain, west of William Sintel's, thence with the main ridge to the top of the high point on the mountain near the Hadden farm, thence a straight line to the mouth of the branch between the Hadden and Justus farms, thence down the French Broad river to the mouth of Bryson's creek, thence a straight line to the top of Pisgah mountain, thence a west direction with the Haywood line to the Jackson line to a point on the Blue Ridge between the head of Indian creek and Toxaway, and running with the dividing ridge between Indian creek and Toxaway river to said river, thence south to the South Carolina line, thence with the South Carolina line to the beginning.

"Sec. 2. Be it further enacted, That this act shall be in force from and after its ratification.

"(Ratified the 15th day of February, 1861.)"

The above act was supplimented and amended by Chapter 11, of which Section 1 reads: "That the county of Transylvania be and is hereby invested with all the rights, privileges and immunities of the other counties of this state, except as hereinafter provided;" The exceptions, covered in sections 2 to 15, make no change in the county lines, but provide only for the transfer of authority and collection of taxes from the changed parts of Henderson and Jackson counties until the new county courts and offices are established, and for the establishment of the county seat at a new town to be named Brevard. See pages 19 to 23 of the Public Laws of North Carolina, 1860-1861.

YANCEY COUNTY

Yancey County was cut off from parts of Burke and Buncombe Counties in the year 1833.

The following is copy of the Act creating Yancey County.

"Revised Statutes of North Carolina, 1836, Vol. 2, Page 170.

"An Act to Erect a New County by the Name of Yancey.

"(Passed in the year 1833.)

"Whereas the large extent of country comprehended in the bounds hereafter described in the counties of Burke and Buncombe, renders the attendance of the inhabitants thereof, to do public duties, extremely difficult and expensive: For remedy whereof,

"Be it enacted by the General Assembly of the State of North Carolina, and it is hereby enacted by the authority of the same, That all that part of the counties of Burke and Buncombe, included within the following bounds, to wit: Beginning on the extreme height of the Black mountain; running thence along said mountain to Ogle's improvement; thence along the dividing ridge to Daniel Carter's fork field; thence a direct course to the mouth of Big Ivy Creek; thence with the Warm Spring road, by Barnard's station, to the three forks of Laurel; thence in a direct line, so as to include James Allen's house, to the Tennessee line; thence with said line to the County of Ashe; thence with the line of said county to the Grandmother mountain; thence a direct course to the extreme height of the Humpback mountain; thence with the Blue Ridge to where it intersects the Black mountain; thence with the ridge of said mountain, to the beginning, be, and the same is hereby erected into a separate and distinct county, by the name of Yancey, with all the rights, privileges and immuniites of the other counties in this state."

"An Act Supplemental to an Act Passed at the Present Session of the General Assembly, Entitled 'An Act to Erect a New County by the Name of Yancey.'

"9. Be it further enacted, That it shall be the duty of the county courts of Buncombe and Yancey, at their spring sessions, to appoint two commissioners respectively, who shall receive such compensation as the said courts shall determine, whose duty it shall be to ascertain and mark the dividing line between said counties, whenever the same shall be necessary.

"10. And be it further enacted, That the said commissioners shall commence their survey at Daniel Carter's fork field, and run a direct line from thence to Barnard's station; from which point the line shall run along the old Warm Spring road to James Allen's road: and with his road, so as to include his house, to the Tennessee line; any thing in the act to which this is supplimental to the contrary notwithstanding."

This concludes my history on land titles to land west of the Blue Ridge in this State, including the Cherokee Land Laws, and I hope that the same will prove valuable to the legal profession and others who may read the same; and I desire here to acknowledge my indebtedness to the Champion Paper and Fibre Company of Canton, N. C., for paying me for my services and most of the expenses incurred in doing this work; and also wish to acknowledge my indebtedness to Hons. Kingland Van Winkle and Joseph F. Ford, Attorneys at Law of Asheville, N. C., and to Hon. J. J. Alexander, one of the title examiners in the United States Forest Service here in Asheville, for information and assistance rendered me in my work; also to Hon. S. W. Black, Attorney at Law of Bryson City, N. C., for information furnished me relative to the Cherokee Indians; also to the Hons. M. W. Bell and Don Witherspoon, Attorneys at Law of Murphy, N. C., and Hon. R. L. Phillips, Attorney at Law of Robbinsville, N. C., for information furnished me relative to the Cherokee Land Laws; also the Hons. Charles A. Webb and Hiden Ramsey of the Asheville Citizen-Times, and to Hon. Marcus Erwin, United States District Attorney for the Western District of North Carolina, and to Messrs. Jones and Ward, Attorneys at Law of Asheville, N. C., for information furnished me and for the interest they have taken in this work.

THE AUTHOR.

June 1, 1938.

INDEX

146

Supplement

To HISTORY By Geo. H. Smathers
on Land Titles in Western North Carolina

To Subscribers To My Book

I find that I may have committed an error in the statement I made on pages 25, 60 and 62 of my book that the Act of 1778, prohibiting the entry and grant of land reserved to the Cherokee Indians by the Treaty of the Long Island of Holston on July 20, 1777, was repealed by the Act of 1782, when, as a matter of fact, the Act of 1778 was not repealed until the Act of 1783, by Chapter 185, entitled: "An Act for opening the land office for the redemption of species and other certifications, and discharging the arrears due to the army."

I also find I may have committed an error in my statement on pages 24 to 26 of my book that the line of Rutherford County running with Burke County did not extend from the top of the Blue Ridge to Pigeon River until the year 1788; and that lands entered and granted as in Rutherford County up about the mouth of Cathey's Creek and up on French Broad River in that locality about five miles above the town of Brevard between the years 1785 and 1788, which are set out on pages 34 to 39 inclusive of my book, were void, while entries and grants in the same locality taken out as in Burke County were valid.

At the time I prepared my book I had not seen a complete copy of the Act of 1783, Chapter 185, above cited, and since the publication of the same I have found a complete copy of this Act set out in Potter's Revisal, issued in 1821, on Pages 435 to 440, inclusive, and until I examined this Act I did not know of Sections 20, 21 and 22 contained therein, and after making a thorough study of the same it now appears to me:

FIRST

That the Act of 1778, prohibiting the entry and grant of land west of the Bue Ridge in this state was repealed by the 20th Section of the Act of 1783, Chapter 185, above cited, and not by the Act of 1782 as stated by me on page 24 of my book.

SECOND

That the line of Rutherford County running with the line of Burke County was extended from the top of the Blue Ridge to Pigeon River, a due West course from the corner of Burke and Rutherford Counties on top of the Blue Ridge, by the 20th Section of Chapter 185 of the

Act of 1783, above cited, and that by Section 21 of said Chapter the land lying south of this line from the top of the Blue Ridge to Pigeon River was made subject to entry and grant as in Rutherford County, and land lying north of this line was made subject to entry and grant as in Burke County, on the First day of August, 1783; and therefore grants set out in my book on pages 33 to 39 inclusive about the mouth of Cathey's Creek and on French Broad River in that locality about five miles above the town of Brevard if taken out as in Rutherford County were valid grants, and those taken out in that locality as in Burke County were void. This is just the reverse of my former opinion as to the validity of grants taken out for land about the mouth of Cathey's Creek and on French Broad River in that locality during the period between the ratification of the Act of 1783 above cited and the year 1788, as set out on page 34 of my book. In cases, however, where entries and grants were obtained as being entirely in either Rutherford or Burke County, and a part of the land actually ran over into the other county, the grants were validated by a later statute, as held by our Supreme Court in the case of Harris vs. Norman reported in 96 N. C. R., pages 59 et seq. I went into a full discussion of this matter on page 26 of my book.

Following are copies of Sections 20, 21 and 22 of the Act of 1783, Chapter 185, above cited:

Repealing Clauses 20. And be it further enacted; that so much of the aforesaid act of the general assembly for establishing offices for receiving entries of claims for land in the several counties within this state, for ascertaining the method of obtaining titles to the same, and for other purposes therein mentioned, and the several amendments thereof, as comes within the meaning of this act, shall be and are hereby repealed and made void.

Certain lands to be entered in Burke and Rutherford. 21. And be it further enacted, That all the lands lying between the Iron mountain and the present Indian boundary, as far as a point opposite to the line already extended between Burke and Rutherford counties, shall be entered in the county of Burke; and all the lands south of the last mentioned line to the south line of this state and the Indian boundary, from the aforesaid point, shall be entered in the county of Rutherford.

When this act to be in force. 22. And be it further enacted, That this act shall be in force, and take effect in the respective counties in this state, on the first day of August next, excepting for the lands appropriated by sundry acts of this assembly, lying to the westward of the present Indian boundary line, which said lands shall not be liable to be entered until the twentieth day of October next."

While Section 21 of Chapter 185 of the Act of 1783 is rather clumsily drawn as to the extension of the line of Rutherford County with the line of Burke County from the top of the Blue Ridge to Pigeon River, and although I have made a thorough examination of the acts of the General Assembly set out in Potter's Revisal between the date of the passage of the first act in 1777 authorizing the entry and grant of lands in this state and the passage of the Act of 1783, Chapter 185, above cited, and fail to find any act extending the line of Rutherford County from the top of the Blue Ridge to Pigeon River, the so-called Indian Boundary; still I think sufficient appears in this Section 21 to show an intention on the part of the Legislature to extend the line between Burke and Rutherford Counties from the top of the Blue Ridge a due west course to Pigeon River, and open up this area to entry and grant in the two counties as above explained. It appears that both the public and the State officials understood that the area between the Blue Ridge and Pigeon River was made subject to entry and grant in the Counties of Burke and Rutherford under the Act of 1783, but at that time the dividing line between Burke and Rutherford Counties from the top of the Blue Ridge to Pigeon River had not actually been run and was not run until Joseph McDowell, Jr., ran the dividing line between the two Counties during the year of 1785 referred to in the Act of 1788, and for want of knowledge as to the dividing line between the two Counties, a number of parties laid entries and obtained grants for land south of the dividing line as being in Burke County up about the mouth of Cathey's Creek and on French Broad River in that locality about five miles above the town of Brevard, when the land in that localty lay in Rutherford County, and as before stated grants issued for land located in Burke County in that locality are void, while grants issued for land located in Rutherford County in that locality are valid, and it may be that some parties laid entries and obtained grants thereon for land as in Rutherford County north of the dividing line between Burke and Rutherford Counties, and if so the same were void excepting cases however where the grants were obtained as being entirely in Rutherford or Burke Counties, and a part of the land actually ran over into the other County, for such grants were validated as before stated in this case, but I fail to find where grants were issued to parties as in Rutherford County north of the dividing line between Burke and Rutherford Counties.

I overlooked sections 20, 21 and 22 of Chapter 185 of the Act of 1783 for the reason that while they are set out in full in Potter's Revisal issued in 1821, on pages 435 to 440 inclusive, they, as well as many other sections of Chapter 185, were not brought forward and incorporated in the Second Volume of the Revised Statutes of 1836, nor in the Second Volume of the Code of North Carolina of 1883, both of which showed other sections of the Chapter under the head of "Cherokee Lands," and I took it for granted that Sections Five and Six, and others which were shown, were the only sections having a bearing on the matter.

Another thing that misled me in this matter was the recital in an act passed in 1788, set out on page 11 of my book, entitled "An Act for Establishing the Dividing Line Between Burke and Rutherford," which began: "Whereas the dividing line between the Counties of Burke and Rutherford hath not yet been 'established'—west of the Blue Ridge—etc." Not having seen Sections 20, 21 and 22 of Chapter 185 of the Act of 1783 at that time, I was naturally led to believe that above recital meant that no line had been legally established or adopted until the passage of this act, whereas I now see that the act meant that no line had been established on the ground until the survey of Joseph McDowell, Jr., in 1785, which this act of 1788 was intended to approve and confirm.

As suggested in my book on page 39, this matter may never be found of legal importance to my readers, since the lands involved were of high agricultural value, and title has been made good by possession; and this applies to the Burke County grants which I now believe were void when located south of the McDowell line, the same as I stated it did to Rutherford County grants I set out as void in the discussion of the matter on page 39 above mentioned.

I will here state that nothing contained in the Act of 1783, Chapter 185, and subsequent acts above discussed, changes my opinion that Rutherford County never did extend west of Pigeon River in this State. (See case of Avery vs. Strother reported in 1 N. C. R., page 558).

I am still of this opinion, although in a talk I recently had with Judge Felix E. Alley in Waynesville, he called my attention to the fact that soon after the passage of the act creating Rutherford County in 1779 a grant was issued by the State of North Carolina for a tract of land now in Tennessee in the locality of Reelsfoot Lake to his great-great-grandfather, and in a suit brought by him and other heirs of his great-great-grandfather to recover possession of this tract against adverse claimants, on the trial of the case the Supreme Court of Tennessee sustained the validity of this grant, and while the plaintiffs recovered a part of the tract they lost a part on account of possession had by the defendants.

I can very well understand why the Supreme Court of Tennessee held this grant valid, for when the grant or certified copy, or record of same, was offered in evidence, although the defendants may have objected to the introduction of the grant, not being in possession of the knowledge of the fact that Rutherford County never extended west of Pigeon River, the Court had a right to presume that the officers of the State had acted within their authority, and the Court of Tennessee had a right to presume that the land lay in Rutherford County and that the grant was authorized by the State of North Carolina.

See case Polk vs. Wendal, 9 Crance (U. S. 87) and cases cited.

I have always heard that North Carolina formerly claimed its western limits as being the South Seas, Pacific Ocean, but later on it became more modest and only claimed as its western limits the Mississippi River.

I have heard also that Burke County created in 1777 claimed its western limits as the Mississippi River, but after making a thorough investigation of this matter, I find that Burke County never extended west of the present western limits of this State, now Graham and Cherokee Counties, and that the area between Graham and Cherokee Counties and the Mississippi River was covered by Washington County, created by act of 1777 covering what is now the State of Tennessee.

See my conclusion as to the western limits of Burke County set out on pages 15 and 16 of my book. It appears that a number of people were under the impression that the western limits of Rutherford County created in the year 1779 extended as far westward as the Mississippi River and grants were taken out indiscriminately in Rutherford County as far west as Tennessee.

I will now call attention to a matter that I did not discuss in my book, and that is this: In the First Volume of Dr. Sondley's History of Buncombe County on pages 375-376, Dr. Sondley states: "In 1763 a Royal British Proclamation or Order prohibited entry and grant of land lying west of the heads of streams which run into the Atlantic Ocean. A line was then partly run and partly agreed on between the North Carolina authorities and representative Cherokees, which divided the Cherokee Country from the country of the white settlers. That line extended from a point on Reedy River in South Carolina, a few miles below the present city of Greenville, north to a marked tree on Tryon Mountain, passing close to what is now the town of Tryon; and from that tree on Tryon Mountain, now in Polk County, North Carolina, it was provided by the agreement that the line should run northward directly to Chiswell's Lead Mine in Southwestern Virginia. This was then supposed to make the line north from Tryon Mountain follow the crest of the Blue Ridge. It prevented settlements in the present North Carolina west of that ridge until some years after the War of the Revolution. However, it did not for a great while prevent troubles to the white settlers on Yadkin and Catawba Rivers coming through the Cherokee inroads."

Mr. Moffett finds, however, that a direct line from the top of Tryon

Mountain to Chiswell's Lead Mine runs about 20 miles east of the Blue Ridge, and it is very evident that the old Cherokee Line referred to in the Act creating Rutherford County in 1779 was this line run in pursuance to the British Proclamation above referred to.

I also find that I committed an error in my statement set out on page 61 of my book, which, however, was corrected in other parts of the book, that the title of the Cherokees for the land on the waters of French Broad River was extinguished by the Treaty of Hopewell, November 28, 1785, and the Treaty of Holston, July 2, 1791, which statement was in words and figures as follows:

"As stated above, the title of the Cherokees was extinguished to the land lying between the Hopewell Treaty line that runs through or a little east of the City of Asheville back to the top of the Blue Ridge by the Treaty of Hopewell of November 28, 1785, and the title of the Cherokees to the remainder of the land on the waters of French Broad River was extinguished by the Treaty of Holston of July 2, 1791."

While it is true that the title of the Cherokees was extinguished to the major part of the land on the waters of French Broad River by the two treaties above mentioned, the title of the Cherokees to the land lying to the south and west of the Holston Treaty July 2, 1791, up to the Meigs & Freeman line was not extinguished until the Treaty of Tellico, October 2, 1798, and the title of the Cherokees lying west of the Meigs & Freeman line on the waters of French Broad River was not extinguished until the Treaty of 1819. This error is corrected, however, in a way by the Royce-Moffett Maps, made a part of my history, and by reference to Pages 80 and 81 of my book, it will be seen that I state that the title of the Cherokees to the land lying between the Meigs & Freeman line and the Tennessee River was not extinguished until the Treaty of 1819.

By reference to pages 60 and 61 of my book, it will be seen that I went into full discussion of the validity of that part of Grant No. 230 issued by the State to George Latimer, that lies on the waters of French Broad River, calling to contain 50,560 acres of land and gave it as my opinion that that part of said grant that lies on the waters of French Broad River is a valid grant and especially so as the land on French Broad River lies on the outside of the boundary reserved to the Cherokees by the 5th Section of the Act of 1783, as defined by the Supreme Court of this State in the case of Brown vs. Smathers, et al, reported in 188 N.C.R., Page 166. Now a lot of confusion has arisen by reason of the Act of 1809 contained in Chapter 774 of Potter's Revisal, and a good many people as well as a number of attorneys seem to think that a grant issued for land anywhere on the waters of French Broad River before the title of the Cherokee was extinguished is void and they refer to numerous decisions of our Supreme Court bearing on this point, and I will now call attention to the fact that every decision of our Supreme Court that held grants void before the title of the Cherokees was extinguished had reference to land that lay inside of the boundary reserved to the Cherokees by the 5th Section of the Act of 1783, Chapter 185, above cited, where the 6th Section of said Act prohibited the entry and grant of lands within that boundary and declared such entries and grants, if so made, to be void, and these decisions had no reference whatever to grants issued for land on the waters of French Broad River outside the boundary reserved to the Cherokees by the 5th Section of the Act of 1783.

It is true that after the joint treaty made and entered into between the states of Virginia and North Carolina and the Cherokees at the Long Island of Holston of July 20, 1777 referred to and set out on pages 5 and 6 of my book all the land lying west of the Blue Ridge in this State was reserved to the Cherokees for a hunting ground or occupancy, and the next Session of the General Assembly of this State following this Treaty prohibited the entry and grant of land reserved to the Cherokees west of the Blue Ridge in this State. But this Act was repealed by the 20th Section of the Act of 1783, Chapter 185, above cited, and by the 21st Section of that Act all the land lying between the top of the Blue Ridge and Pigeon River on the waters of French Broad River were laid open to entry and grant in Burke and Rutherford Counties, and a great many grants were issued for land on the waters of French Broad River between the date of the passage of this Act up to and during the year of 1787, which were valid grants as there was no prohibition against the entry and grant of lands within this area during this period.

Grant No. 226 issued by the State to William Cathcart on July 20, 1796 calling to contain 49,920 acres, which was made the subject of the litigation in the case of Latimer vs. Poteet, 39 U.S.R. (14th Pet.) Page 4, lay inside the boundary reserved to the Cherokees by the 5th Section of the Act of 1783, Chapter 185, above cited, and the Court held in that case as the 6th Section of the Act of 1783 prohibiting the entry and grant of land within this boundary was in full force and effect, and that every foot of Grant No. 226 to William Cathcart was void. The Court however held in that case that the State of North Carolina could have granted the fee in the land subject to the Indian right of occupancy, and that when the Indian title was extinguished it would relieve the land of the encumbrance. It was only by reason of the 6th Section of the Act of 1783 that the Court held this grant void.

While under Section 20 of the same Act of 1783 (Chapter 185) all the land lying on the waters of French Broad River whether valley or mountain land, was made subject to entry and grant after August 1, 1783 under the 21st Section, as there was no prohibition against the entry and grant of land on the waters of French Broad River after the Act of 1783, I am of the opinion that all grants issued for land within this area after that date, if laid in the proper county, and if properly described and properly authenticated, were valid grants without regard to the question as to whether the title of the Cherokees had been extinguished or not.

I will here call attention to the fact as shown on the Moffett Map that about two-thirds of the land embraced in Grant No. 230 to George Latimer on July 2, 1776, calling to contain 50,560 acres lay inside of the boundary reserved to the Cherokees by the 5th Section of the Act of 1783, and this part of said grant was declared void by our Supreme Court in the case of Avery vs. Strother reported in 1st N.C.R., page 558, and later on in the case of Strother vs. Cathey, 1st Murphy (5th N.C.R.) page 152, and several later cases, including Latimer vs. Poteet, 39th U.S.R. (14th Pet.) page 4, and the recent decision of our Supreme Court in the case of Brown vs. Smathers, 188th N.C.R. page 172, but about one-third of the grant lies on the waters of French Broad River outside of the boundary reserved to the Cherokees by the 5th Section of the Act of 1783 as defined by our Supreme Court in the case of Brown vs. Smathers et al, reported in 188th N.C.R. page 172, and I am of the opinion that that part of Grant No. 230 to George Latimer that lies on the waters of French Broad River is a valid grant.

A grant may be valid in part and void in part.

See case of Hough vs. Dumas, 20 N.C.R. page 473.

It will be presumed that all preliminary steps required by law to validate a state grant of lands have been taken, statutory regulations relating thereto being directory.

See case Polk vs. Wendal, 9 Cranche (U.S.) page 871.

See case Westfelt vs. Adams, 159 N.C.R. page 420.

See case Waldo vs. Wilson, N.C.R. 173, pages 690 etc.

It is only in cases where the entry and grant of land is prohibited by a statute as provided in the 6th Section of the Act of 1783 and where the officers of the State had no authority for issuing such grants that the grant could be attacked collaterally on the trial of the cause.

See case Waldo vs. Wilson, N.C.R. 173, page 690, above cited.

See case of Johnson vs. Lumber Company, reported in 144th N.C. R. page 717, and my comment on the decision of the Supreme Court in this case set out on pages 97 and 98 of my book. According to the principle enunciated in this case, while that part of Grant No. 230 to George Latimer that lies inside of the boundary reserved to the

Cherokees by the 5th Section of the Act of 1783 could be attacked collaterally on account of the 6th Section of the Act prohibiting the entry and grant of same, that part of said grant that lies on the waters of French Broad River could not be attacked collaterally, as there was no prohibition against the entry and grant of this part of said Grant No. 230 to George Latimer.

Now referring again to the contention of parties and some attorneys that all grants issued by the State to parties for land on the water of French Broad River before the title of the Cherokees was extinguished is void. If this contention should be sustained, then all of the early grants issued by the State to parties for land on the waters of French Broad River south and west of the Holston Treaty line of July 2, 1791, between the years of 1783 and 1791, prior to the creation of Buncombe, Henderson and Transylvania Counties, would be void, including the grants issued to parties at the mouth of Cathey's Creek and on French Broad River in that locality about five miles above the town of Brevard, as set out on pages 34 to 39 inclusive of my book.

According to this contention then two of the oldest grants for land in what is now Buncombe County would be void, to-wit: Grant No. 1031 issued by the State to William Moore on the 7th day of August, 1787 for 450 acres of land on Hominy Creek, then in Burke, now in Buncombe County, N. C. (See copy of this grant set out on pages 31 & 32 of my book, and see also my reference to this grant set out on page 50 of my book), and Grant No. 912 issued by the State to William and James Davidson on the 7th day of August, 1787 for 640 acres of land in Burke County on both sides of Swannanoa River, (See copy of this grant and my comments on same set out on pages 32 etc. of my book), as the title of the Cherokees had not been extinguished to these two grants and a number of other grants issued by the State to parties on the waters of French Broad River lying west of and in between the Hopewell Treaty line of November 28, 1785, and the Holston Treaty line of July 2, 1791 until the Treaty of Holston of July 2, 1791. Also the title of the Cherokees had not been extinguished to a number of grants issued by the State to parties for land on the waters of French Broad River west of and in between the Holston Treaty line of July 2, 1791 and the Tellico Treaty line of October 2, 1798 shown on maps as Meigs & Freeman line until the Treaty of Tellico of October 2, 1798, and as before stated the title of the Cherokees was not extinguished to land lying west of the Meigs & Freeman line on the waters of French Broad River until the Treaty of 1819. After the creation of Buncombe County in 1791 a number of grants were issued by the State for land lying west of Meigs & Freeman line on the waters of French Broad River, among others, Grant No.

230 to George Latimer, before the title of the Cherokees was extinguished in 1819.

I went into a brief discussion on pages 119 and 120 of my book of when the U. S. Courts would follow the decisions of the highest court of the States in litigation over land, and in commenting on the decision of the U. S. Circuit Court of Appeals of Richmond, Virginia, in an opinion rendered by Judge Parker on June 17, 1931, in the case of Wood, Forest Supervisor, vs. R. L. Phillips, et al, I use the following language:

"But by reference to the decision of Judge Parker of the United States Circuit Court of Appeals, rendered in the case of Arthur A. Wood, Forest Supervisor, vs. R. L. Phillips et al, rendered on June 17, 1931, it will be seen that Judge Parker held that in that case under the equity practice of the United States Courts, a plaintiff cannot sustain an action against a defendant to remove a cloud upon his title under the Act of 1893 of North Carolina, unless the plaintiff is in possession of the land, which to my mind is a case in which the United States refuses to follow the decisions of the State courts on land matters, and it appears to me also that the decision of Judge Parker in this case on the question of possession is contrary to the decisions of the Supreme Court of North Carolina. And while, as above stated, the general rule is that the United States Court will follow the decisions of the State Courts in cases involving the title to land within the states, this will depend very largely upon whether the United States Courts want to follow the decisions of the State Court, and if they don't want to follow the same, they will find some excuse for not doing so."

Since the publication of my book, Hon. Mark Squires, Attorney-at-Law of Lenoir, N. C., one of the subscribers to my book, after reading certain parts of the same, calls my attention to the following recent decisions of the Supreme Court of the U. S., not yet published, bearing on this point, namely:

"Erie Railroad Co. v. Tompkins, decided April 25, 1938, page 787;

Ruhlin v. New York Life Ins. Co., decided May 2, 1938, page 823;

Rosenthal v. New York Life Ins. Co., decided May 16, 1938, page 933."

In a letter writter to me by Senator Squires in reference to these decisions, he says:

"You will note by careful reading that the old rule of Justice Story to the contrary has been overruled and that on matters of general law, the Federal Court must follow the decisions as well as the statutes of the State. These decisions have created quite a discussion among law teachers and will not probably be overruled in our life time."

Now, as I understand it, Senator Squires gives it as his opinion that under these decisions the U. S. Courts are required to follow the decisions of the highest State Courts and Statutes of the States in all controversies over title to land in the states in both law and equity; and after reading over carefully the Advance Sheets containing these decisions, I concur in the opinion of Senator Squires as to the legal effect of the same. I decided to call the attention of the readers of my history and this Supplement to this matter, and let them decide for themselves what construction to place on these decisions.

The Author,

GEO. H. SMATHERS.

This August 4th, 1938.

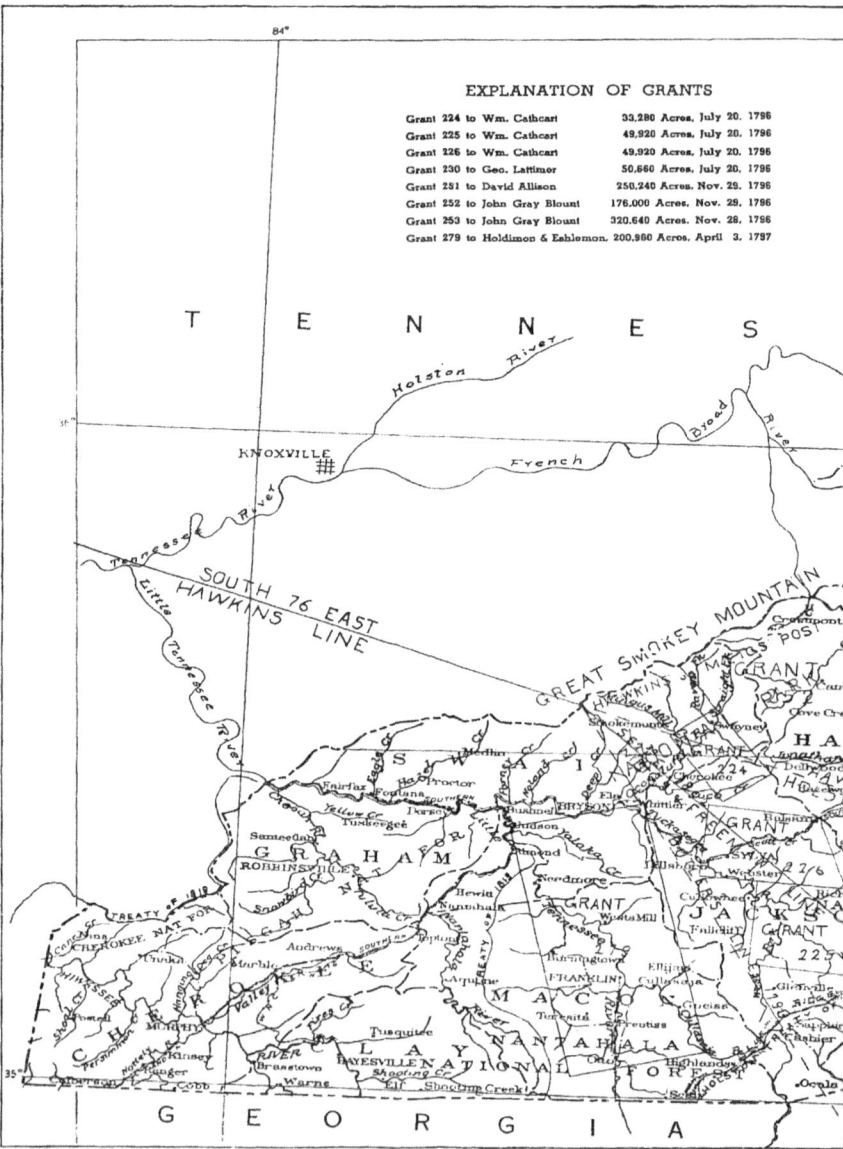

EXPLANATION OF GRANTS

Grant 224 to Wm. Cathcart   33,280 Acres, July 20, 1796
Grant 225 to Wm. Cathcart   49,920 Acres, July 20, 1796
Grant 226 to Wm. Cathcart   49,920 Acres, July 20, 1796
Grant 230 to Geo. Lattimor   50,660 Acres, July 20, 1796
Grant 251 to David Allison   258,240 Acres, Nov. 29, 1796
Grant 252 to John Gray Blount   176,000 Acres, Nov. 29, 1796
Grant 253 to John Gray Blount   320,640 Acres, Nov. 28, 1796
Grant 279 to Holdimon & Eshlemon, 200,960 Acres, April 3, 1797

BY E. M. MOFFETT. F. E. OF
PART OF NORTH CAROLINA
T OF THE BLUE RIDGE
SHOWING
NDARIES OF VARIOUS TREATIES
H THE CHEROKEE INDIANS, AND
AIN EARLY LAND GRANTS: AS
OUT IN REPORT ON THE SAME
GEO. H. SMATHERS. ATTORNEY.
EMBER. 1937.

87°

SOUTH-CAROLINA